The Symphony™ Book

The Symphony™ Book

Edward M. Baras

Osborne **McGraw-Hill**
Berkeley, California

Published by
Osborne **McGraw-Hill**
2600 Tenth Street
Berkeley, California 94710
U.S.A.

For information on translations and book distributors outside of the U.S.A., please write to Osborne **McGraw-Hill** at the above address.

The Symphony™ Book

234567890 SLSL 898765

ISBN 0-07-881160-0

Cynthia Hudson, Acquisitions Editor
Fran Haselsteiner, Copy Editor
Jean Stein, Technical Editor
Steven E. Miller and Rick Finocchi, Technical Reviewers
Jan Benes and Richard Cash, Text Design
Rhonda L. Smith, Composition
Yashi Okita, Cover Design

To Dan Israel and Joshua Noam Baras

Acknowledgments

I would like to acknowledge the following individuals for their advice and assistance:

Steve Miller of Lotus Development Corporation, whose review of the manuscript profoundly enhanced the quality of this book. A master of metaphor, common sense, and clarity, Steve's suggestions were, without exception, constructive and insightful.

Rick Finocchi, who reviewed the manuscript, giving generously of his time and expertise.

Jean Stein, whose editorial assistance went beyond the call of duty, and whose efforts helped keep the book on schedule.

Cindy Hudson, Acquisitions Editor, who guided this project skillfully.

Sondra Oster Baras, who reviewed the manuscript before it even left my pen, and who postponed (cancelled?) my household responsibilities during the manuscript preparation.

EB

Contents

Introduction

In the past, software users had to choose between power and ease. The most powerful programs were also the most complex and difficult to use, while "user-friendly" programs were often limited in power and scope.

Symphony erases this contradiction between capability and simplicity. Symphony's power is two-dimensional. Its capabilities are so broad that you can use the program for nearly any business project appropriate for a personal computer. Remarkably, Symphony's breadth does not detract from its power. Each of Symphony's business programs, or *environments*, offers as much capability as you would expect from a program dedicated to a single task. This book shows you how to make the most of those capabilities.

Five Integrated Environments

Symphony's five environments are the spreadsheet, database management, word processing, telecommunications, and graphics.

A *spreadsheet* is a grid of cells made up of columns and rows. Cells contain data in the form of words, numbers, or formulas. Symphony supports a spreadsheet of up to 8,192 rows and 256 columns (more than four times the potential capacity of the Lotus 1-2-3 spreadsheet). The size of Symphony's spreadsheet does not detract from its speed, however. Change some numbers, and the spreadsheet recalculates formulas instantly, so that you can test alternatives without waiting for an answer.

The Symphony spreadsheet includes more than 70 *functions*, built-in formulas that perform a variety of calculations — financial, statistical, calendar, logical, mathematical, and text-related. Furthermore, Symphony has extensive formatting capability to control the appearance of the spreadsheet, and its printing options provide complete control over reports.

Another strength of Symphony is *database management*. Database management lets you manage and manipulate information stored in electronic files. Subject to your computer's memory constraints, Symphony can store over 8,000 records of information (a record is a grouping of related information, such as an invoice or a library catalog card). Symphony can sort the information you store; it also lets you locate, extract, or delete information, and produce reports with subtotals and statistical summaries. You can even create an electronic form for entering or retrieving individual data records. Forms-oriented data entry and retrieval makes it easy to control the information stored in a database.

Don't get the impression that Symphony restricts you to numbers, formulas, and files. You can use Symphony's *word processor* to write memos, letters, or lengthy documents. Word processing is an important use of your personal computer, and Symphony makes word processing far more productive and simple than ordinary typing.

Reports, spreadsheets, and data files are not the only way to present data, however. Symphony includes an excellent *graphics program* that generates business-quality charts from data in the spreadsheet or database. If you change the data that underlie the graph, Symphony automatically revises the graph on the screen. Symphony also provides an impressive array of styles and features that let you produce professional-looking printouts.

The fifth Symphony environment is *communications*. With a modem and a phone line, your desktop computer has access to the world outside. Not only can you use Symphony to exchange files with other Symphony users at remote locations; you can also communicate with large computers, with electronic mail services, or with information services that provide access to vast sources of data. You can capture the information into the spreadsheet, or a printer, or both.

Individually, Symphony's five work environments provide the depth of capabilities that you would expect from five independent software products. Taken together, they give you the versatility you need for a wide range of applications.

Integration makes Symphony magical. It means that a single project can use more than one work environment. For example, you can use Symphony to manage a customer database, and integrate a word processed document with the customer file to create a form letter personalized for each individual in the database. This book will show you how.

Then again, you might create a manuscript that includes text, spreadsheets, and graphs, and submit it to your publisher via modem using the communications environment—which is precisely how this book was developed!

Integration works nicely in Symphony for a few reasons. First, data is shared among the separate environments in a single storage area, called a *worksheet*. Thus, if you create files in the database environment, you can also view them in the spreadsheet. Second, Symphony uses the same commands, wherever possible, in the different environments. That makes it easier to move from one environment to another.

A third feature that makes integration so easy in Symphony is *windows*, divisions of the screen that let you view more than one portion of the worksheet at a time. You can use windows to keep track of what happens in two different areas of one environment, as when you change a number in the upper corner of a spreadsheet and see what effect it has on the grand total, several rows down.

You can also use windows to view several different environments on your screen at once. For instance, you could display part of a database in one corner of the screen, reserve another corner for a spreadsheet summary of statistics derived from the database, use a word processing window to write a table based on the spreadsheet results, and display a graph in still another window on the same screen. As you might have guessed, if you change the information in the database window, the changes will be automatically reflected in the other windows. Even the graphs are redrawn.

When you add up all of Symphony's features, you can see just how much Symphony has to offer. Taken singly, each aspect of Symphony is easy to use. But there are so many facets that it is difficult to make the most of Symphony without a carefully structured approach.

Using This Book

Learning to use Symphony requires time, diligence, patience, and experience. That last ingredient, experience, is the key to this book. In the following chapters, you will gain experience using Symphony's commands and functions as you recreate the spreadsheet, database, graphics, and word processing examples presented here. You will also learn how integration works, as you move from one environment to another and begin using windows.

This book begins at an introductory level and moves quickly to cover many advanced Symphony concepts. It is written for both beginners and experienced users of Symphony. Beginners should start with the first chapter and proceed sequentially through the text. Readers who are familiar with Lotus 1-2-3, or who have some familiarity with Symphony, can skim through the first chapter and then work through the applications tutorials in the remainder of the book. Many commands and techniques will seem familiar, especially in the first five chapters, but there is also a lot that is new.

You will be learning to use Symphony by building applications one step at a time. Since the spreadsheet environment is the cornerstone of the Symphony program, the first application will make use of the spreadsheet. It is a *pro forma* income statement that projects costs and revenues over a period of five years. As you create this financial forecast in Chapters 2 through 6, you will be learning many basic commands and techniques, including copying, inserting columns and rows, setting titles, using windows, and printing. Chapter 7 teaches graphing, using the income statement as the basis for building a graph.

Chapters 8 and 9 use another spreadsheet application, a purchase order tracking system, to present some more advanced spreadsheet techniques. These chapters show you how to use the DOS add-in program, a program that lets you temporarily extend Symphony's capabilities to include the disk operating system commands. You will learn to use the @VLOOKUP function to tell Symphony to look for information in one part of the spreadsheet and use it in another area. You will also learn to use strings, string functions, conditional formulas, and several other @ functions.

Chapters 10 through 16 introduce database management. You will begin in Symphony's database environment, creating an electronic data entry form and learning to store and sort records and check their validity. You will also learn to use the spreadsheet environment to manipulate the database in sophisticated ways. By the time you have finished these chapters, it will seem quite natural to go back and forth between the database and spreadsheet environments. You will also have mastered several complex database management tasks, including querying, using multiple criteria to extract data, and creating a database report.

In the last two chapters, you will learn to use Symphony's word processor and then put to use your accumulated skills as you create an electronic form letter that automatically inserts information from the database each time it prints.

Finally, Appendix A shows you how to use *keystroke macros* — cells that store the keystrokes of Symphony commands and entries exactly as you would type them to execute a task. Macros are great time-savers for repetitive tasks: instead of entering the same keystrokes over and over again, you can simply invoke the macro you have stored, and Symphony will go through the paces for you. The macro application presented in Appendix A is designed for the model developed in Chapters 8 and 9, but the general procedure for creating and invoking macros is carefully explained.

By the time you finish this book, you should be an accomplished Symphony user, applying the concepts and techniques you've learned here to your own computer projects. Symphony can do much more for you, however. A second book, *Symphony™ Master: The Expert's Guide* (Edward M. Baras, Osborne/McGraw-Hill, 1985), will begin where this book ends, giving special attention to macros and the Command Language, the telecommunications environment, and many advanced techniques.

Chapter 1
Getting Started
With Symphony

Before You Start:
The Install Program

Booting Symphony:
Two Methods

The SHEET Environment

Menu Commands
And Services Commands

Checking Disk Storage:
The File Bytes Command

Exiting Symphony

As you prepare to use Symphony for the first time, keep one thing in mind: It will take time to become an advanced user, but you will get there. You will begin slowly, but by Chapter 2 you will be ready to begin developing a spreadsheet model.

In this chapter you will load Symphony and become acquainted with the Symphony worksheet. You will learn about the Access program, which provides access to three parts of the Symphony package: the Symphony program itself; the PrintGraph program, which produces hard-copy graphs; and Translate, the utility that allows Symphony to exchange data with other programs. You will also learn how to enter the spreadsheet environment and how to issue commands. In addition, you will find out how Symphony uses computer memory and disk storage and how to issue the commands that report the amount of space available in memory and on disk.

Before You Start: The Install Program

If you are the first person to use your Symphony package, you will have to prepare the program disks for use by going through a procedure called *Install.* The primary tasks of Install are to customize your Symphony program to work with your particular set of hardware and to tell Symphony how to treat graphics and text on the monitor during a Symphony session. This book will not attempt to guide you through the Install procedure; you should instead consult the Symphony *Introduction* manual. The actual steps differ from one computer's version of Symphony to another, and they are spelled out clearly in the manual.

Even if someone else has already installed your disks, read on. You will find it helpful to understand how Symphony creates Setup files with the information provided during the Install procedure.

Setup Files

After you give Install all the answers to the questions it asks about your system, it creates a *Setup file*—a special file that Symphony reads each time you load the program into your system. Without the Setup file, Symphony would not recognize what kind of system, printer, or monitor you are using.

Setup files have another purpose. Suppose you owned several computer systems. One has a monochrome monitor and a letter-quality printer. Another has a color monitor, an IBM Color Adapter, and a dot-matrix printer. The third has a high-resolution color adapter and a pen plotter. No doubt you would not want to go through the Install procedure every time you switched from one computer system to the other—and you don't have to. All you have to do is use Install to create three Setup files—one for each of your systems.

Even if you do not have multiple computer systems, Setup files can be useful. For example, if you have an IBM Color Adapter, there may be times when you want black-and-white graphics in *Shared Mode* (where graphics and worksheet share the screen) and other times when you want color graphics in *Toggle Mode* (where you toggle back and forth between the two). Setup files speak to this need.

Each of your Setup files must have a name, which either you or Symphony supply during installation. The Setup file that you use most often (or your original Setup file, if you have only one) should be named LOTUS.* When you go through the procedure, Install will request a name for the Setup file; and it will inform you

---

*The full name will be LOTUS.SET. Symphony automatically assigns the .SET extension to all Setup file names. When you enter a Setup file name, however, you only need to specify the first part of the name.

that if you don't supply a name yourself, it will automatically call the Setup file LOTUS. Install will otherwise use whatever name you specify. It is practical to choose a name that helps you remember the Setup file's function. For instance, you might name your file SHARED or TOGGLE.

The bottom line is that you should be aware of what names belong to what Setup files on your Symphony program disks. You will need to know these names and what their associated Setup files contain when you *boot*, or start, the Symphony program.

Booting Symphony: Two Methods

There are two ways to enter Symphony. Before you actually work with the spreadsheet, you will want to try both methods to see which one to use under what circumstances. The material in this section assumes that you are working with an IBM PC or PC-compatible computer with two floppy disk drives. If you own an IBM PC XT or some other computer, consult the Symphony *Introduction* manual for details on booting the program.

Before you can issue the command to enter Symphony, you must load the disk operating system of your computer. Note that if you are using an IBM PC, your version of DOS must be 2.0 or above in order to use Symphony.

better if reversed

1. With your computer off, place the DOS (Disk Operating System) disk in drive A.*

2. Next turn on your computer.

Turning on the computer and loading a program into it (such as the DOS program) is called *booting the system.* Depending on the type of computer you are using, you may be able to boot the system with the Symphony disk; and you should do so if possible. This would enable you to turn on the computer with the Symphony Program Disk in drive A and to enter Symphony without having to put in the DOS disk first. The Symphony *Introduction* manual explains how to install DOS on the Symphony Program Disk so you can boot Symphony automatically.

After a few moments, the drive will whirr and a message on your screen will request the current date (unless someone has placed a special startup program on your DOS disk that circumvents this prompt). You may inform the system of the date if you wish, or you may take a shortcut. Let's do the latter.

3. Press the RETURN key (the key marked ↵ on the right side of the PC alphabetic keyboard).

As you use Symphony with this book and on your own, you will need to use many keys that you may not be familiar with. To reduce the time you might later spend in searching the keyboard for an F6 or a PG DN, you should take a moment now to read "The IBM PC Standard Keyboard" (see box), which introduces the IBM standard keyboard and the notations used in this book.

---

*Throughout this book, all instructions that require you to type or enter commands are presented as numbered steps. To construct any of the application models quickly, you need only follow the numbered steps.

THE IBM PC STANDARD KEYBOARD

TAB   BACKSPACE RETURN

Function-   *Function*   SHIFT   *Typewriter keyboard*   SHIFT   *Numeric*
key   *keys*   *keypad*
template

Database,
spreadsheet
Spreadsheet
Communications
Spreadsheet,
word processing,
database

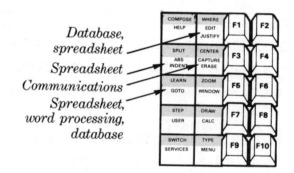

Shaded areas indicate that
you hold down ALT and press
the key.

    The illustration shows the IBM standard keyboard labeled to show several special keys used by Symphony.

    This book will use small capital letters whenever it refers to these special keys. For example, the "enter" or "return" key (the key marked ↵ on the right side of the keyboard) is represented in this book as the RETURN key. The key marked ⇥ is referred to as the TAB key, and ← is the BACKSPACE key. Other special key names will also be printed in small capital letters. For example, HOME is the key marked "Home" on the IBM PC keyboard, and PG UP is the "Page Up" key. The four directional arrow keys (←, →, ↑, and ↓ on the far right of the keyboard) are described in this book as the left, right, up, and down arrow keys.

    There are ten keys labeled F1 through F10 on the IBM PC keyboard. These are the *function keys*, and they have the special meanings that may

continued

vary depending on the environment that you are in. The plastic function-key template that comes with the Symphony package identifies what the various function keys do, both alone and in combination with the ALT key. Each function key will be explained later in the book.

The numeric keypad on the far right of the standard IBM keyboard serves two functions: it can be used to move the pointer or to key in numbers. However, the keyboard can perform only one of these two functions at a time. (Pressing the NUM LOCK key in the upper-right portion of the keyboard causes the numeric keypad to toggle back and forth between the two functions.) As a rule, it is best to reserve the numeric keypad for pointer movement only and to use the keys on the top row for entering numbers.

Pressing RETURN in response to the DOS date prompt brings another prompt from the system, this one for the current time. Again, ignore the prompt and

4. Press the RETURN key.

The DOS "A>" prompt is now displayed on the screen. This is the operating system's way of saying, "Your wish is my command."

5. Replace the DOS disk with the Symphony Program Disk in drive A.*

The Access Command

Your wish is to get into Symphony. One of the commands that do this is called the Access command. You enter it as you would enter a DOS command, by typing the command name in capital letters—but don't type it just yet.

Here is where those Setup files come in. The purpose of the Access command is to open the appropriate Setup file. If you are going to use the standard LOTUS Setup file, typing ACCESS by itself is enough. However, if you want to use a different Setup file created by Install, you must type ACCESS *setupname*, where *setupname* is the name of the Setup file you want. For example, typing ACCESS PLOTTER would tell Symphony to read the PLOTTER.SET file you customized to use Symphony with your pen plotter. If you make a typing error in the following step, press the BACKSPACE key to back up and erase it. Now,

1. Issue whichever Access command is appropriate for your needs, and press RETURN. (Pressing RETURN sends what you've typed to the computer.)

---

*Again, IBM PC XT users should consult the Symphony *Introduction* manual for the procedure that applies to the hard disk.

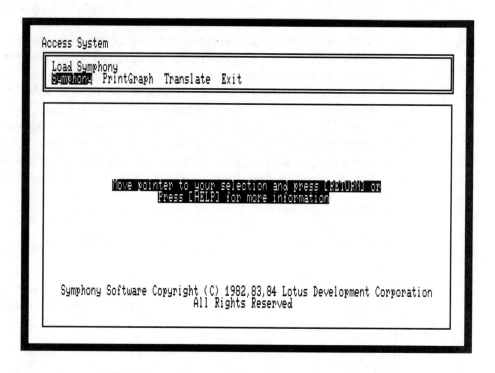

Figure 1-1. The Access System screen

The Access Program: What It Does

In response to the Access command, the screen clears and displays the Access System menu shown in Figure 1-1. You're not in Symphony yet, but you're standing on the front porch. From the Lotus Access System you can enter Symphony itself, print a hard copy of a graph created in Symphony (the PrintGraph option of the menu), transfer files between Symphony and some other program (the Translate option), or return to DOS (the Exit option).

Let's look more closely at the screen portrayed in Figure 1-1. The top line of the display indicates that you are in the Access System. Skipping to the third line, you see a menu of Access System commands, with a highlight (called the *menu pointer*) on the Symphony command option. The caption above the menu is a brief description of the command currently being highlighted. A message at midscreen informs you that selecting a menu option involves moving the menu pointer to an option and pressing the RETURN key. The arrow keys at the right side of your keyboard are the ones used to move the menu pointer.

1. Press the right arrow key (→) to move the pointer to the PrintGraph option.

The menu pointer moves to PrintGraph, and the caption above the menu changes from "Load Symphony" to "Load PrintGraph Program." Press the left arrow key (←); the pointer returns to the Symphony command.

Bear in mind that you will be seeing many menus like this one since Symphony is a menu-oriented system. The options in a menu may be selected by moving a menu pointer to the option you want and pressing RETURN. You may also select a menu option by typing the first letter of the option you want.

In a moment you will select the Exit option. But first, note that if you had chosen the Symphony option of the menu, you would have entered the spreadsheet environment. This is the second of a two-step process that brings you directly to the spreadsheet with the Access command: first you issue the Access command to enter the Access program; then you select Symphony to enter the spreadsheet.

2. Move the pointer to the Exit option and press RETURN.

You have returned whence you came: at the "A>" prompt of the operating system.

The Symphony Command:
An Easier Way

Using the Access command to enter the Symphony program gives you the opportunity to print graphs or translate files instead of going directly into the spreadsheet or some other Symphony work environment. It may have occurred to you by now that unless you need to print a graph or exchange a file between Symphony and another program, the Access System is superfluous. Most of the time you won't need Access. After you start up the system with the DOS disk and get the "A>" prompt, you'll want to bypass the Access System and enter Symphony directly. For this reason, there is another command to begin Symphony. It is the Symphony command, and it puts you directly into Symphony.

Typing SYMPHONY by itself (with the DOS "A>" prompt on the screen) loads the program with the default Setup file (named LOTUS). To use a different Setup file, type SYMPHONY *setupname* (again, *setupname* is the name of the Setup file).

1. Type **SYMPHONY**, followed by a Setup file name if you want to use one other than LOTUS.SET. Press RETURN.

Note that throughout this book, **boldface** print will be used to highlight character keys that you should type. Thus, **SYMPHONY** in the previous step appears in boldface.

Pressing RETURN causes the disk drives to whirr, and after a few moments, a copyright message appears. When the disk-drive light turns off,

2. Press RETURN again to get rid of the copyright message.

The SHEET Environment

Symphony has now opened the spreadsheet environment, called the *SHEET environment* for short. Figure 1-2 shows what your display should look like.*

Recall that there are five environments in Symphony: spreadsheet, word processing, database management, graphics, and communications. When you purchase Symphony, the Program Disk is already configured to establish certain *defaults* (options that are assumed by Symphony unless you instruct it otherwise). One of these factory-installed defaults is automatic entry into the SHEET environment. You will see that these default assumptions can be overridden if you choose. For now, though, SHEET is precisely where you want to be.

The large rectangle on your screen is the border of the SHEET window. The actual spreadsheet is far too large to be displayed in this window. Instead, the window shows a small portion of a vast expanse of columns and rows. You'll soon see just how vast the spreadsheet is.

Windows have names in Symphony. This one is called MAIN, a name supplied as a default by Symphony and displayed in the lower-right corner of the window border.

Two aspects of the display verify that you are indeed in the spreadsheet. First, the indicator at the top right of the screen says "SHEET". Second, the window contains column and row names, for a spreadsheet is made up of columns and rows. The top border of the window contains the letters A through H, identifying the leftmost screenful of columns in the spreadsheet. The numbers 1 through 20 along the left edge of the window are row indicators that identify the first 20 rows in the spreadsheet.

The Cell Pointer and the Control Panel

The cell in column A, row 1 is highlighted in reverse video. This highlight is called the *cell pointer.* It functions much like the menu pointer used in the Access System. The cell pointer points to a particular cell of the spreadsheet. You will use this pointer to explore the limits of the spreadsheet. First, though, you will learn about one more part of the display, the *control panel.*

The control panel occupies the top two lines of the display. One item of the control panel has already been pointed out: the indicator that says which environment you are in. In the left corner, the control panel displays the current address of the cell pointer. A cell's *address* is a coordinate that consists of two parts: the cell's column position and its row position. The coordinates must specify the column first and then the row. Thus, with the cell pointer in column A, row 1, the control panel displays "A1:". You will soon see that the control panel displays other information about cells. It is also used to display command menus, to make data entries into the spreadsheet, and to display and enter command prompts.

---

*If your display is different, your Symphony disk has probably been changed so that an environment other than SHEET appears on the screen when you first load the Symphony program. Consult the person who originally installed the Symphony system disks.

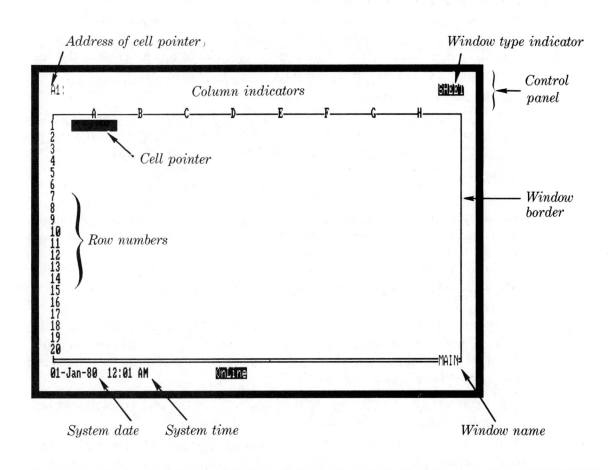

Figure 1-2. The SHEET window

Exploring the Spreadsheet

You will become more familiar with the control panel as you proceed through the steps in this book. It is also important to acquaint yourself with the spreadsheet, so turn your attention to that task now.

1. Begin by pressing the right arrow key once.

Look at the address in the top line of the control panel; it has changed to "B1:".

2. Press the right arrow key until the pointer reaches column H ("H1:" will appear in the control panel).

There's no more room on the right to move and still retain the same columns on the screen. To see what happens when you go past column H,

3. Press the right arrow key again.

Column I appears in the window; the pointer is in I1. However, because there is no room on the display for an extra column, column A scrolls off the screen at the left.

4. Press the right arrow key again.

You gain column J but lose column B. The right arrow key moves the cell pointer, which in turn pulls the window to the right.

Holding down an arrow key causes the keystroke to repeat. (This is the case with almost any key on the keyboard.) To see how this works,

5. Hold down the left arrow key.

The pointer moves to the left, eventually causing the window to shift to the left. The pointer cannot go beyond column A, though. If you try to move the pointer beyond any of the spreadsheet's limits, Symphony will sound a beep.

The up and down arrow keys move the pointer vertically.

6. Hold down the down arrow key until you reach row 30.

You can see that this arrow key can cause the window to scroll vertically downward. The up arrow key has the opposite effect.

Moving the Pointer Quickly

You could continue to use the arrow keys to move the cell pointer up, down, right, or left, but this would soon become tedious. There is a better way to travel. Luckily, Symphony has some nifty pointer-movement capabilities that transform the pointer into a speeding bullet.

1. Press the END key (located at the bottom left of the pointer-movement keypad, on the right side of the keyboard).

Nothing happens yet, but an "END" indicator appears at the bottom right corner of the display. The END key endows the arrows with temporary superpowers.

2. Press the down arrow key.

You will see the pointer instantly jump to the bottom row of the screen. If you look at the left border of the window, you will see the vertical limit of the spreadsheet: 8192 rows. Notice that the "END" indicator has disappeared from the display. Pressing an arrow key now moves the pointer just one cell over. The arrow keys react normally when the "END" indicator is absent.

The END-arrow sequence of keys causes the pointer to skip over a vertical or horizontal group of cells. If the pointer is on a blank cell, pressing the END key followed by an arrow key transfers the pointer to the next nonblank cell in the direction of the arrow. If the pointer is on a nonblank cell, pressing the END key followed by an arrow key moves the pointer to the nonblank cell before the next blank cell.

Since you have not entered any data into this spreadsheet, all cells are empty. Therefore, the END-down arrow sequence caused the pointer to skip down to the lower limit of the sheet.

Now try END with the right arrow.

3. Press END to get the "END" indicator to appear.

4. Press the right arrow key.

The pointer skips to column IV. How many columns is IV? To answer this question, you must know how Symphony uses the alphabet to identify spreadsheet columns. And to find this out, you must travel back to the beginning cell of the sheet and roam a bit more casually across the columns.

You have used the END key to move quickly through the spreadsheet. There's an even quicker way to move to the first cell, A1 (which is also called the *home* position): with the HOME key on the pointer-movement keypad.

5. Press the HOME key.

The cell pointer instantly moves to the home position. Your next step is to move across the worksheet by scrolling toward the right a screenful at a time.

Locate the CTRL key, toward the left side of the keyboard.

6. Hold the CTRL key down, and while doing so, press the right arrow key.

Now examine the column indicators. The screen has moved a *page*, or screenful, over to the right and now displays columns I through P. Try the same step again:

7. Hold down CTRL and press the right arrow key.

Now the screen displays columns Q through X. CTRL combined with a left or right arrow key moves the screen horizontally a page at a time. CTRL-right and CTRL-left are important key sequences to remember, since you will be creating models that use more than a window's width of columns.

You are up to column X, in the vicinity of the end of the alphabet.

8. Press the right arrow key by itself a few times, until you just pass column Z.

When Symphony has finished using the letters of the alphabet to indicate the first 26 columns, it begins the next sequence of columns with AA, AB, AC, ... AZ. The next sequence is BA...BZ, then CA...CZ, and so on through IA...IV. In all, there are 256 columns. The theoretical limits of the spreadsheet are 256 columns by 8192 rows, a total of more than 2 million cells.

If Symphony provides a page-left and page-right capability, it stands to reason that there is a page-up and page-down key sequence that moves the window vertically one windowful (20 rows) at a time. Actually, paging up and down is easier than paging horizontally, because a single key is assigned to each direction of vertical paging. The PG UP and PG DN keys (on the pointer-movement keypad) respectively move the window upward and downward a page at a time. Try them out.

The GOTO Function Key

Thus far you have explored six keys or key sequences that affect pointer movement: the four arrow keys, the END-arrow combination, the CTRL-arrow combination, PG UP, PG DN, and HOME. Before you move on to commands and menus, let's investigate one more means of moving the pointer: the GOTO key, which is F5 on the IBM PC keyboard.

GOTO asks you for a specific coordinate to send the pointer to and sends the pointer to the place that you specify. You will use GOTO to move to the bottom right of the spreadsheet.

1. Press the GOTO (F5) key.

Here and later in this book, a keyname from the IBM PC keyboard is placed inside parentheses after the Symphony keyname.

Symphony prompts you for the address to go to and suggests that you go to the address where the pointer is currently positioned. Nice try, Symphony, but that's not where the pointer is supposed to go. Its destination is column IV, row 8192. This translates into an address of IV8192. (*Note:* Do not use commas in row specifications greater than 999.) As soon as you type the I of IV8192, Symphony will remove its original recommendation.

2. Type **IV8192** and press RETURN.

Instantly, the pointer is in cell IV8192.

Menu Commands
And Services Commands

No matter what Symphony environment you are in, there is a single, uniform way of telling Symphony what to do. As you saw in the Access System, you issue commands by choosing an option from a menu of commands. To invite a command menu to the screen within Symphony, you must press a special key. Actually, there are two such keys, because there are two command menus available for your use in any Symphony environment.

Each of the five environments has its own specific *Menu commands*—commands that are particular to the context of the environment. The spreadsheet has a set of Menu commands, word processing has a different set of Menu commands, and so forth. The Menu commands are accessed by pressing a special key (appropriately, the MENU key), as you will see shortly.

In addition, there are certain commands, or services, that you can take advantage of no matter what environment you are in. These options are called *Services commands*, and they are accessed by pressing another key on the keyboard.

Invoking the SHEET Menu
Commands

Let's examine the SHEET environment's Menu commands first. To invoke the Menu commands for any environment, you press the MENU key (F10 on the IBM PC keyboard). Try it now:

1. Press the MENU (F10) key.

The second line of the control panel now contains the SHEET Menu commands:

Copy Move Erase Insert Delete Width Format Range Graph Query Settings

A menu pointer highlights the first command, Copy, and a brief description of the Copy command appears on the control panel's first line.

Move the menu pointer to the various commands, and read the description of each in order to get an idea of what you can do in the spreadsheet. Don't worry if the command descriptions aren't clear just yet; in the next chapter you will begin to work with the spreadsheet commands. Meanwhile, let's examine the Services commands.

In order to withdraw from the SHEET command menu, you must

2. Press the ESC key (at the top right corner of the IBM keyboard).

ESC is short for "escape," and as you work with Symphony, you will see that ESC can get you out of trouble in numerous instances and contexts. In general, think of ESC as the key that you can use to backtrack a step to the previous state of affairs. Before you invoked the SHEET commands with the MENU (F10) key, you were free to move the cursor around the spreadsheet. Pressing ESC now removes the menu from the control panel and restores the screen to the way it was before.

Invoking the Services Commands

To see what options are included in the Services commands,

1. Press the SERVICES key (F9 on the IBM keyboard).

A new menu leaps to the control panel:

Window File Print Configuration Application Settings New Exit

Once more the menu pointer highlights the first option, Window, and its description appears on the top line. This time let's satisfy our natural craving for power and issue a firm command.

2. Move the menu pointer to the Settings option and press RETURN.

The Settings option of the Services menu invokes a submenu of options that control some of the ways in which Symphony goes about its business. You are not going to alter these settings just yet; however, one result of selecting the Settings option should be noted right now. Beneath the control panel a new rectangular window has displaced the spreadsheet. Examine the first line of the new window; it tells you how much computer memory is available for use with Symphony and how much you have already used up. It even tells you how much memory is available as a percentage of the disk.

Memory is an important concept to understand in Symphony, since you must be able to gauge how much information you can store with this program. "Symphony and Your Computer's Memory" (see box) examines the relevance of computer memory and information storage to your everyday use of Symphony.

To return to the SHEET window, you have a few options. Pressing ESC will take you back one step; you would need to press the ESC key twice to clear the Services command menu from the screen. Alternatively, you can select the Quit option from the command menu.

3. Move the menu pointer to Quit and press RETURN.

Checking Disk Storage: The File Bytes Command

Turning off your computer will erase all the information in RAM, including any work you've done since you began the Symphony session. How do you store work permanently? By saving data onto a formatted diskette (or hard disk).

SYMPHONY AND YOUR COMPUTER'S MEMORY

In certain respects, a computer "remembers" very much as you do.

Suppose you are asked to write down all of the telephone numbers listed in Elyria, Ohio. You probably don't know any of the numbers, but there is an Elyria telephone book on your bookshelf. You open to the first page and read the first phone number; it jumps from the page into your memory. Once the number is in your memory, your main processing unit (sometimes known as your brain) can instruct the output device (your hand) to copy the contents of your memory onto a piece of paper. Next you find another number, load it into memory, and output it onto the list. When you get to the fifth number, you will probably have forgotten the first one. This happens because your short-term memory is transitory.

Your computer's memory is also transitory. Before you switch it on, its *random-access memory (RAM)* is blank. You may wish to use Symphony, but your machine doesn't recognize the program until you load the Symphony system from the Program Disk. Loading the program makes your computer the world's greatest expert in Symphony—but only temporarily. Turning off your computer or exiting from Symphony produces severe amnesia. All traces of the program are erased from RAM, and you must reload Symphony from disk in order to run it again.

Just as your computer's memory is temporary, it is also finite. The amount of memory available for Symphony, as reported with the Services Settings command described in this chapter, depends on how much memory has been installed in your computer. To function at all, Symphony requires a minimum of 320K of RAM (1K equals 1024 characters). The Symphony program itself takes up a majority of this amount. The remaining free memory (which is the amount shown in the Memory Available line of the Settings window) is used to store data and formulas in Symphony. If your worksheets are going to be large, they may not fit into the free memory remaining, in which case you may want to increase the amount of RAM installed in your machine.

Because of this memory constraint, you won't be able to realize the full potential of the 8192-row by 256-column spreadsheet. You may be able to use all of the rows but only some of the columns, or all of the columns but only some of the rows. The important point to remember is that memory limits the size of the worksheet that you can actually use in Symphony.

If memory is temporary storage, a disk is permanent storage. Even if memory is erased, you can retrieve your work by loading the disk back into memory. A disk records data just as a tape records sound. Unfortunately, the analogy between a disk and a tape goes further. As with tapes, it is possible to erase information from a disk, either deliberately or accidentally. A disk is also subject to damage.

Therefore, it is important to save your work often and to make backup copies of important files.

Let's see how much space is available for data storage on a typical floppy disk (or on your fixed disk).

1. Invoke the Services menu by pressing the SERVICES (F9) key.

2. Choose the File option.

Among the many things the File command can do is tell you the amount of space in bytes that is available on disk.

3. Choose the Bytes option of the File menu.

Symphony inspects the disk drive and reports the amount of free disk space that it has found. After taking note of the available disk space,

4. Press any key to continue the Symphony session.

On an IBM PC with a blank, formatted floppy disk in the disk drive, File Bytes detects 362,496 bytes. This means that before you put anything on a diskette, there is room for about 362,496 characters of information. It is highly unlikely that you would ever have a worksheet in memory that is larger than this number of bytes. As you fill the disk with files, though, the amount of free space on the disk will decrease. The File Bytes command will let you know when you are running out of space on a particular diskette.

Exiting Symphony

Now that you have loaded Symphony and gained a little experience with its commands, let's end this chapter by learning how to exit from the program.

Since ending a Symphony session is something you might do from any environment, it is logical that the Exit command is in the Services menu.

1. Press the SERVICES (F9) key and select Exit.

A prompt will ask whether you are sure you want to leave the current work session.

2. Select the Yes option.

If you used the Symphony command to enter Symphony from DOS, you will be returned to DOS (provided that the disk in the main drive is a system disk containing the COMMAND.COM file). If you entered Symphony through the Access program, you will be returned to the Access System menu.

Note that you don't have to select the Exit command to leave Symphony. If you are finished with a Symphony session and you have no need to exit into either Access or DOS, simply remove your diskettes and turn off your machine. The purpose of the Exit option is really to enable you to continue doing something else with your computer. If you have nothing else to do, there's no need to stand on formalities.

In this chapter, you learned how to begin a Symphony session, use menus, issue commands, and determine available storage space in memory and on disk. You also explored the limits of the spreadsheet environment and took a brief tour through the spreadsheet command menu.

The next chapter looks at the spreadsheet in detail. Never mind the fact that you haven't used the spreadsheet yet—the material to follow is much more ambitious. You will begin a comprehensive model that takes you deep into the labyrinths of spreadsheeting.

Chapter 2
Using
The Symphony Spreadsheet

Yorick Headgear Income
Statement: First Steps

A Formula for
Numeric Column Headings

Introducing
The Copy Command

Repeating Labels
And Underscores

Saving, Listing,
And Retrieving Files

This chapter, together with the next few chapters, develops a financial tool for forecasting the revenues, expenses, and profits of a business or service enterprise. In the process, these chapters serve as an introduction to basic spreadsheet concepts. You will learn how to enter and edit data, develop formulas, save and retrieve worksheets, copy cells from one part of the spreadsheet to another, format cells, and insert columns.

INCOME STATEMENT
YORICK HABERDASHERY, INC.
($ IN THOUSANDS)

Row	A	B (0)	C (1)	D (2)	E (3)	F (4)	G (5)	I (NOTES)
6	REVENUE	10000	12000	15600	18720	20592	22651	
7	% GROWTH OVER PREVIOUS YEAR		20.00%	30.00%	20.00%	10.00%	10.00%	
9	COST OF GOODS SOLD							
10	MATERIALS		2040	2652	3182	3501	3851	% OF SALES
11	WAGES		1680	2184	2621	2883	3171	% OF SALES
12	FRINGE BENEFITS		252	328	393	432	476	% OF WAGES
13	OTHER		100	108	117	126	136	% GROWTH RATE
15	GENERAL & ADMINISTRATIVE EXPENSE							
16	COMPENSATION: OFFICE		1200	1320	1452	1597	1757	% GROWTH RATE
17	COMPENSATION: SALES		960	1248	1498	1647	1812	% OF SALES
18	FRINGE BENEFITS		367	437	501	552	607	% OF OFFICE & SALES COMP
19	ADVERTISING & PROMOTION		300	390	468	515	566	% OF SALES
20	DEPRECIATION		20	20	20	20	20	DIRECT INPUT
21	MISCELLANEOUS		10	20	30	40	50	CONSTANT GROWTH
23	TOTAL OPERATING EXPENSES	6400	6929	8706	10282	11313	12446	
25	INTEREST EXPENSE	10	10	10	10	10	10	DIRECT INPUT
27	PRE-TAX INCOME	3590	5061	6884	8428	9269	10196	
29	TAX	1867	2632	3580	4383	4820	5302	% OF PRE-TAX INCOME
31	NET INCOME	1723	2429	3304	4045	4449	4894	

Figure 2-1. A preview of Yorick Haberdashery's income statement

Completing these chapters will give you a working knowledge of the spreadsheet environment, as well as a working model to use in forecasting the income statement of an organization. More important, you will have the necessary tools to develop your own spreadsheets for such applications as personal financial planning, budgets, cost projections, and checkbook registering.

Yorick Headgear Income Statement: First Steps

Congratulations! You've just been appointed Financial Oracle of Yorick Headgear, Inc., a manufacturer of dress hats to fit every skull. As Financial Oracle, you are responsible for predicting the financial performance of Yorick for the next five years.

One barometer of financial performance is the *pro forma income statement*, which is an enumeration of the revenues and expenses associated with an organization's operation in one or more future periods. The model will be based on assumptions relating to the change in each line item of the income statement over time. While your initial forecast will be reasonable, you must build a model that allows you to easily change the assumptions built into the forecast, since you will be trying out more than one set of predictions to see how the company is doing. The model will be applicable to many organizations, though it will focus on Yorick in particular.

Figure 2-1 gives you a preview of the type of pro forma income statement you will be developing. Step by step, you will make assumptions about Yorick's financial performance and use those assumptions to create the formulas that underlie the pro forma income statement. If the statement you develop on your screen does not always match the figure, don't worry. You will be making a number of adjustments as you go along.

Entering Labels Onto the Spreadsheet

Load Symphony as described in Chapter 1, and be sure that you have a formatted disk handy to store your work on. The first step in building Yorick's pro forma income statement is to enter titles that describe the information you are entering.

1. Use the arrow keys to move the cell pointer to cell C1.

Here you will enter the spreadsheet title INCOME STATEMENT. The words INCOME STATEMENT constitute a *label*, which is defined as a string of characters that form the contents of a cell. Before entering the label into cell C1, notice that the indicator at the top right of the control panel says "SHEET". This will change in a few moments. For now, though, Symphony is ready to accept data or to receive a command.

2. Press the CAPS LOCK key near the bottom right of the IBM PC keyboard.

The word "CAP" appears in inverse video at the bottom of the screen. While the "CAP" indicator is on, every letter you type will appear in uppercase. If you press the CAPS LOCK key again, the "CAP" indicator will vanish from the screen, and typing will revert to lowercase except when the SHIFT key is used.

When entering this label, it is most convenient to remain in uppercase mode. That way you need not bother with the SHIFT key to capitalize each letter. Note that CAPS LOCK affects only letters, not numbers or other keys.

3. Type the letter **I**.

Observe the mode indicator: it has switched from "SHEET" to "LABEL," because Symphony has guessed that you have begun to enter a label into a cell. The letter I is on the second line of the control panel, followed by a blinking cursor that indicates where the next character you type will appear.

4. Finish typing the title **INCOME STATEMENT** and press the RETURN key.

Pressing RETURN stores the label in cell C1 and restores the mode indicator to "SHEET", indicating that Symphony is once more on the alert for your next command or data entry.

If you discover a typing error before pressing RETURN, you can correct it by using the BACKSPACE key. If there are too many errors to bother correcting and if you have not yet pressed RETURN, you may escape from the situation by pressing the ESC key at the top left corner of the IBM PC keyboard. The ESC key totally negates the entry, as if you had never begun it in the first place.

Chapter 1 introduced ESC as a way to backtrack from an erroneous menu selection. Here ESC functions in a similar way but in a different context.

Once you press RETURN, the entry is stored in the cell. If you find an error in the entry, simply leave the pointer on the cell and retype the entry. Whatever you type will replace the previous contents of the cell when you press RETURN again. The next section shows another way to edit an entry that has already been stored in a cell.

Initially, each cell in the spreadsheet has a width of 9 characters. The INCOME STATEMENT title, however, is 16 characters wide, and so it does not fit entirely into cell C1. The last 7 characters spill over into the next cell, D1.

Notice the first line of the control panel. It displays the location of the pointer, cell C1, as well as the contents of this address. An apostrophe precedes the label. The apostrophe is called a *label-prefix*, and it serves as proof that the cell contains a label. You will learn more about label-prefixes later in this chapter ("Repeating Labels and Underscores").

To identify this spreadsheet further, you will add a second title line giving the name of the company to which this income statement pertains.

5. Go to cell B2 by pressing the GOTO (F5) key, typing **B2**, and pressing RETURN.

6. Type **YORICK HEADGEAR, INC.**, and then press RETURN to store the label in the cell.

Using Edit Mode

Perhaps you made a typing error somewhere in the second title. Even if you didn't, the board of directors has just decided to change the name of the firm from YORICK HEADGEAR, INC., to YORICK HABERDASHERY, INC. To change the contents of a cell, or in this case the spreadsheet title, you can use *Edit Mode.* You begin Edit Mode by pressing the EDIT key (F2 on the IBM PC keyboard).

1. With the pointer remaining on cell B2, press the EDIT (F2) key to begin Edit Mode.

Two changes immediately take place. The first is that the mode indicator now reads "EDIT". Edit Mode permits you to add to, delete from, or otherwise alter the contents of the current cell.

The second change is that the cell contents appear on the second line of the control panel, along with the blinking *edit cursor.* The edit cursor indicates the point at which the next editing action will take effect.

The edit cursor initially appears at the end of the cell contents. To change the contents of a cell, you need to position the edit cursor beneath the portion you want to edit and then type the characters to be added to the cell contents. When the edit cursor is at the end of the cell contents, the characters you type are appended to the end of the current contents.

There are several ways to move the cursor in Edit Mode. The left arrow key moves the underscore one space to the left; the right arrow key one space to the right. The TAB key moves the edit cursor five characters to the right. To tab left, hold down the SHIFT key while pressing the TAB key. The END key makes the cursor skip to the last character of the cell, whereas the HOME key skips to the first character.

2. Press the left arrow key 14 times to position the edit cursor beneath the H of HEADGEAR.

First remove the word HEADGEAR from the label. In Edit Mode, the DEL key (on the bottom right of the IBM keyboard) removes characters from a label. Pressing DEL deletes the character above the edit cursor. Thus, to delete HEADGEAR,

3. Press the DEL key until the word HEADGEAR disappears from the label in the control panel. (You will be pressing DEL eight times).

This leaves the cursor directly under the comma. To insert characters in Edit Mode, simply type the insertion. The characters you type will be inserted *before* the position where the cursor was pointing—that is, before the space.

4. Type **HABERDASHERY** and press RETURN.

This ends the edit and restores the "SHEET" indicator. The second title line is not quite centered beneath the first, but you'll fix that in the next chapter.

Entering Column Headings

The pro forma income statement will include six columns of data, as was shown in Figure 2-1. The first column will contain actual revenue and expense figures for the current year of operations. This period is referred to as Year 0. The next five columns will contain the forecasted results for the next five years of operations. Column A will be used for the row heading REVENUE. Therefore, Year 0 figures will be stored in column B, Year 1 in column C, and so forth.

You'll enter the headings for these columns in row 4 of the spreadsheet. Each heading will consist of the number corresponding to the year: 0, 1, 2, 3, 4, or 5.

1. Use the GOTO (F5) key to move to cell B4.

Here you will enter the heading for Year 0.

2. Type **0** with the zero key on the top row of the keyboard.

The character 0 is numeric, and Symphony considers it a value rather than a label. Notice the mode indicator. Symphony enters Value Mode because it knows that you pressed the number 0, not a character. The important distinction between Value Mode and Label Mode is explained in "Label Mode vs. Value Mode" (see box).

3. Press RETURN to complete the data entry.

Look at the control panel. Its first line reads "B4: 0." Observe that Symphony does not insert a prefix for values as it does for labels.

LABEL MODE VS. VALUE MODE

You can store two types of entries in a cell: *labels*, which contain text, and *values*, which contain numbers and formulas. Labels and values are treated in distinct ways. Label cells cannot contain formulas, and Symphony has particular ways of displaying labels on screen and on paper that differ from the way it displays values. Because the distinction between labels and values affects what Symphony can do with a cell, Symphony classifies each and every cell entry as either a label or a value.

Symphony uses the first character you type to decide whether your cell entry is a label or a value. For example, if your cell entry is the label REVENUE, you will begin the entry by typing R. When Symphony sees that you began the entry with a letter, it assumes your entry will be a label; so Symphony goes into *Label Mode*—anything you type for the rest of the cell entry is considered part of a label.

Conversely, if your intention is to store the number 100 in a cell, then as soon as you type the number 1, Symphony enters *Value Mode*, because it assumes that an entry beginning with a number is intended to be a value.

The following characters, when typed as the first character of an entry, place Symphony in Value Mode:

$$0\ 1\ 2\ 3\ 4\ 5\ 6\ 7\ 8\ 9$$
$$+ - .\ \$\ (\ @\ \#$$

All other characters put Symphony in Label Mode.

A Formula
For Numeric Column Headings

The heading for Year 1 could be entered in the same way that you entered Year 0's heading, by typing the number. This time, however, you will use a different method to see how Symphony uses formulas.

There are two types of values. One is a *number*, such as the zero you entered in cell B4. The other type of value is a *formula*. Think of a formula as an instruction for Symphony to perform a computation. When a formula is placed in a cell, Symphony stores the instruction, carries out the calculation according to the formula, and displays the results of the calculation in the cell. You will be learning to develop complex formulas to tell Symphony to carry out tasks for you. For the purposes of introduction, you'll develop a simple formula here to tell Symphony to fill in the remaining Year column headings. (This may be the easiest formula you'll ever use!)

1. Move to cell C4.

Because the income-statement years are sequential, the formula for each year after Year 0 can be expressed as 1 plus the previous year. Thus, the heading for Year 1 is derived from the formula 1+0=1. In terms of cell coordinates, the formula for the Year 1 heading can be entered as 1+B4. Upon receiving this formula, Symphony examines the value of cell B4 (which is 0), adds 1 to it, and stores the result of 1 at the current position of the pointer, C4.

2. Type the **1** key on the top row of the keyboard.

Notice that the mode indicator shows that Symphony has entered Value Mode, because the first key pressed for the entry is a number. Now continue entry of the 1+B4 formula:

3. Type **+B4** and press RETURN.

Pressing RETURN stores the formula, displays the result in cell C4, and resumes Ready Mode. The control panel indicates that the formula 1+B4 has been assigned to the cell.

If you were to use formulas to enter the headings for Years 2 through 5, you would find that the formulas are nearly identical. In each cell, the formula is 1 plus the value of the previous cell. The formulas are not *exactly* the same; the formula 1+B4 for Year 1 differs slightly from 1+C4, the formula for Year 2. However, because the formulas are similar, the *Copy command* can be used to copy the formula in C4 to another cell or to several other cells.

Introducing the Copy Command

The *Copy command* replicates a range of cells from one location of the spreadsheet (the *FROM range*) to another (the *TO range*). Ranges of cells are used frequently in Symphony commands and functions, so before you go on to experiment with copying, you should take a moment to read "Cell Ranges" (see box) to find out what Symphony considers a range and to learn how to refer to cell ranges.

CELL RANGES

A *cell range* is a rectangle of cells. This rectangle can be a row of two or more adjacent cells, a continuous column of cells, or a block containing two or more rows and columns. A single cell also qualifies as a range; it is a block made up of a single row and a single column.

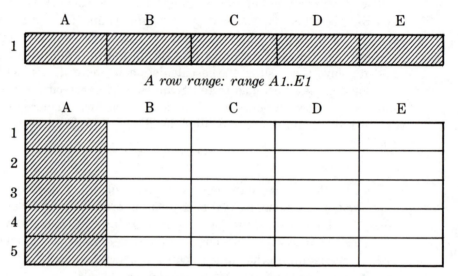

A row range: range A1..E1

A column range: range A1..A5

Symphony identifies a range by its first and last coordinates. As you will see later, there are several ways to specify a range. The row of cells from A1 through E1 is entered as A1.E1. The column from A1 to A5 is entered as A1.A5. Symphony allows you to type one, two, or three periods between the two addresses of the range. Thus, A1.E1, A1..E1, and A1...E1 all have the same meaning.

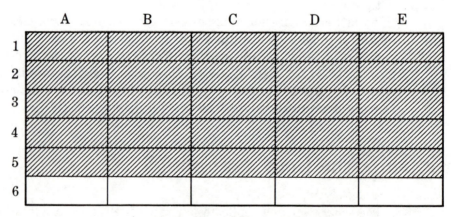

A rectangular range: range A1..E5

continued

A rectangular block of cells is fully described by specifying any two of its diagonally opposite corners. For example, a rectangle whose corners are A1, E1, E5, and A5 could be entered as A1.E5, E1.A5, A5.E1, or E5.A1. When Symphony sees one of these sets of coordinates, it realizes that the range's width spans columns A through E and that its length spans rows 1 through 5.

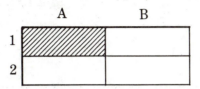

A one-cell range: range A1..A1

There is little choice in how to designate a single-cell range. The cell's address is both the beginning and the end of the range. For example, the range consisting only of cell A1 would be entered as A1.A1. Note that the cell address A1 is different from the range address A1.A1. In commands and formulas that require ranges, you would use A1.A1 to refer to a single cell as a range. In commands and formulas that do not require ranges, you would use the address A1, which is not a range.

These examples illustrate cell groups that are not single ranges. The first example doesn't qualify because it is not rectangular; the second, because the cells are not all contiguous.

How the Copy Command Works

The Copy command copies a source, called the FROM range, to a target called the TO range. Figure 2-2 summarizes the various types of replications you can produce with the Copy command.

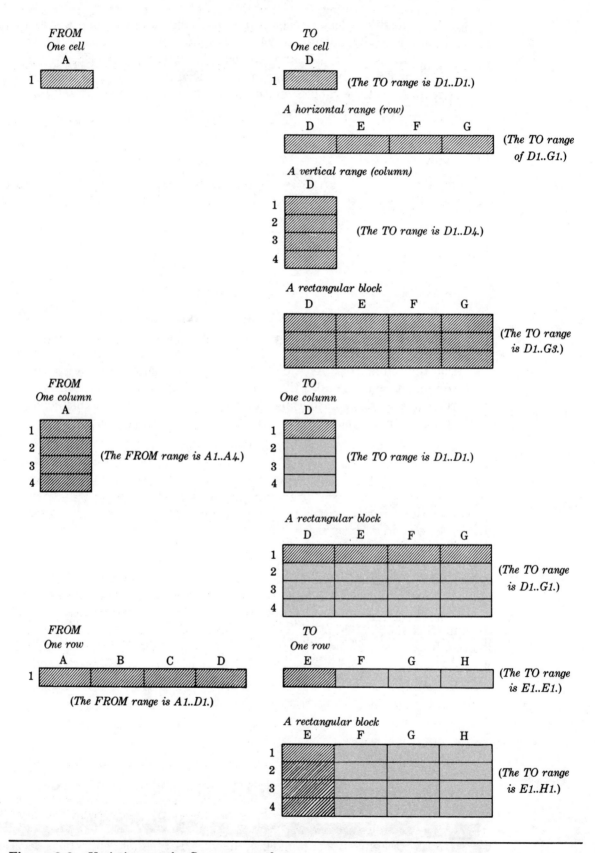

Figure 2-2. Variations on the Copy command

The Copy command generally involves four steps.

- First, move the pointer to the FROM range. If the FROM range is a single cell, position the pointer at that cell. If the FROM range is a range of cells, position the pointer at the top left cell of the range.
- Next, initiate the Copy command by pressing the MENU (F10) key to invoke the spreadsheet command menu* and then selecting the Copy command from the menu.
- Third, identify both the FROM and TO ranges in response to Symphony prompts.
- Finally, press the RETURN key to activate the copy procedure.

The simplest type of copy is from one cell to another cell. This is the type of procedure you will use to copy the formula stored in cell C4 (1+B4) into cell D4.

Copying to a Single Cell

To implement the four steps just described,

1. Position the pointer at cell C4, the FROM range.
2. Press the MENU (F10) key to invoke the spreadsheet command menu:

Copy Move Erase Insert Delete Width Format Range Graph Query Settings

The menu pointer highlights the Copy command.

There are two ways to select a command from a Symphony menu. You have already used the most intuitive method: pressing the arrow keys to move the menu pointer to the desired selection and then pressing RETURN. The other way is to type the first letter of the desired command. As you become more accustomed to Symphony, you will probably prefer the second method since it usually requires fewer keystrokes. For now, though, since the highlight is already on the command that you want to pick,

3. Press RETURN to select the Copy option.

Now Symphony gives the response "Range to copy FROM: C4..C4". (When Symphony displays a range, it always uses two dots between the two addresses, even though it allows you to use one, two, or three dots.) Symphony automatically assumes that the beginning of the FROM range is the cell where the pointer is located. It also recommends the same cell as the end of the FROM range. In other words, Symphony recommends a FROM range of a single cell, in this case C4. This is precisely the desired source, so

4. Press RETURN to lock in the FROM range.

---

*Lotus 1-2-3 users will note that the MENU (F10) key invokes the Menu command list in Symphony, whereas in 1-2-3 the / key has this function. Actually, you may use the / key to invoke the spreadsheet menu in Symphony as well. However, you may not use the / key for this purpose in other environments.

By the way, this is just one of many instances in which Symphony attempts to predict your next step. When you began the Copy command, there was no need for you to specify the beginning of the FROM range; Symphony supplied it for you. The assumption was that you placed the pointer at the beginning of the FROM range before initiating the command.

Now that Symphony knows the FROM range, it awaits the designation of the TO range by prompting "Range to copy TO: C4". By default, Symphony recommends the current pointer position (C4), but this is not what you want. The cell you would like to copy to is D4. One way of overriding Symphony's recommendation is to type the address of the TO range yourself.

5. Type **D4**.

This tells where you want the TO range to be. To signal to Symphony that you have finished entering the TO range,

6. Press RETURN.

The sum of 1+C4, which is 2, instantly appears in cell D4. The pointer remains at C4, its position prior to the Copy procedure. Move the pointer to cell D4 and inspect the control panel. The first line, indicating the contents of the cell, shows the cell's value to be a formula, 1+C4. Always remember that the spreadsheet cell shows the *results* of a formula. To see the formula itself, you must move the pointer to the cell and inspect the control panel.

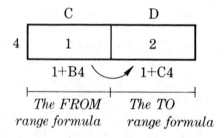

You may have noticed that Symphony's Copy command does not necessarily copy exactly. Although the FROM cell contained 1+B4, the TO cell contains 1+C4 after the copy. This is because Symphony performed a *relative copy* by replicating the *relative* positions of cells referenced in the source's formula. Relative copying is an important concept to understand. The boxed discussion, "Relative Copying," explains the concept in familiar terms.

Copying to a Range of Cells

To obtain the headings for Years 3, 4, and 5, simply use the Copy command to replicate cell D4's formula to cells E4 through G4. You do this by copying from a single-cell FROM range to a multiple-cell TO range. The first step is to move the pointer to the source of the copy, cell D4.

1. Move the pointer to cell D4.

Next begin the command.

2. Press the MENU (F10) key, and select the Copy option by either pressing RETURN or typing C (the first letter of the command).

RELATIVE COPYING

When someone stops you to ask directions to a street in your neighborhood, do you reply "78.634 degrees longitude, 42.981 degrees latitude"? It's not likely. You would be more apt to say something like "three blocks up, then two blocks to the right" than to give precise geographic coordinates for the destination. Your instructions would be *relative* to your present location.

Unless you tell it otherwise, Symphony also thinks in relative terms. That is why in "Copying to a Single Cell" Symphony interpreted the contents of the source cell in the Copy procedure as 1 + *the contents of the cell to the left of the source*, not as 1 + *cell B4*. The cell referenced in the source formula (B4) is interpreted in terms of its position relative to the source cell (C4). Therefore, when the formula is copied to the TO range (D4), it is copied as *1 + the contents of the cell to the left of D4*, so the target cell's contents become 1+C4.

Symphony recommends D4..D4 as the FROM range. Symphony's assumption is correct, so

3. Press RETURN.

The desired TO range is E4..G4, but Symphony is suggesting D4 in the control panel. There's no way for Symphony to make a reasonable assumption about where you want to copy to. In general, you will have to override Symphony's suggestion when you enter a TO range.

To type in a range explicitly, type the top left corner of the range first (E4). Next type a period, which signals to Symphony that you have finished specifying the beginning of the range and are about to type the end of the range. Last, type the address of the bottom right of the range (G4).

The period that you type between the two addresses of the range is called an *anchor*, because it has the effect of "anchoring" the first address as the beginning of the range.

4. Type **E4.G4** to specify the TO range.

5. Press RETURN.

The column headings for the forecasted years are now complete, and the cell contents should look like the following illustration.

	D	E	F	G
4	2	3	4	5
	1+C4	1+D4	1+E4	1+F4

The FROM range formula   *The TO range formulas*

Using formulas and the Copy command to produce these column headings may have seemed an unduly complicated substitute for entering numbers. However, the

Copy command is the cornerstone of electronic spreadsheets. Once mastered, it acts as a significant timesaver in applications development, as will be demonstrated in the next section.

Repeating Labels and Underscores

A good way to set off the column headings from the rest of the spreadsheet is with a line of hyphens. You can't put a series of hyphens within the heading cells themselves because the characters would replace the heading characters. However, it is possible to put a row of hyphens in the cells beneath the headings.

1. Press the GOTO (F5) key; then type **B5** and press RETURN.

This will place the pointer at cell B5, the cell beneath the heading for Year 0.

To fill the cell with hyphens, you would expect to press the - key several times. Try pressing the - key once and then examine the mode indicator.

2. Type the - key.

Note that Symphony is in Value Mode, even though you think you are entering a label. Remember that Symphony classifies a data entry by examining the first key typed—in this case, the - key. When Symphony sees a - as the first character of an entry, it assumes that you are about to enter a negative value (for example, −5). Here is an instance when you do not intend to enter a numeric character, but Symphony assumes a value. Therefore, you must override the default assumption.

First you must exit Value Mode. To do this,

3. Press the ESC key.

To override the program's default assumption that your - entry is a value, you must begin the entry by typing a label-prefix character.

Which label-prefix character? The apostrophe has already been introduced. When you entered titles earlier in this chapter, Symphony assumed they were labels and automatically inserted the apostrophe label-prefix. However, it is permissible to type the label-prefix yourself. Thus, one way to enter a string of hyphens would be to type '-----. Symphony would recognize the initial apostrophe as a label-prefix, enter Label Mode, and display only the hyphens in the cell entry. You could type as many hyphens as you wished.

Symphony provides an easier way using a different label-prefix. The \ (backward slash) label-prefix is used to make any characters that follow it repeat. For example, \- would cause the hyphen character to repeat, filling the cell with hyphens.

With the pointer still on B5,

4. Type the \ key.

Symphony enters Label Mode (check the mode indicator) and awaits a repeating label. Any character(s) you type before pressing RETURN will be repeated until the cell is full.

5. Type the - key and then press RETURN.

The \- could be used in each of cells C5 through G5 to underscore the rest of the headings. But you already know an easier way: the Copy command can be used to

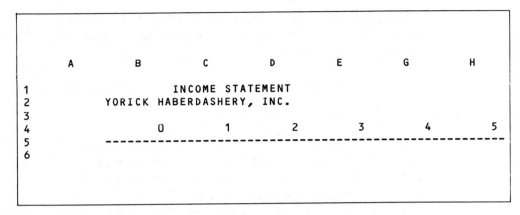

Figure 2-3. The income statement after the Copy command

save some keystrokes. (Copy can be used for labels as well as values.) The pointer is already on the source, so proceed with the command:

6. Press the MENU (F10) key and select the Copy command.

7. Press RETURN to accept B5 as the source.

The TO range is the range of C5 through G5, so

8. Type **C5.G5** and press RETURN.

Your spreadsheet should look like Figure 2-3.

Copy is an extremely powerful command. Imagine how useful it would be if the forecast covered 20 years instead of only 5.

Saving, Listing, and Retrieving Files

If you lose something valuable for no good reason, you have been "zapped." You might be zapped with a $45 ticket because you forgot to renew your automobile registration. Likewise, your worksheet might be zapped if the computer malfunctions or the electricity is interrupted even for a second, and you have neglected to save your file onto disk periodically as you developed your worksheet. Recall that the computer's internal memory is a temporary storage area that is automatically erased when you end a Symphony session. The only way to save a session permanently is to save it on a permanent storage medium like a floppy or hard disk.

The File Save Command

Like all zaps, the worksheet variety can be prevented with due care. The Services menu, which includes commands that are relevant to each of Symphony's environments, has a *File Save command* to store your work onto disk. File Save takes a "snapshot" of the worksheet at a particular point in time and stores the snapshot onto disk.

1. Press the SERVICES (F9) key to invoke the Services menu.

2. Select the *File command* either by moving the pointer to the File option and pressing RETURN, or by typing **F**. This brings the File submenu to the screen:

Save Retrieve Combine Xtract Erase Bytes List Table Import Directory

3. Select the Save option of the File menu.

In response to the program's "Save file name:" request, you must enter a file name. File names may be up to eight characters long, and they may include the letters A through Z, the digits 0 through 9, and some other characters, including the underscore (_). Spaces are not allowed.

Let's choose the name INC_STA, short for "income statement." Note that the underscore character (_) is a good substitute for a space, since the space character is not permitted in file names.

4. Type **INC_STA** and press RETURN.

It takes only a few seconds to copy the worksheet from memory onto disk. If your work is important to you, save it often.

Now there is a copy of the spreadsheet on disk as well as in RAM. Soon you will be making changes to the spreadsheet on the screen. Bear in mind that these changes will not be saved on disk until you explicitly resave the file with the File Save command.

The File List Command

How do you know for certain that the file was saved? One way is to issue the *File List command*, a Services option that lists the names of files stored on the data disk.

1. Press the SERVICES (F9) key to invoke the Services menu.
2. Select the File command; then choose the List option of the File menu.

This brings yet another submenu to the control panel:

Worksheet Print Graph All

Symphony has a special way of storing a worksheet file. Files can have first names and last names, known more technically as *prefixes* and *extensions*. The last name of the file (the extension) usually indicates a type of file, while the first name is a unique identifier of the file. When Symphony asked you for a file name in the File Save command, the name you supplied (INC_STA) was the file's prefix. However, Symphony automatically adds the extension WRK to the first name, so the full name of the file is INC_STA.WRK. When you actually use the file name in a Symphony command, you only refer to the first name. However, when you see a list of file names, you will see the extensions Symphony has assigned to them.

Choosing the Worksheet option of the File List menu would list files that have an extension of .WRK. Symphony also stores other types of files, called print and graph files, which have unique extensions of their own. However, the Print and Graph options of the menu do not concern you at present. The All option of the menu lists all files on the disk, regardless of their extensions. Let's try the Worksheet option for now.

3. Select the Worksheet option of the menu.

The screen temporarily clears and then shows a list of worksheet files. If INC__STA is the only worksheet on disk, it will be the only file listed. The control panel contains information about the file: its name, the date and time it was last modified (Symphony uses the system date and time, which you supplied when you first booted the system), and the size of the file in bytes.

To return to the SHEET screen,

4. Hold down the CTRL key (on the left side of the IBM PC keyboard) and press BREAK (on the top right corner of the IBM PC keyboard). Alternatively, you can press the ESC key several times until the "SHEET" indicator appears.

The File Retrieve and New Commands

If a file is listed in the file directory, it exists on the disk. Therefore, there's no harm in erasing the worksheet from memory, because you can always retrieve the file from disk. To see how this works, let's first erase the current worksheet from memory and then retrieve the file. The command to erase the worksheet from memory is New, and it is part of the Services menu.

1. Press SERVICES (F9) and select the New option.

Since using the New command carelessly is one of the primary causes of worksheet zap, Symphony tries to prevent a mishap by asking if this is really what you want to do. Let's take the plunge.

2. Select the Yes option.

This clears the screen. You may try as you will to scroll around the window in search of the Yorick spreadsheet, but it is gone. Alas, poor Yorick...

There is life after death, however, in the form of the File Retrieve command.

3. Press SERVICES (F9); select File; then select Retrieve.

Symphony requests the name of the file you want to fetch. It also looks at the list of worksheet files on the disk, reproduces this list in the control panel, and places a highlight on the first (and perhaps the only) file name in the list. Now you have a choice. If you like, you may type the name of the file you want to retrieve. Alternatively,

4. Place the highlight on the file you want to retrieve (if it's not there already) by using the arrow keys. Then press RETURN to load the file from disk into memory. Yorick lives again!

Chapter 3
Using Formulas
And the Copy Command

———————————————————————————————

———————————————————————————————

———————————————————————————————

Building Yorick's Revenue
Forecast

Improving the Spreadsheet's
Appearance

Calculating the Cost
Of Goods Sold

Absolute Versus Relative
Copying

Saving the Worksheet

In this chapter you will continue to develop the income statement forecast that you began in Chapter 2. Here you will learn how to enter cell addresses in formulas and commands by pointing to cells, how to recalculate projections automatically, and how to change the format of the spreadsheet. You will also learn how to change a column's width and erase spreadsheet cells. In addition, you will increase your familiarity and dexterity with the Copy command.

If you do not have the Income Statement worksheet on your screen currently, retrieve it from disk by pressing the SERVICES key (F9), selecting File Retrieve, typing **INC—STA**, and pressing RETURN. Your screen should look like Figure 2-3. Thus far, you have entered the title and column headings of the spreadsheet; you will continue by forecasting the revenue of Yorick Haberdashery, Inc.

Building Yorick's Revenue Forecast

The stream of revenues that a company receives for its product depends on various factors. Demand, of course, is a primary factor; the state of the economy is another. Price increases must also be taken into account in predicting sales, and returns of merchandise must be deducted from sales to arrive at a net figure. If historical figures are available, past trends can be used to forecast revenue. Inasmuch as you have no historical data on Yorick, you must make your own assumptions as to how revenues will grow.

For the first run of the model you will assume high growth in the first two years, less growth in the third year, and stabilized growth in the fourth and fifth years.

Management predicts that year-to-year revenue growth will be as follows:

YEAR	% GROWTH OVER PREVIOUS YEAR
1	25%
2	30%
3	20%
4	10%
5	10%

This scenario may be an optimistic one, particularly considering the high growth rates in the first three years. Later you may choose to change these growth rates. It is therefore important to build the spreadsheet with a liberal amount of flexibility so that changing assumptions won't require you to build another model.

To begin the revenue forecast,

1. Press CAPS LOCK, move to cell A6, and then enter the row label **REVENUE**.

You don't necessarily have to press RETURN to store a formula. Pressing an arrow key to move to another cell also stores the formula. Since you are going to move to another cell anyway, you can omit pressing RETURN.

2. Move the pointer to Year 0 REVENUE (cell B6).

3. Enter **10000** (no commas).

The figures used in this statement are expressed in thousands of dollars, so that 10,000 actually means $10 million. To make this clear, you will need to put the label ($ IN THOUSANDS) in the right corner of the spreadsheet. Since the label begins with a parenthesis, which Symphony interprets as the beginning of a formula or value, you must precede the label with a label-prefix, the apostrophe.

4. Move to cell F1.

5. Type **'($ IN THOUSANDS)** and press RETURN.

As soon as you enter the apostrophe, Symphony enters Label Mode. Any further alphabetic or numeric entries are treated as part of a label.

Projected growth for Year 1 is 25 percent of the previous year's net sales of $10,000. Year 1 sales are therefore 1.25*$10,000, or $12,500. (Symphony uses an asterisk, *, to indicate multiplication and a slash, /, to indicate division.) In fact, each year's sales can be expressed by the formula (1 + *percentage rate*) * *previous year's revenues.*

Parentheses enclose the first term of this formula to avoid ambiguity. If there were no parentheses, it would not be clear whether the rate is first added to 1 and the result multiplied by the previous year's revenue (correct), or whether the rate should first be multiplied by the previous year's revenue and the result added to 1 (incorrect). In fact, without the parentheses, Symphony would not interpret the formula the way you intended. Its reference manual describes what Symphony does when parentheses are omitted. You will find it wise to cultivate the habit of using parentheses whenever there is any ambiguity in a formula.

Each period's revenue will be derived in a similar way—a situation that implies that you can use the Copy command. If you were not worried about later changes in annual growth rates, you could input equations into each year column, such as 1.25*B6 for Year 1, 1.30*C6 for Year 2, 1.20*D6 for Year 3, and so forth. However, you may decide that Yorick's revenue will grow at 20 percent in Year 1 instead of at 25 percent. This would require you to change the Year 1 formula by either reentering it or editing it. If you decided to change several growth rates or to investigate several sets of growth rates, you would have to reenter the formulas each time you wanted to make a change. This kind of inconvenience is not what you are looking for in a flexible model.

A different approach allows such alterations. Instead of putting the rate inside the revenue formula (as you would by storing 1.25*B6 in Year 1), you will store the growth rate in a separate cell of the spreadsheet and create a revenue formula that refers to the rate cell. For example, if you stored the Year 1 growth rate of 25 percent (0.25) in cell C7, the Year 1 revenue formula would be rewritten as (1+C7)*B6. The revenue formulas for the other years would be constructed in a similar way.

If a rate must be changed, the rate cell will be altered, but none of the formulas referring to that cell will need revision. For example, to change the growth rate for Year 1 from 25 to 20 percent, you would only have to put 0.20 in cell C7, the rate cell. Symphony would then do the work of figuring out the new revenue based on the revenue formula (1+C7)*B6. In this way, the revenue growth rates can easily be varied.

Let's place the rate for Year 1 just below the cell containing Year 1 revenue.

6. Move the pointer to cell C7, the cell beneath Year 1 REVENUE.

7. Type **.25** and press RETURN to store a 25 percent growth rate.

The revenue formula, stored in the Year 1 REVENUE cell, should be (1 + *cell below revenue amount*) * *previous year's revenue.* With Symphony, it is easy to enter such a formula.

Entering Formulas by Pointing

When you are dealing with a small spreadsheet, it is no effort to specify cell coordinates in formulas or commands. Larger spreadsheets present a problem, however. Unless your mind is equipped with 5 megabytes of RAM, you may have trouble remembering the exact address of a particular cell when you need it.

Suppose you were developing this income statement with pen and paper and someone asked you to show where Year 0 REVENUE is listed. You would not say "second column, sixth row," even though this is a valid way of describing the location. Instead, you would point to Year 0 REVENUE and say, "Here."

Electronic spreadsheets are supposed to be at least as easy to use as manual ones, and cell referencing should be no exception. This is true of Symphony. It allows you to reference cells by *pointing* to them rather than by specifying their addresses. When you need to refer to a cell, use the arrow keys to place the pointer on that cell. Symphony knows where the pointer is and figures out its address. Once you know how to use the pointer to refer to cells, you rarely have to think in terms of column letters and row numbers. You will use pointing to enter the formula for Year 1 REVENUE.

1. Move to the Year 1 REVENUE cell (C6).

The formula is (1 + *cell below*) * *cell to the left*, so

2. Type **(1+**.

Now instead of typing the address of the cell below, use the arrow keys to move the pointer to the cell below.

3. Press the down arrow key once to move the pointer to the annual growth rate cell (C7).

Do not type anything else yet. First examine the mode indicator. The word "POINT" means that Symphony understands that it is in Point Mode; you can now use the arrow keys to position the pointer to the cell whose address you would otherwise have had to type. Now look at the second line of the control panel. So far it contains (1+C7.

Note that Symphony itself supplied the address C7; there was no need for you to know the cell address. Pointing is a very natural way of using the spreadsheet. With pointing, you think in terms of "Year 1 REVENUE" rather than "C6."

The formula (1 + *rate*) * *Year 0 REVENUE* has not been completed.

4. Type **)** to complete the first expression of the formula.

The pointer returns to its initial position at the Year 1 REVENUE cell.

5. Type * to indicate multiplication.

Once more you must refer to a cell, and again you can utilize the pointing capability.

6. Press the left arrow key once to point to the Year 0 REVENUE cell (B6).

The control panel now shows (1+C7)*B6. This is what you want, so

7. Press RETURN to conclude the formula entry.

The result is 12500, or $12.5 million revenue in Year 1.

Copying to a Range by Pointing

To complete the revenue forecast, you must enter the other annual rates in the cells below the annual revenues, and then copy the Year 1 REVENUE formula to Years 2 through 5.

1. Enter the annual growth rates **.3, .2, .1,** and **.1** into the annual growth rate cells (D7, E7, F7, and G7, respectively).

Notice that Symphony displays .3 rather than .30. Unless you tell it otherwise, Symphony displays only the digits necessary to show the number accurately. You will tell it otherwise later on.

Now you're ready to copy the rest of the revenue formulas.

2. Move the pointer to the Year 1 REVENUE cell (C6), the source of the copy.

3. Press MENU (F10); then select Copy.

4. Press RETURN to designate the Year 1 REVENUE cell (C6..C6) as the FROM range.

Symphony is now awaiting the target, which is the range of revenue cells for Years 2 through 5. Instead of trying to determine the beginning and ending coordinates of the range, you can simply point to them. You do this by pointing to the beginning of the TO range, typing a period to anchor the beginning of the range, and then pointing to the end of the range.

5. Move the pointer to the Year 2 REVENUE cell (D6), the first cell in the row of TO range cells.

6. Type a . to anchor the range.

7. Move the pointer to the Year 5 REVENUE cell (G6), the last cell in the range.

Notice how the pointer expands to highlight the entire TO range. This is how Symphony lets you know exactly where the TO range is.

8. Press RETURN to activate the Copy command.

Figure 3-1 shows the forecasted revenue stream along with the underlying rates.

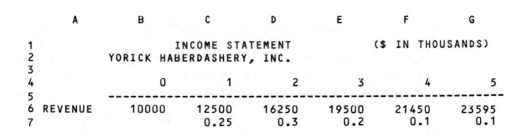

	A	B	C	D	E	F	G
1			INCOME STATEMENT			($ IN THOUSANDS)	
2		YORICK HABERDASHERY, INC.					
3							
4			0	1	2	3	4	5
5							
6	REVENUE	10000	12500	16250	19500	21450	23595
7			0.25	0.3	0.2	0.1	0.1

Figure 3-1. Revenue forecast for Yorick Haberdashery

Recalculating Projections
Automatically

One of the principal features of an electronic spreadsheet is *automatic recalculation*. When the contents of a cell are altered, other cells that depend on the altered cell automatically reflect the change. Suppose you decide that 25 percent growth in Year 1 is too optimistic a projection. Changing the revenue growth rate in Year 1 necessitates changing the rest of the forecasted revenues, because each year's revenue depends on the previous year. The growth rate can be changed simply by placing the pointer at the appropriate rate cell in row 7 and entering the revised growth assumption. For example:

1. Move the pointer to Year 1's rate cell (C7).
2. Type .2 and press the RETURN key.

This will change the growth rate of Year 1 to 20 percent.

Look at the new revenue numbers on your screen. As soon as you pressed the RETURN key, the numbers changed. Year 1 REVENUE became 12,000, a 20 percent increase. Without any further instructions, Symphony automatically recalculated the revenue growth projections for Years 2 through 5.

You might want to try out some other growth rates. If so, make sure that you conclude by entering the same set of rates that you have used up to this point: 0.2, 0.3, 0.2, 0.1, and 0.1.

Improving the Spreadsheet's
Appearance

The spreadsheet works quite well now, accommodating yearly variations in growth rates. The income statement's appearance could be improved, however. It is time to use two of Symphony's features, the Format command and Edit Mode, to improve the spreadsheet's appearance.

Using the Format % Command

Although the growth rates should be in decimal form for purposes of the revenue formulas, you might prefer to display them in percentage format (for example, 20% instead of 0.2). This may seem to be a matter of aesthetics, but it is also important for clarity. With Symphony, it is easy to make this change.

The *Format command* assigns display characteristics to one or more cells.

1. Move to the first cell to be formatted, the Year 1 growth rate (C7).
2. Press the MENU (F10) key and select Format.

The Format menu will appear in the control panel. This menu consists of a variety of display formats:

Currency Punctuated Fixed % General Date Time Scientific Other Reset

You will experiment with many of these formats in this book. For now you will use the % option, which formats a cell by multiplying its contents by 100 and appending a percent sign (%) to it. For example, a cell containing 0.200333 can be displayed as 20%. You can even control how many decimal places are displayed in the formatted number (for instance, 20.0, 20.03, or 20.0333 percent).

3. Select %.

Now Symphony requests the number of decimal places to be displayed *after* the cell contents are multiplied by 100. The default recommendation of two decimal places will serve nicely, so

4. Press RETURN.

Now you must designate the range of cells you want to format as percentages. The control panel displays "Range of format: C7..C7". Notice that Symphony assumes that the beginning of the range is the cell where the pointer was located prior to the Format command.

All Symphony needs is the end of the range. If the end were the same as the beginning—that is, if you wanted to format only one cell—you would press the RETURN key at this point to complete the command. Otherwise, you can point to the end of the range, as you shall do next.

When you explored the spreadsheet's borders in Chapter 2, you used the END key to move through the spreadsheet quickly. Pressing the END key causes the "END" indicator to appear in inverse video on the bottom right of the screen.

When this indicator appears, the arrow keys take on a different function. If the pointer is on a blank cell, pressing the END key followed by an arrow key transfers the pointer to the next nonblank cell in the direction of the arrow. If the pointer is on a nonblank cell, pressing the END key followed by an arrow key moves the pointer to the nonblank cell before the next blank cell. Once the END-arrow key sequence has been entered, the "END" indicator vanishes, and the arrow keys resume their normal functions.

5. Press the END key.

6. Press the right arrow key.

The pointer expands to the end of the row of consecutive nonblank cells; in this instance, the pointer shifts to the annual growth rate for Year 5.

7. Press RETURN to activate the Format % command.

Figure 3-2 shows the new format. Do not be deceived by looks: the actual contents of the cells are decimal numbers that have *not* been multiplied by 100. The Format command affects only the *display* of the cell; it does not affect its actual contents. Thus, Year 1 REVENUE is still computed as $(1+0.25)*10000$ rather than $(1+25.00)*10000$.

Using the Width Command

As a measure of clarity, you will next assign a row label to identify the row of growth rates. The label will be % GROWTH OVER PREVIOUS YEAR, and it should be indented three spaces.

1. Move the pointer to the cell beneath the REVENUE label (A7).

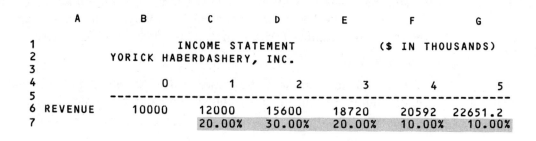

Figure 3-2. Rate cells after the Format % command

2. Press the space bar three times.

3. Type % **GROWTH OVER PREVIOUS YEAR.**

4. Press RETURN.

Something is rotten in the state of Denmark. The label is truncated on the spreadsheet, even though the control panel shows that the entire label was accepted into cell A7. Why was the label shortened here, whereas nothing like this occurred when you entered the income statement titles?

Recall that each column of the spreadsheet is nine characters wide. If a label is longer than nine characters, the remaining part of the label spills over into the cells to the right—if the cells to the right are blank. Cell C7 is not blank, so the label is truncated in the spreadsheet display.

You will need to enter other long labels into this column later on, so it would be best to expand column A. The *Width command* is used to expand or contract the width of any column in the spreadsheet.

With the pointer in the column whose width is to be changed (column A),

5. Press the MENU (F10) key and select the Width option.

The Set and Restore options of the resulting menu permit you to set the width to a new value or to reset the width to the default value. Currently, the *global*, or general, column width defaults to nine characters (although even this default can be changed with the Settings option of the spreadsheet command menu).

6. Choose the Set option.

Now Symphony requests the new width and suggests the current setting of 9. To maintain the current setting, you would press RETURN.

There are two ways to revise the current width. One is to enter the new width explicitly (for instance, type 30 and press RETURN); the other is to use the pointing method.

With the pointing method, pressing the right arrow key expands the pointer to a new width. As you continue to press the right arrow key, the control panel displays the new width of the pointer (and of the column). When the width is

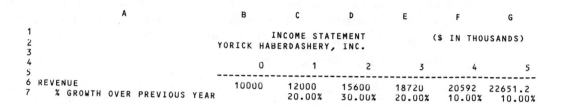

	A	B	C	D	E	F	G
1			INCOME STATEMENT			($ IN THOUSANDS)	
2		YORICK HABERDASHERY, INC.					
3							
4			0	1	2	3	4	5
5		--					
6	REVENUE		10000	12000	15600	18720	20592	22651.2
7	% GROWTH OVER PREVIOUS YEAR			20.00%	30.00%	20.00%	10.00%	10.00%

Figure 3-3. Expanded column A after the Width command

suitable, pressing RETURN assigns the new width to the column. When changing the column width significantly, as you are, typing the new width explicitly is more convenient.

7. Type **30** and press RETURN.

Column A's width is now wider than the default of nine characters, and the entire label is visible in cell A7, as shown in Figure 3-3.

Using Edit Mode to Center a Label

Before you continue with the income statement, let's make one final change to the appearance of the current spreadsheet. You will use Edit Mode to center the label YORICK HABERDASHERY, INC., beneath the first title line, INCOME STATEMENT.

Because the second title line is longer than the first, you began it one column to the left (in Column B) so that it would end up centered beneath the first title line. Unfortunately, the company name is not quite long enough to be perfectly centered below the INCOME STATEMENT title. The label INCOME STATEMENT is 16 characters long, while YORICK HABERDASHERY, INC., is 25. The difference of 9 characters means that the second title line must begin 4 spaces to the left of the top line in order to be centered. However, you placed the second title line in the column preceding the first title line, and because each column of the spreadsheet has a default width of 9 characters, you began 5 spaces too far to the left. You need to insert 5 spaces in front of the YORICK HABERDASHERY, INC., label. This is accomplished by using Edit Mode.

1. Move to cell B2 and press the EDIT (F2) key to enter Edit Mode.

You want to insert spaces at the beginning of a label, so you must move the edit cursor to the far left of the cell's contents.

2. Press the HOME key.

The edit cursor now appears at the beginning of the cell's contents, under the label-prefix. Any entry you make at this point will be inserted before the apostrophe, causing the apostrophe and all characters to its right to shift to the right. However, it is not your intention to insert spaces before the apostrophe. Because the label actually begins after the apostrophe, you must position the edit cursor after the apostrophe, beneath the letter Y of YORICK.

3. Press the right arrow key once.

Now insert the spaces:

4. Press the space bar five times.

5. Press RETURN to conclude editing.

So far you've been happily projecting revenues, but now it's time to come down to earth. There are expenses in this company, and they have deleterious effects on its beloved profits. These expenses fall into a few broad categories, including cost of goods sold, general and administrative expenses, and taxes. In the remainder of this chapter and in Chapter 4, you will be figuring these expenses into your projections.

Calculating the Cost of Goods Sold

Expenses that are clearly associated with the goods produced are classified under *cost of goods sold*, which is defined as the sum of costs that directly enter into the production of the items sold. Production materials are a significant manufacturing cost for Yorick. The wages and fringe benefits paid to factory workers are the second and third ingredients in the cost of goods sold. In the model, you will include the three major expenses, and you will add an "other" category to include the remaining cost of sales.

Materials used in production are generally a function of sales. If sales are high, more goods are sold and more material is used to produce the goods. Low sales dictate less use of materials. It is reasonable, therefore, to forecast material expenses as a percentage of sales. For example, based on the opinions of market analysts, the past performance of Yorick, and the history of similar manufacturing firms, Yorick expects material costs to amount to 16 percent of sales in each of the five forecast years.

Cost of Goods Sold as a Fixed Percent

One way of setting material expenses at 16 percent of revenue is to enter the appropriate formula into the Year 1 material-expense cell and then to copy this formula to the material-expense cells of Years 2 through 5. Because materials represent a cost of goods sold, you will first enter the COST OF GOODS SOLD heading. Then you will enter the label MATERIALS, indented three spaces.

1. Move to cell A9 and enter the label **COST OF GOODS SOLD**.

2. Move to cell A10.

3. Press the space bar three times, type **MATERIALS**, and press RETURN.

The formula for Year 1 MATERIALS is 0.16 * *Year 1 REVENUE*. Use the pointing facility to enter the formula as follows:

4. Move to the Year 1 MATERIALS cell (C10).
5. Type **.16*** to begin the formula.
6. Move the pointer to the Year 1 REVENUE cell (C6).
7. Press RETURN.

Next you will replicate this formula into the remaining forecast years in the same way that you copied the revenue formula. With the pointer already positioned on the FROM range (cell C10),

8. Press the MENU (F10) key and select Copy.
9. Press RETURN to accept the present pointer position (C10) as the FROM range.
10. Move the pointer to the beginning of the TO range (Year 2 MATERIALS, at cell D10).
11. Type a . to anchor the range.
12. Move the pointer to the end of the TO range (Year 5 MATERIALS, at cell G10).
13. Press RETURN.

The results are displayed in Figure 3-4.

A Variable-Rate Formula for Cost Of Goods Sold

The method you just used is one way of calculating material expenses. However, it is always worthwhile to make a spreadsheet as flexible as possible, and the method you used is not the most flexible. What will happen if Yorick's 16 percent

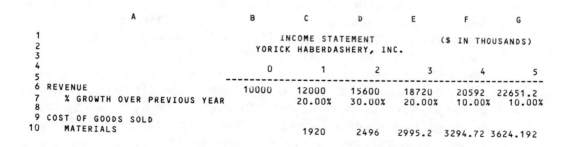

Figure 3-4. Income statement showing materials expense

estimate for material expenses is unrealistic? You will then have to reenter the entire Year 1 MATERIALS formula and then recopy it to the remaining years. There is a more efficient way to design the model.

When you developed the forecasting method for revenue, you used two rows: one for the revenue itself and the other for entering growth rates. This strategy permits you to change any one year's growth without having to change its revenue formula. The revenue formula itself refers to a rate cell whose contents can be varied without affecting the formula.

You can apply a similar concept to the material-expense formula. Instead of entering a fixed-rate formula like 0.16 * *revenue*, you will enter a variable-rate formula: the rate cell times the revenue cell.

Storing the percent of revenue in a cell and referring to that rate cell in the material-expense formula allows you to alter the rate without altering the formula. However, because the percent of revenues is going to be the same for all years (for example, 16 percent for Years 1 through 5), it is not necessary to create an entire row of rate cells as you did for revenue. Instead, you can designate a single cell to contain the percent of revenues that determines material expenses for all five years.

Material expenses are not the only expenses that you will treat this way as you continue to develop Yorick's pro forma income statement. As a matter of foresight, you will next create a column of cells to the left of the income statement that will serve as a rate column, such as the one shown in Figure 3-6 later in this chapter. When any given row of the income statement utilizes a consistent rate, you can store that rate in the corresponding cell of the rate column.

However, there is no room on the left side of the income statement. The row headings already occupy column A. If this model were being designed with pencil and paper instead of an electronic spreadsheet, it would be a thankless job to shift all columns to the right in order to make room for the rate column. One advantage of using Symphony is that revisions to the model's format are easy, even after the model has been stored in the worksheet. In this instance, you can add the column with the Insert command from the spreadsheet command menu.

Using Insert to Create Extra Workspace

The *Insert command* is used to insert columns or rows in the spreadsheet. Before using the command, you must position the pointer at the place where the rows or columns are to be inserted. If you wish to insert a column, you must place the pointer in any cell of the column to the left of which the blank column will be inserted.

For example, to insert a blank column before column D, you would position the pointer anywhere in column D (cell D2, for example) and issue the Insert Column command. Data stored in column D and in columns to the right of D would be shifted over to make room for the new blank column.

A row insertion is made in the same way as a column insertion. To insert a row, place the pointer in any cell of the row above which the blank row is to be inserted. For example, to insert a blank row at row 6, you would move the pointer to a cell in row 6 and invoke the Insert Row command. The current contents of row 6 and any rows below it are shifted downward, leaving a blank row at row 6. No further alterations are necessary: any formulas that referred to cells in the shifted rows or columns are automatically adjusted to address the new cell coordinates.

It may take some practice to remember where the new row or column goes relative to the pointer's location. Rows and columns are always added above and to the left of the pointer. Otherwise, with the pointer at A1, how could you add rows or columns at the top or left of the spreadsheet?

Back to the task at hand: inserting a blank column in which variable rates can be stored.

1. Move the pointer to a cell in column A (this can be done in a single keystroke by pressing the HOME key).
2. Press the MENU (F10) key, and select Insert.

The Insert submenu is

Columns Rows Global

The Global option will be described in a later chapter. For your purposes, the Columns option is what you need.

3. Select the Columns option of the Insert submenu.

Now you have the option of inserting one or several columns. You communicate your intentions to Symphony by indicating a column insert range. Following its prompt of "Column insert range:", Symphony suggests a range of a single cell, for example, A1..A1. As usual, Symphony assumes you will want to make a change at the current location of the pointer.

A dash appears inside the pointer, indicating that you may use the pointing facility to expand the pointer over more than one column. To see how this works, press the right arrow key once; the pointer widens to span columns A and B, and the insert range automatically changes to A1..B1. By expanding the pointer over more than one column, you can insert multiple blank columns beginning at column A. Naturally, the current spreadsheet will shift right as many columns as it takes to make room for the insertions. Press the left arrow key to shrink the pointer so that it includes only column A. The insert range also reverts to one cell, A1..A1.

4. Press RETURN to execute the insertion.

The former contents of column A now reside in column B, and all other columns have been shifted to the right. Formula references have also been adjusted. If you move the pointer to Year 1 MATERIALS at D10, you will find that the formula has changed to 0.16*D6.

5. Move to cell A4 and enter the label RATES.
6. At A5, type \- RETURN to underscore the label.

Using the Erase Command

With the variable-rate column in place, you can now revise the formula for material expenses.

1. Move to the rate cell corresponding to MATERIALS (cell A10).
2. Enter the rate of **.16**.
3. Place the pointer at the Year 1 MATERIALS cell (D10).

Before you enter the new formulas, you might get rid of the old ones. This is not really necessary because you will be entering revised formulas that would overwrite the old ones. For demonstration purposes, though, you will delete the original formulas by using the *Erase command.*

4. Press the MENU (F10) key and select Erase.

Symphony prompts for a range to erase, suggesting the single-cell range of D10..D10. However, you want to erase the entire row of formulas. To indicate this to Symphony,

5. Press the END key, and then press the right arrow key to expand the pointer to the end of the range.
6. Press RETURN to complete the command.

The RATE formulas are erased.

Using + to Activate Value Mode

Recall that the new formula for material expenses is the rate cell (A10) times the revenue cell for the appropriate year. For example, the formula for Year 1 would be A10*D6. To allow you to point to the rate cell as the first step in entering the formula, Symphony must comprehend that you are entering a formula. This is because Symphony allows you to enter formulas with pointing only when it is in Value Mode, that is, when Symphony thinks you are entering a formula. After all, it would not make sense to point when you are entering a label. Somehow you must force Symphony into Value Mode so that it expects a formula.

Symphony enters either Value Mode or Label Mode depending on the first character typed in an entry. For example, you saw that typing a letter or a label-prefix invokes Label Mode. Typing a number, such as 5, throws Symphony into Value Mode. Other symbols that have a mathematical connotation, like +, −, ., and (, also invoke Value Mode when they are typed as the first character of an entry. For purposes of pointing, typing + is a good way to begin the entry, even if you are not going to do addition.

Even if you choose to type coordinates directly instead of pointing to them, you may still need to start the formula with a special arithmetic character to force Symphony into Value Mode.

Consider the formula A10*D6. If you begin entering the formula by typing A, Symphony defaults to Label Mode because A is a character. Instead, enter + to activate Value Mode, and then enter the formula.

1. With the cell pointer still in cell D10, type + to begin the formula.

The mode indicator shows "VALUE," and you may now point to a cell.

2. Move the pointer to the rate cell (A10).
3. Type * to continue the formula.
4. Move the pointer up to the Year 1 REVENUE cell (D6).

5. Press RETURN.

The new formula, +A10*D6, gives the same result (1920) as that obtained with the old formula in Figure 3-4. The next step is to copy the Year 1 formula to the other years.

Absolute Versus Relative Copying

When you used the Copy command to replicate the revenue formula, you copied formulas in a relative manner. If the revenue for Year 1 equaled the previous year's revenue times Year 1's growth rate, the revenue for Year 2 was copied as the previous year's (Year 1) revenue times Year 2's growth rate.

Actually, Symphony does not understand the terms "Year 1" or "growth rate." To Symphony, the formula for Year 1 revenue was *one cell to the left * one cell below*, so that when the formula was copied, it was copied in terms of relative positions. Most uses of the Copy command are for relative replications like the one used for revenue (and the one used to create the column headings 1 through 5).

However, there are times when relative copying is not desired, and the materials formula is one such case. The materials formula is a mixed breed with regard to copying. On the one hand, the reference to REVENUE should be relative. As the formula is copied from one cell to another, the target of the copy should always search four rows above itself to find the correct REVENUE amount. For example, the Year 1 MATERIALS formula in cell D10 should multiply the rate cell by the Year 1 REVENUE cell four cells above (in cell D6); Year 2 should multiply the rate by Year 2 REVENUE four cells above, in cell E6; and so forth. The problem is the rate cell. If the materials formula were copied relatively, Symphony would interpret the source formula for Year 1 as "the cell three positions to the left" (cell A10) times "the cell four positions above" (cell D6). This formula works for Year 1, but if you apply it to the other years, the rate cell will be lost from the formula.

Your intention is not to copy the entire formula relatively, but rather to make the copied reference to the rate cell nonrelative, or *absolute*. Instead of "the cell three positions to the left," you want "the cell in column A, row 10." Returning to the analogy of someone asking you for directions to a street in your neighborhood, an absolute address would be equivalent to giving the geographical latitude and longitude of the street. No matter where in the world you are, you can identify the precise coordinates of the street. A relative address of "three blocks up, two blocks to the right" does not lead a person in Bangkok to the same street as it does a person in New York. An absolute address works for both people. Figure 3-5 illustrates the difference between copying a formula relatively and copying with an absolute cell address.

To specify an absolute address in Symphony, you must alter the Year 1 source formula and designate A10, the MATERIALS rate cell, as an *absolute reference* to be copied in nonrelative terms.

Symphony uses the special character $ to make a column or row reference absolute. The dollar sign must appear before the column letter or before the row number of the coordinate or in both positions. For the cell A10, $A$10 will always be copied without changing the A or the 10 in the TO range.

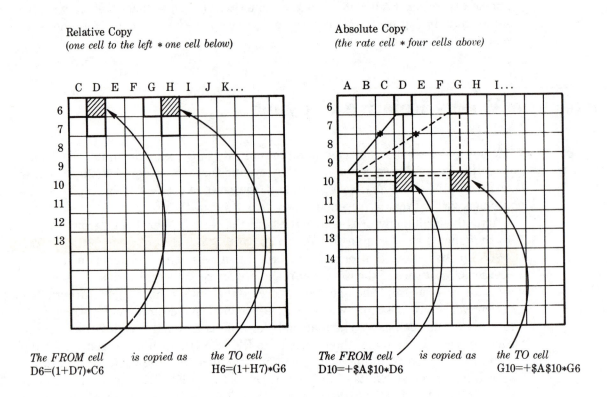

Figure 3-5. Relative copying versus absolute copying

As far as Year 1 is concerned, it makes no difference whether or not the formula A10*D6 contains any dollar signs. The difference comes into play only with regard to copying, when the appearance of a dollar sign in one or more references of the FROM cell affects the formula copied to the TO range.

This is a very important point. Symphony requires you to have the correct placement of dollar signs in the formulas contained in the FROM range, *before* you initiate the Copy command. If you forgot to put in the dollar signs before you copied, go back and use Edit Mode to put them in, as you are about to do with the material-expense formula.

In the material-expense formula, the column of the address of the rate cell must be copied absolutely, not relatively. Therefore, the formula should be $A$10*D6. No matter where the cell is copied to, the first term of the formula is copied absolutely as A10, not as a relative reference.

One way of inserting a dollar sign into the formula is by using Edit Mode:

1. Press the EDIT (F2) key.

The blinking edit cursor appears immediately to the right of the formula.

2. Press the HOME key to position the edit cursor at the left side of the formula.

3. Press the right arrow key once to place the edit cursor below the A of the A10 reference.

4. Type the $ to insert the absolute symbol before the A.

5. Press the right arrow key to move the edit cursor below the 1, and type the $. Press RETURN to conclude the edit.

The formula in the control panel should be +$A$10*D6. Now copy this formula from Year 1 to the rest of the row.

6. Press the MENU (F10) key and select Copy; then press RETURN to accept Symphony's suggestion that the FROM range be D10..D10.

7. Move right once to Year 2 MATERIALS (cell E10) to designate the first cell of the TO range.

8. Type the . to anchor the range.

9. Use the right arrow key to move to Year 5 MATERIALS (cell H10), the end of the TO range.

10. Press RETURN.

Compare the results to those derived originally in Figure 3-4, and examine the formulas underlying the cells.

Now you can take full advantage of your new flexibility. For instance, when Yorick finds that the cost of materials has increased, forcing material expenses to rise to 17 percent of sales, all you have to do is

11. Move to the MATERIALS rate cell (A10), type .17, and press RETURN.

The model immediately recalculates the material-expense line, yielding the results shown in Figure 3-6.

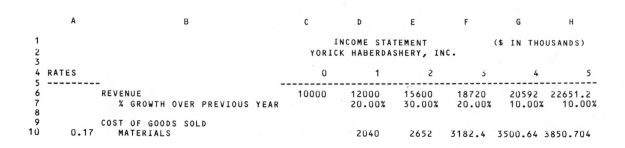

	A	B		C	D	E	F	G	H
1					INCOME STATEMENT			($ IN THOUSANDS)	
2					YORICK HABERDASHERY, INC.				
3									
4	RATES			0	1	2	3	4	5
5	--------								
6		REVENUE		10000	12000	15600	18720	20592	22651.2
7		% GROWTH OVER PREVIOUS YEAR			20.00%	30.00%	20.00%	10.00%	10.00%
8									
9		COST OF GOODS SOLD							
10	0.17	MATERIALS			2040	2652	3182.4	3500.64	3850.704

Figure 3-6. Income statement showing new rate calculations

Saving the Worksheet

You have completed a significant portion of the pro forma income statement for Yorick Haberdashery, Inc. In the next chapter, you will complete the model and explore the Copy command even further. Before you leave this exercise, though, remember to save the current version of your model.

1. Press the SERVICES (F9) key and select File; then select Save.

Symphony anticipates that you probably want to replace the old version of this model with the new one, recommending that you use the same file name in the control panel. Using the same file name causes Symphony to erase the old file on the disk and to replace it with the new file under the same name, INC_STA. To accept Symphony's recommendation,

2. Press RETURN.

Before it begins saving the updated version, Symphony ascertains whether you truly intend to overwrite the old one. After all, this is another way to zap the worksheet. We know what you're doing, though, so go ahead and

3. Select the Yes option to replace the previous model.

Your updated worksheet is now saved on disk, ready for you to retrieve it when you begin work in Chapter 4.

Chapter 4
Advanced Copying
And the @SUM Function

Calculating the Remaining
Costs of Goods Sold

Using Copy for General
And Administrative Expenses

Totaling Operating Expenses:
The @SUM Function

Calculating Interest Expense
And Income

This chapter continues the income statement forecast of Chapters 2 and 3. To complete the model, you will explore additional applications of the Copy command, use the @SUM function to total a group of cells, and finish your calculations with a few keystrokes.

In order to follow this chapter's instructions, you must have the model developed in the last chapter (see Figure 3-6). If you already have the model on the screen, skip to the next paragraph. If you saved the model, retrieve it again by pressing the SERVICES (F9) key and then selecting File and Retrieve. Now Symphony will prompt you for the name of the file to be retrieved, displaying the names of worksheets currently stored on the data diskette. With the pointer on INC—STA, press RETURN.

Calculating the Remaining Costs Of Goods Sold

In Chapters 2 and 3 you began Yorick Haberdashery, Inc.'s income statement by forecasting revenues; then you proceeded to the first cost of goods sold, material expenses. Many more costs are involved in making hats, however. You will work with those costs in this chapter, starting with the second cost of goods sold, factory wages.

Copying Wage Formulas With the ABS (F3) Key

Like materials, the wages of factory workers can be assumed to depend on sales. As more units are sold, more workers are employed and more wages paid. Assume that Yorick spends 14 cents of every sales dollar on wages. The formula for wages is essentially the same as that for materials: the rate cell at the left of the WAGES line multiplied by the revenue cell. Now that you are aware of the implications of absolute versus relative copying, you will not make the same mistake twice: when you enter the wages formula, you will make an absolute reference to the rate cell. With the "CAP" indicator on,

1. Move to cell B11, beneath the MATERIALS label, and enter the indented label WAGES by pressing the space bar three times and typing **WAGES**.

2. Move left once to the rate cell (A11), and enter **.14** as the rate.

3. Move right to the Year 1 WAGES cell (D11).

The formula to be input here is *rate * revenue*.

4. Type + to begin the formula.

5. Move the pointer to the rate cell (A11).

The control panel shows +A11 thus far. You could complete the formula and then backtrack by editing the formula, changing +A11 to +$A$11. However, Symphony provides a means for evading this roundabout method by allowing you to transform the cell reference to absolute form while remaining in Point Mode, *before* the formula has been completed. The ABS key (F3) is used for this purpose.*

6. Press the ABS (F3) key once.

The formula in the control panel has now been changed from +A11 to +$A$11, the absolute form for copying purposes. At this point you can proceed with the formula, as if you had originally entered the absolute address.

7. Type * to continue the multiplication formula.

8. Move the pointer to the Year 1 REVENUE cell (D6).

9. Press RETURN.

1-2-3 users: This is different from 1-2-3, which uses F4 as the ABS key instead of F3.

The formula for wages is +$A$11*D6 which evaluates to 1680. The formula may now be copied to the rest of the row.

10. Press the ___ ___ ___ ___ ___ ___ ___ N to use the current cell (D11)

11. Move righ ___ ___ ___ ___ ___ ___ as the beginning of the TO ra ___

12. Type a . t ___

13. Move the ___ ___ ___ ___ nd of the TO range.

14. Press RET ___

The cost of wag ___ ___ ___ ___ ___ ___ ___ ther costs that must be estimated. ___

Calculatin ___

On page 55, need
to do the problem
w/o $ before 6.
Then, he makes
you correct it on
page 63.

10-7-89

Fringe benefits for factory workers can be approximated as a percent of wages because the more people employed, the greater the fringe benefits expense will be. Again, you use the rate cell to make the percent variable. Fringe benefits are 15 percent of wages at Yorick.

1. Enter the indented label FRINGE BENEFITS beneath the WAGES label. (Move to cell B12, press the space bar three times, and type **FRINGE BENEFITS**.)

2. Move to the left and enter **.15** in the rate cell (A12).

3. Move to the Year 1 FRINGE BENEFITS cell (D12).

4. Type **+** to begin formula entry.

5. Move the pointer to the rate cell (A12).

6. Press the ABS (F3) key to make the cell reference absolute.

7. Type ***** to continue the multiplication formula.

8. Point to the Year 1 WAGES cell (D11) by moving the pointer up one space.

9. Press RETURN.

Now copy the formula to the other years:

10. Press MENU (F10), select Copy, and press RETURN.

11. Move the pointer to the Year 2 FRINGE BENEFITS cell (E12).

12. Type a . to anchor the beginning of the target range.

13. Move the pointer to the Year 5 FRINGE BENEFITS cell (H12).

14. Press RETURN.

Because fringe benefits is a function of wages, which in turn is a function of revenue, the fringe benefits expense (shown in Figure 4-1) grows at the same annual rate as revenue. Thus, the Year 2 fringe benefits of 327.6 exceeds the Year 1 expense of 252 by 30 percent, which equals the revenue growth from Year 1 to Year 2.

	A	B	C	D	E	F	G	H
1				INCOME STATEMENT			($ IN THOUSANDS)	
2				YORICK HABERDASHERY, INC.				
3								
4	RATES		0	1	2	3	4	5
5	---------		---------					---------
6		REVENUE	10000	12000	15600	18720	20592	22651.2
7		% GROWTH OVER PREVIOUS YEAR		20.00%	30.00%	20.00%	10.00%	10.00%
8								
9		COST OF GOODS SOLD						
10	0.17	MATERIALS		2040	2652	3182.4	3500.64	3850.704
11	14.00%	WAGES		1680	2184	2620.8	2882.88	3171.168
12	15.00%	FRINGE BENEFITS		252	327.6	393.12	432.432	475.6752

Figure 4-1. Yorick income statement, FRINGE BENEFITS expense

Calculating Other Expenses

You will next label the remaining cost of goods sold as OTHER. The OTHER category incorporates production-related expenses (such as supplies, factory, heating, lighting, and power) and miscellaneous expenses. Because this category of cost of goods sold is primarily associated with the factory as a whole, it does not change as a function of sales. No matter what quantity of hats are produced, factory expenses remain unaffected except by factors like inflation or plant expansion. You will therefore assign an annual growth rate to this category, assuming that it increases by a constant percentage each year.

The rate cell can be used to store the growth rate, but the formula for other expenses differs from those for the costs of goods sold considered thus far. The formula is (1 + *growth rate*) * *previous year's expense*. Assume that OTHER expense starts at 100 and grows by 8 percent per year. A start-up value must be input for the first year.

1. Move to the cell below the FRINGE BENEFITS label (B13), press the space bar three times, and type **OTHER**.
2. Move to the rate cell (A13) and enter **.08** as the growth factor.
3. Move the pointer to the Year 1 OTHER cell (D13).
4. Enter **100** as the start-up value.
5. Move the pointer to the Year 2 OTHER cell (E13).
6. Type **(1+** to begin the formula.
7. Move the pointer to the rate cell (A13).

Additional items will be forecast by using a growth rate, so it is important at this point to consider all the possible uses for copying this formula. The rate cell's column reference, A, must be absolute because no matter where you copy the formula to, the rate cell will remain in column A. However, the row reference must be relative because if you copy the formula to another row, the target's rate will be contained in the target's row.

Consider the Year 2 OTHER formula. It is either (1 + *the rate cell*) * *Year 0 OTHER expense* or (1+$A$13)*D13. Suppose you were going to copy this formula down to the Year 2 cell (column E) of a different expense, hypothetically called Mystery Expense, in row 20. If you copied the formula (1+$A$13)*D13 to cell E20, you would get (1+$A$13)*D20. The $A$13 does not change because the cell reference is entirely absolute. The D13 is copied as D20 since the reference is entirely relative.

What you really need in Year 2 Mystery Expense is (1 + *the Mystery Expense growth rate*) * *the previous year's Mystery Expense*. The Mystery Expense growth rate is in cell A20, yet you would have copied $A$13—the right column, but the wrong row.

The problem lies in the absolute reference, $A$13, in the FROM range formula. The column reference, A, should be absolute and therefore should have a $ symbol preceding the A. However, since you want the row reference (13) to change as you copy the formula to another row, the row reference should not be absolute—it should not have a $ symbol in front of it. In other words, the cell reference to the rate cell should be a *hybrid*. Part of the reference should be absolute, part should be relative. The correct hybrid reference in the FROM range formula should be $A13 (without a $ symbol in front of the 13).

You can use the ABS (F3) key to obtain this hybrid absolute reference.

8. Press the ABS (F3) key, so that the formula appearing in the control panel is (1+$A$13.

Next,

9. Press the ABS (F3) key once more.

The control panel now shows (1+A$13. This is not yet what you want because the $ precedes the wrong part of the address.

10. Press the ABS (F3) key one more time.

The formula in the control panel changes to (1+$A13, the way you want it.

11. Type)* to continue the formula.

Incidentally, if you had pressed the ABS (F3) key a fourth time, the formula in the control panel would have changed to (1+A13, with no $ symbols. Pressing ABS (F3) causes Symphony to cycle through all the forms of a cell reference, one step at a time.

12. Move the pointer to the previous year's OTHER expense cell (D13).

This cell reference should be left relative. As you copy the formula to other columns, the column reference should change; and as you copy the formula to other rows, the row reference should change.

13. Press RETURN.

The Year 2 value of 108 is 8 percent higher than the Year 1 value. Copy the Year 2 formula to the rest of the row.

14. With the pointer at E13, press MENU (F10), select Copy, and press RETURN.

15. Press the right arrow key once.

16. Type a . to anchor the range.

17. Move the pointer to the Year 5 OTHER cell (H13).

18. Press RETURN.

Figure 4-2 shows what you have accomplished thus far in the model. Let's pause for a moment and review what it shows.

You have created a forecast of revenue growing at a rate that you can specify for any year of the forecast. Cost of sales has been dissected into four parts: materials, wages, fringe benefits, and other expenses. Materials and wages change as a percent of sales. Fringe benefits are a function of wages, while the other category grows at a constant rate. For each of these expenses, the associated rate can be changed simply by revising the rate cell.

Within the general assumptions of the model it is quite easy to generate alternative scenarios. If one of the general assumptions changes, however, the underlying formulas may have to be altered. Still, with the aid of the powerful Copy command you can usually make such changes without expending much energy or time. You will be using the Copy command to apply the percent of sales and growth rate assumptions to the line items that follow. Before you proceed, however, let's take a moment to make the spreadsheet clearer.

Annotating the Spreadsheet

Looking at Figure 4-2, no one could tell what assumptions or formulas this forecast is based on. Even if you are the only person using the spreadsheet, you may not remember how you derived the numbers. For this reason, it is a good practice to set aside an area of the spreadsheet where you can annotate what you have done.

To make your model clearer, you will add one more column to the right of the income statement for annotation. The column should be wide enough to contain the notes, so you will begin by selecting the Width command from the SHEET Menu commands list to override the default width of 9.

	A	B	C	D	E	F	G	H
1				INCOME STATEMENT			($ IN THOUSANDS)	
2				YORICK HABERDASHERY, INC.				
3								
4	RATES		0	1	2	3	4	5
5	---------		----------	----------	----------	----------	----------	----------
6		REVENUE	10000	12000	15600	18720	20592	22651.2
7		% GROWTH OVER PREVIOUS YEAR		20.00%	30.00%	20.00%	10.00%	10.00%
8								
9		COST OF GOODS SOLD						
10	0.17	MATERIALS		2040	2652	3182.4	3500.64	3850.704
11	14.00%	WAGES		1680	2184	2620.8	2882.88	3171.168
12	15.00%	FRINGE BENEFITS		252	327.6	393.12	432.432	475.6752
13	8.00%	OTHER		100	108	116.64	125.9712	136.0488

Figure 4-2. Yorick income statement, OTHER expenses

1. Move the pointer to cell J4.

2. Press MENU (F10), select Width, select Set, and type **30**.

3. Press RETURN.

The heading for this column is NOTES. If you enter the heading as is, Symphony will insert an apostrophe label-prefix before the heading, causing the label to be left-justified within the 30-character cell. As mentioned earlier, there are other label-prefixes that format a label differently. The ^ (caret) label-prefix centers the label within the cell, and the ″ (double quotes) label-prefix justifies the label on the right.

4. Type ″**NOTES** and press RETURN.

The label is right-justified. On second thought, though, the heading would look better in the center.

5. Type ^**NOTES** and press RETURN.

Notice that the previous contents of cell J4 are overwritten automatically.
Next use the repeating label-prefix (\ ) to underscore the heading.

6. Move down one space to cell J5, type \-, and press RETURN.

Now you can document the assumptions for the four cost-of-goods-sold expenses in the NOTES column.

7. Move to cell J10 and enter the label **% OF SALES**; then enter the same label in J11.

8. Move down the NOTES column to the FRINGE BENEFITS row (J12), and enter the label **% OF WAGES**.

9. Move down the NOTES column to the OTHER row (J13), and enter **% GROWTH RATE**.

Now the forecast is almost self-explanatory.
Column I was left blank in order to set the NOTES column off from the model. But the column does not need to be nine characters wide. Let's shrink it down to two characters.

10. Go to cell I1 (or any cell in column I), press MENU (F10), select Width, select Set, type **2**, and press RETURN.

Using Copy for General And Administrative Expenses

Unlike the cost of goods sold, certain company expenses do not relate directly to production (at least in the short term). For example, as Yorick's Financial Oracle you are going to receive your $500,000 salary next year whether the company sells 5 hats or 5 trillion hats. Compensation for managerial and sales staff, as well as advertising and depreciation, comes under the heading GENERAL & ADMINISTRATIVE EXPENSE, the next set of deductions from revenue in the income statement.

Calculating Managerial Compensation

You begin by calculating the costs of compensating the managerial staff over the next five years. The first step is to enter labels.

1. Move to cell B15 and enter the label **GENERAL & ADMINISTRATIVE EXPENSE** (not indented).

2. Move down once to cell B16, press the space bar three times to indent the label, and type **COMPENSATION: OFFICE**.

The compensation of company management is not primarily a function of sales. Office compensation is more a function of inflation and the state of the job market. You can therefore assume that office compensation grows at some rate that reflects increases in the same factors that affect salaries. Since this assumption is the same as the one you used to forecast the OTHER cost-of-sales line, that intuitive urge to use the Copy command should be welling up within you.

Copying From a Range to a Range

Until now you have used the Copy command to replicate one cell to another cell or to several other cells. Here, however, you want to copy more than a single cell. Except for different amounts in the Year 1 cost cell and in the rate cell, the row of formulas in the OTHER cost-of-sales line will be used for calculating COMPENSATION: OFFICE expenses. To Symphony, copying a range of cells is just as easy as copying a single cell.

Copying from one row of cells to another involves the same steps as the previous copies. First, position the pointer at the beginning of the FROM range; then invoke the Copy command; identify the FROM range; identify the TO range; and execute the copy. Instead of containing a single cell, the FROM range will encompass a range, the row of consecutive cells to be copied.

In specifying the TO range, however, you need not always identify a multiple-cell range. In this case, Symphony requires only the address of the first cell in the TO range. Why? The program knows what the FROM range is, and it knows the exact dimensions of the rectangle that makes up the FROM range. With only the beginning address of the TO range (the top left cell), Symphony has sufficient information to copy the FROM range, in its exact dimensions, to the target. There is no need to specify the end of the TO range in this instance, because the dimensions of the FROM range determine the dimensions of the TO range. Once you tell Symphony what the FROM range is (and, implicitly, what shape it is), let Symphony figure out the shape of the TO range. As you saw in Figure 2-2, you just have to show Symphony where to begin.

Assume that office compensation in Year 1 amounts to $1200 thousand.

1. Move to the Year 1 COMPENSATION: OFFICE cell (D16) and enter the value **1200**.

Next set the annual growth rate to 10 percent:

2. Move to the rate cell (A16) and enter **.1**.

Now for the copy.

3. Move to the beginning of the FROM range, the Year 2 OTHER cell (E13).

4. Press MENU (F10) and select the Copy command.

Now Symphony suggests a one-cell FROM range of E13..E13, and it highlights this range on the spreadsheet. Moving the pointer will expand the range. To expand the range to the end of the OTHER row,

5. Press the END key, followed by the right arrow key, to transfer the pointer to the Year 5 OTHER cell (H13).

6. Press RETURN to set the FROM range.

Next you must respond to Symphony's prompt, "Range to copy TO:", by pointing to the beginning of the target.

7. Move the pointer to the Year 2 COMPENSATION: OFFICE cell (E16).

8. Press RETURN to activate the copy.

Finally, don't forget to document the assumption:

9. Move to the NOTE cell (J16) and type **% GROWTH RATE**.

Figure 4-3 identifies the source and target ranges of the Copy procedure, and it also shows the underlying formulas.

Calculating Sales Compensation

Unlike office compensation, sales compensation is closely linked to revenues. As sales increase, so does the need to expand the marketing staff. The forecast assumption for sales compensation is the same as that for wages (calculated earlier under the COST OF GOODS SOLD heading), so you can use the Copy command to set sales compensation at 8 percent of sales.

1. Move to cell B17 and enter the indented label **COMPENSATION: SALES**.

2. Enter **.08** in the rate cell (A17).

3. Move to Year 1 WAGES, the beginning of the FROM range (cell D11).

4. Press MENU (F10) and select the Copy command.

Symphony prompts you for the end of the FROM range.

5. Press the END key, followed by the right arrow key, to transfer the pointer to the Year 5 WAGES cell (H11).

Since the assumption for sales compensation is the same for wages, you can copy the note for WAGES also:

6. Press the right arrow key twice to expand the source range to encompass the note cell (J11).

7. Press RETURN to set the FROM range.

8. Move down to the Year 1 COMPENSATION: SALES cell (D17), the beginning of the TO range.

9. Press RETURN.

Now wait—something has gone wrong. Check the Year 1 COMPENSATION: SALES number. It should be 8 percent of Year 1's $12,000 thousand revenue, which comes to 960 thousand. The actual result, 35.28, misses the mark rather miserably. Something's wrong, but where is it?

When errors like this one occur, the first place to look is in the formula.

	A	B	C	D	E	F	G	H
				INCOME STATEMENT				
				YORICK HABERDASHERY, INC.				
				($ IN THOUSANDS)				
1								
2								
3								
4	RATES			0	1	2	3	4	5
5	----------							
.								
.								
13	8.00%	OTHER		100	(1+\$A13)*D13	(1+\$A13)*E13	(1+\$A13)*F13	(1+\$A13)*G13
14		GENERAL & ADMINISTRATIVE EXPENSE						
15		COMPENSATION: OFFICE						
16	10.00%			1200	(1+\$A16)*D16	(1+\$A16)*E16	(1+\$A16)*F16	(1+\$A16)*G16

The FROM range (row 13)

The TO range (row 16)

Figure 4-3. Underlying formulas in the TO and FROM ranges

10. Move the pointer to Year 1 COMPENSATION: SALES (cell D17).

The control panel shows the formula to be $A$11*D12. The Copy command did not work quite the way you intended. The formula you wanted was the COMPENSATION: SALES rate cell, A17, times Year 1 REVENUE, cell D6. Instead you obtained the address of the rate cell of the FROM range, A11, and the row portion of the revenue address is six rows farther down than what you aimed for.

The problem is due to using incorrect absolute and relative references in the FROM range formulas when you first entered the wage formulas. It would not have occurred if, when you created the wage line, you had used the formula $A11*D$6 for Year 1 WAGES. The row reference of the rate cell should be relative, and the row reference of the revenue cell should be absolute. Copying this formula down to Year 1 COMPENSATION: SALES in cell D17 would have produced $A17*D$6, the correct formula.

This mistake underscores the importance of being aware of possible future copying when you enter formulas in a spreadsheet. It also shows that correcting the problem is easy. You can use Edit Mode to change the original Year 1 WAGES formula and then recopy that formula to the COMPENSATION: SALES row.

11. Move the pointer to cell D11, Year 1 WAGES.

12. Press the EDIT (F2) key, and change the formula from $A$11*D6 to $A11*D$6; then press RETURN.

13. Press MENU (F10) and select Copy.

14. Press RETURN to designate D11..D11 as the FROM range.

15. Move to Year 1 COMPENSATION: SALES, the beginning of the TO range (D17).

16. Type a . to anchor the range.

17. Press END, then the right arrow key to move to the end of the range (H17).

18. Press RETURN to conclude the copy.

Your results should coincide with Figure 4-4.

	A	B	C	D	E	F	G	H
1				INCOME STATEMENT			($ IN THOUSANDS)	
2				YORICK HABERDASHERY, INC.				
3								
4	RATES		0	1	2	3	4	5
5	---------		--					
6		REVENUE	10000	12000	15600	18720	20592	22651.2
7		% GROWTH OVER PREVIOUS YEAR		20.00%	30.00%	20.00%	10.00%	10.00%
8								
9		COST OF GOODS SOLD						
10	0.17	MATERIALS		2040	2652	3182.4	3500.64	3850.704
11	14.00%	WAGES		1680	2184	2620.8	2882.88	3171.168
12	15.00%	FRINGE BENEFITS		252	327.6	393.12	432.432	475.6752
13	8.00%	OTHER		100	108	116.64	125.9712	136.0488
14								
15		GENERAL & ADMINISTRATIVE EXPENSE						
16	10.00%	COMPENSATION: OFFICE		1200	1320	1452	1597.2	1756.92
17	8.00%	COMPENSATION: SALES		960	1248	1497.6	1647.36	1812.096

Figure 4-4. Income statement showing COMPENSATION: SALES

Entering the Remaining
Year 1 Expenses

Copying from row to row is a great timesaver once you get accustomed to it. But the Copy command has even greater potential — it also allows you to copy from one column to another. Better yet, you can copy from one row to many rows or from one column to many columns.

There are four additional line items pertaining to general and administrative expense: fringe benefits for office and sales staff, advertising and promotion, depreciation, and miscellaneous. You will develop the formulas for these items in Year 1 only. Then, in one command, you will copy the Year 1 formulas to Years 2 through 5.

Fringe Benefits

You can assume that fringe benefits of administrative and marketing employees will be a percentage of office and sales compensation. Because these employees receive additional "perks" above and beyond those of the factory wage earners, you will apply a higher fringe rate than the 15 percent allotted at line 12. In this example, a rate of 17 percent should be about right.

1. At cell B18, enter the indented label **FRINGE BENEFITS**.

2. Move to the rate column (cell A18) and enter **.17**.

3. Move to the Year 1 FRINGE BENEFITS cell (D18).

The formula is *rate * (office compensation + sales compensation)*.

4. Type + to begin formula entry.

5. Move left to the rate cell (A18).

6. Press the ABS (F3) key three times to form $A18, a reference suitable for copying.

7. Type *(.

8. Move the pointer to the Year 1 COMPENSATION: OFFICE cell (D16).

9. Type + to continue the formula.

10. Move the pointer to the Year 1 COMPENSATION: SALES cell (D17).

11. Type) and press RETURN.

The result is $367.2 thousand.

Advertising and Promotion

Advertising and promotion expense is directly related to sales. The higher the sales, the greater the justification for increasing this expense. Yorick plans to spend 2.5 percent of sales on advertising and promotion.

1. Move to cell B19 and then enter the indented label **ADVERTISING & PROMOTION**.

2. Store **.025** in the rate cell (A19).

Instead of entering the Year 1 formula from scratch, you can use the Copy command to duplicate the Year 1 WAGES formula you entered earlier, for this also depends on revenue.

3. Move to the Year 1 WAGES cell (D11), the FROM range.
4. Press MENU (F10), select Copy, and press RETURN.
5. Move down to the Year 1 ADVERTISING & PROMOTION cell (D19).
6. Press RETURN to start the copy.

Your results should show $300 thousand in advertising and promotion expenses for the first year.

Depreciation

Depreciation is different from the other types of expenses you have encountered so far. No cash actually leaves the corporate till because of depreciation. Equipment is depreciated in order to reflect its decreasing value over time. Moreover, depreciation depends on several other factors, including the value of the depreciable assets, the useful life of these assets, and the accounting method that the company uses to apportion depreciation over the life of the assets.

If information about currently depreciable assets and future purchases of depreciable assets were available, you could develop a subsidiary spreadsheet to derive the forecast of depreciation expense (or you could input the line directly into this model). No such details are provided for Yorick, but company management assures you that depreciation will amount to a constant $20 thousand per year. Therefore,

1. Move to cell B20 and enter the indented label **DEPRECIATION**.
2. Store the value **20** in the Year 1 DEPRECIATION cell (D20).

Miscellaneous Expenses

The miscellaneous classification of general and administrative expenses is independent of revenue. It is assumed to grow, but not at a percentage rate; so in this case assume that miscellaneous expenses increase at a constant rate, such as $10 thousand per year. In each year, miscellaneous expenses are $10 thousand greater than the year before.

The percentage growth was a multiplicative rate, but the constant increase is an additive rate. That is, each year's increase in miscellaneous expenses is simply added to the previous year's total. You can store the value 10 in the rate cell and refer to it in the miscellaneous expense formula. In this way, it will be possible to change the additive rate at a later time.

1. Move to cell B21 and enter the indented label **MISCELLANEOUS**.
2. Move to the rate cell (A21) and type **10**.
3. Move to the Year 1 MISCELLANEOUS cell (D21).

The formula for each year's miscellaneous expense is *rate + previous year's miscellaneous expense.*

```
          A        B                              C        D        E        F        G        H          I         J

                                              INCOME STATEMENT
                                         YORICK HABERDASHERY, INC.        ($ IN THOUSANDS)

 1
 2
 3
 4  RATES                                         0        1        2        3        4        5        NOTES
 5  -------                               ---------------------------------------------------------------   -------
 6         REVENUE                          10000    12000    15600    18720    20592   22651.2
 7         % GROWTH OVER PREVIOUS YEAR               20.00%   30.00%   20.00%   10.00%   10.00%
 8
 9         COST OF GOODS SOLD
10   0.17  MATERIALS                                 2040     2652    3182.4  3500.64  3850.704  % OF SALES
11  14.00% WAGES                                     1680     2184    2620.8  2882.88  3171.168  % OF SALES
12  15.00% FRINGE BENEFITS                            252    327.6    393.12  432.432  475.6752  % OF WAGES
13   8.00% OTHER                                      100      108    116.64  125.9712 136.0488  % GROWTH RATE
14
15         GENERAL & ADMINISTRATIVE EXPENSE
16  10.00% COMPENSATION: OFFICE                      1200     1320     1452    1597.2  1756.92   % GROWTH RATE
17   8.00% COMPENSATION: SALES                        960     1248    1497.6  1647.36  1812.096  % OF SALES
18  17.00% FRINGE BENEFITS                          367.2   436.56   501.432 551.5752 606.7327
19   2.50% ADVERTISING & PROMOTION                   300      390      468     514.8   566.28
20         DEPRECIATION                               20       20       20       20       20
21   10    MISCELLANEOUS                              10       20       30       40       50
```

The FROM range

The TO range

Figure 4-5. Copying from one column to several columns

4. Type + to begin the formula.

5. Move the pointer to the rate cell (A21).

6. Press the ABS (F3) key three times to make the column reference absolute (+$A21).

7. Type + to continue the formula.

8. Move the pointer to the Year 0 MISCELLANEOUS cell (C21).

9. Press RETURN.

Even though the Year 0 MISCELLANEOUS cell is blank, Symphony considers it a numeric zero for purposes of calculation. Thus, the Year 1 result is 10 + 0, or 10.

Copying From Year 1 To the Remaining Years

Now that you have entered the basic formulas for the last four general and administrative expense categories, all it takes to forecast Years 2 through 5 is a single Copy command.

The FROM range of the copy will be the Year 1 cells for fringe benefits, advertising and promotion, depreciation, and miscellaneous (cells D18 through D21).

For the TO range you need only specify E18..H18 (Year 2 FRINGE BENEFITS through Year 5 FRINGE BENEFITS). This TO range refers only to the first row of the columns to which the Year 1 formulas will be copied, but it gives Symphony enough information to do the entire job. Symphony knows that the FROM range is a column of four cells. It sees that E18 is the beginning of the TO range, so it copies the D18..D21 range to column E beginning in row 18. The dimension of the FROM range (four vertical cells) determines that the formulas will be copied from E18 to E21. Similarly, Symphony sees F18, G18, and H18 in the TO range, so it copies the FROM range to the columns F18..F21, G18..G21, and H18..H21.

1. Move the pointer to D18, the beginning of the FROM range.

2. Press MENU (F10) and select Copy.

3. Move the pointer down to the Year 1 MISCELLANEOUS cell (D21) to designate the end of the FROM range.

4. Press RETURN.

5. Move the pointer to the Year 2 FRINGE BENEFITS cell (E18), the beginning of the target range.

6. Type a . to anchor the range.

7. Move the pointer to the Year 5 FRINGE BENEFITS cell (H18).

8. Press RETURN.

With a single Copy command you have just developed 16 forecast formulas and completed the operating expense section of the income statement. Figure 4-5 shows the results with both the FROM and TO ranges highlighted. For good measure you should annotate these items in the NOTES column.

9. In cells J18, J19, J20, and J21, enter the following labels consecutively: **% OF OFFICE & SALES COMP**, **% OF SALES**, **DIRECT INPUT**, and **CONSTANT GROWTH**.

Totaling Operating Expenses: The @SUM Function

The next step is to total the operating expenses by combining the cost of goods sold and general and administrative expenses. Begin by putting an underscore in the row below MISCELLANEOUS:

1. Enter an underscore in the Year 0 column (cell C22) by typing \- and pressing RETURN.

2. At B23, enter the label **TOTAL OPERATING EXPENSES** indented three spaces.

You did not need Year 0 expenses in order to derive the Year 1 predictions. For informational purposes, however, include the total Year 0 expenses in the model. According to Yorick's accounting books, there were $6.4 million of expenses in Year 0.

3. Move to cell C23, the Year 0 TOTAL OPERATING EXPENSES cell, and type **6400**.

4. Move to the Year 1 TOTAL OPERATING EXPENSES cell (D23).

Using @SUM to Total Year 1 Expenses

Total operating expenses in each of Years 1 through 5 is the sum of the materials through miscellaneous expenses of each year. Is it necessary to reference each and every expense cell in the formula to find the sum? Fortunately, the answer is no.

Symphony provides a function called @SUM that totals the contents of a range of cells. The format of the function is @SUM(*list*), where *list* is a cell, a range, or a list of cells and ranges separated by commas. For example, @SUM(D1..D100) totals the column of cells from D1 to D100. @SUM(A1..Z1) adds the row of cells from A1 to Z1. As usual, the range for the @SUM function can be specified by pointing to the beginning and ending coordinates.

1. With the pointer in cell D23, type **@SUM(**.

2. Point to the beginning of the range to be summed, the Year 1 MATERIALS cell (D10).

3. Type a . to anchor the range.

4. Move the pointer to the Year 1 MISCELLANEOUS cell (D21).

Notice that Symphony highlights the range, as it does whenever ranges are specified in Point Mode.

5. Type a) to close the range of the @SUM function.

6. Press RETURN.

Using Copy to Total Remaining Expenses

Year 1 operating expenses amount to $6929.2 thousand. You will next copy both an underscore and the Year 1 formula to the other years.

1. Move the pointer to cell D22, and enter an underscore by typing \- and pressing RETURN.
2. Press MENU (F10) and select Copy.
3. Expand the pointer to the Year 1 TOTAL OPERATING EXPENSES cell (D23), the end of the FROM range.
4. Press RETURN to complete the FROM range entry.
5. Point to the beginning of the TO range in the Year 2 column, cell E22.
6. Type a . to anchor the range.
7. Expand the pointer to the Year 5 column (cell H22).
8. Press RETURN to activate the command.

Calculating Interest Expense And Income

You will be developing lines for pre-tax income, tax expense, and net income, but first there is one more pre-tax expense to deal with: interest expense. Interest expense represents the amount of interest that the firm is required to pay in the current period. It includes interest payments due for notes, bonds, and both short- and long-term loans. Like depreciation, interest expense is difficult to predict — it depends on the interest rate of each type of debt that the company owes. In your model you will not attach an assumption to interest expense; rather, you will use a simple estimate. Later you may wish to adapt more complicated formulas and input them directly.

Much to its credit, Yorick obtains most of its funding from its own profits. However, it has a $100 thousand long-term loan, on which the firm pays 10 percent interest throughout the forecast period. No additional borrowing is anticipated, so interest expense will be a constant $10 thousand for all years of the forecast.

Interest expense, and the line items that follow it, is available for Year 0. Therefore, you will enter only Year 0 figures for the next few items. You will later copy the Year 0 formulas to the forecast years with a single Copy command.

1. Move to cell B25 and enter the indented label **INTEREST EXPENSE**.
2. Move to cell C25 and enter the value **10**.
3. Now move to the note cell for INTEREST EXPENSE (J25) and type **DIRECT INPUT**.

Calculating Pre-Tax Income, Year 0

Pre-tax income can be calculated by subtracting both operating expenses and interest expense from revenue.

1. Move to cell B27 and type the label **PRE-TAX INCOME**.
2. Move to Year 0 (cell C27).
3. Type + to begin the formula entry.
4. Move the pointer to the Year 0 REVENUE cell (C6).
5. Type a − to continue with the subtraction of operating expenses from revenue.

6. Move the pointer to the Year 0 TOTAL OPERATING EXPENSES cell (C23).

7. Type the − key, and move the pointer to the Year 0 INTEREST EXPENSE cell (C25).

8. Press RETURN.

Year 0 pre-tax income is $3590 thousand.

Calculating Taxes and Net Income, Year 0

Net income is, of course, pre-tax income minus tax expense. This is probably the most important line item of the income statement for owners, creditors, and investors. You will first calculate tax expense and then use these figures to calculate net income.

In Year 0, the company's tax expense came to 52 percent of pre-tax income. This percentage includes federal, state, and local taxes. Taxes are often forecast as a percent of income, and for Yorick you can assume that this rate will remain constant throughout the forecast horizon. As you probably guessed, the rate cell can store the effective tax rate, so that the rate can be altered if the assumption changes.

1. Move to cell B29 and enter the indented label **TAX**.

2. Move to the TAX line of the rate column (cell A29) and store **.52**.

3. Move to the Year 0 TAX cell (C29).

4. Type + to begin the value entry.

5. Point to the rate cell (A29).

6. Press the ABS (F3) key once to make the rate reference absolute (+$A$29) for future copying.

7. Type * to multiply this rate by pre-tax income.

8. Move the pointer to the Year 0 PRE-TAX INCOME cell (C27).

9. Press RETURN.

Taxes are $1866.8 thousand in Year 0.

10. In the notes cell (J29), type **% OF PRE-TAX INCOME**.

11. Move to cell B31 and type **NET INCOME**.

12. Move to the Year 0 NET INCOME cell (C31) and type + to begin the formula.

13. Point to the Year 0 PRE-TAX INCOME cell (C27).

14. Type a − to continue.

15. Point to the Year 0 TAX cell (C29).

16. Press RETURN.

Of the $10 million of revenue in Year 0, $1723 thousand was net income, making for a profit of over 17 cents on every dollar of sales—a good performance. What about the other years?

	A	B	C	D	E	F	G	H	I	J
					INCOME STATEMENT					
				YORICK HABERDASHERY, INC.			($ IN THOUSANDS)			
4	RATES		0	1	2	3	4	5		NOTES
6		REVENUE	10000	12000	15600	18720	20592	22651.2		
7		% GROWTH OVER PREVIOUS YEAR		20.00%	30.00%	20.00%	10.00%	10.00%		
9		COST OF GOODS SOLD								
10	0.17	MATERIALS		2040	2652	3182.4	3500.64	3850.704		% OF SALES
11	14.00%	WAGES		1680	2184	2620.8	2882.88	3171.168		% OF SALES
12	15.00%	FRINGE BENEFITS		252	327.6	393.12	432.432	475.6752		% OF WAGES
13	8.00%	OTHER		100	108	116.64	125.9712	136.0488		GROWTH RATE
15		GENERAL & ADMINISTRATIVE EXPENSE								
16	10.00%	COMPENSATION: OFFICE		1200	1320	1452	1597.2	1756.92		% GROWTH RATE
17	8.00%	COMPENSATION: SALES		960	1248	1497.6	1647.36	1812.096		% OF SALES
18	17.00%	FRINGE BENEFITS		367.2	436.56	501.432	551.5752	606.7327		% OF OFFICE & SALES COMP
19	2.50%	ADVERTISING & PROMOTION		300	390	468	514.8	566.28		% OF SALES
20		DEPRECIATION		20	20	20	20	20		DIRECT INPUT
21	10	MISCELLANEOUS		10	20	30	40	50		CONSTANT GROWTH
23		TOTAL OPERATING EXPENSES	6400	6929.2	8706.16	10281.99	11312.85	12445.62		
25		INTEREST EXPENSE	10	10	10	10	10	10		DIRECT INPUT
27		PRE-TAX INCOME	3590	5060.8	6883.84	8428.008	9269.141	10195.57		
29	52.00%	TAX	1866.8	2631.616	3579.596	4382.564	4819.953	5301.699		% OF PRE-TAX INCOME
31		NET INCOME	1723.2	2429.184	3304.243	4045.443	4449.187	4893.876		

Figure 4-6. Completed Yorick income statement

Using Copy
For Remaining Years' Profits

Using just one Copy command, you can derive five years of data for the last four income statement items (20 formulas) by copying the Year 0 formulas to Years 1 through 5. The FROM range consists of the five Year 0 formulas in column C; the TO range is the row of pre-tax income, Years 1 through 5.

1. Move the pointer to the first cell of the FROM range, the Year 0 INTEREST EXPENSE cell (C25).

2. Press MENU (F10) and select Copy.

As always, Symphony assumes that the beginning of the source range is the current position of the pointer. Move the pointer to the end of the source range:

3. Move to the Year 0 NET INCOME cell (C31).

4. Press RETURN to set the FROM range.

5. Move the pointer to the Year 1 INTEREST EXPENSE cell (D25), the first cell of the TO range.

6. Type a . to anchor the beginning of the TO range.

7. Move the pointer to the Year 5 INTEREST EXPENSE cell (H25).

8. Press RETURN to activate the Copy command.

If you did not use the Copy command, the cumulative number of keystrokes you would need would be quite impressive. Imagine the work involved if this forecast were a monthly statement, and you can see why the Copy command is perhaps the most important command of the spreadsheet. Figure 4-6 shows the significant growth expected by the company: from $1.795 million in Year 0 to more than $5 million in Year 5.

Don't forget to save the worksheet.

9. Press the SERVICES (F9) key and select File Save; then select INC_STA as in previous chapters. In Chapter 5 you will add some finishing touches to the income statement and then print it.

Chapter 5
Formatting and Printing
The Income Statement

Formatting Numeric Displays
With the Settings Option

Printing
The Income Statement

Saving Print Settings

Now that you have completed the analytical part of the income statement forecast for Yorick Haberdashery, Inc., you will want to produce a presentable copy on paper. In this chapter you will enhance the appearance of the spreadsheet on screen, examining some additional numeric formats along the way. Then you will study the *Print command*, which not only allows you to print the spreadsheet, but also gives you a measure of control over the features of your printer.

You will need the INC_STA worksheet file that you have been developing over the last few chapters. If it is not yet on screen, load it from disk with the File Retrieve command. Also, make sure that the "CAP" indicator is on.

Formatting Numeric Displays
With the Settings Option

Before you print this model, there is a matter of neatness that you must attend to. The use of growth rates has led to a mixture of numeric displays. Some numbers have no decimals, while others have one, two, three, or even four decimal places. Unless the numbers can be formatted differently, the printed output will look as inconsistent as the display.

In Chapter 3 you used the Format % command to format the revenue listed in the % GROWTH OVER PREVIOUS YEAR line. It would be best to show the other income statement line items rounded to the nearest integer or some fixed number of decimal places. You could accomplish this with the Format command, but it would take several command sequences to format various ranges of the report. You will take an easier route here and set up a default format that will apply to all numeric cells *except* those specially formatted with the Format command.

Formatting is one of several settings that Symphony allows you to control. These settings are called *global settings* because they affect the entire spreadsheet. Symphony initially sets up its own default settings. As you've seen, it sets columns to a default width of 9 characters. You can change the width of a particular column with the Width command, but you can also change the default global setting from 9 to some other width.

The initial global format is called the General format. In General format, numbers appear with as many decimal places as it takes for Symphony to display them accurately, subject to the width of the column. To change the default to some other type of format, you choose the Settings option of the spreadsheet menu.

1. Press MENU (F10) to invoke the spreadsheet Menu commands.

2. Select the Settings option.

The spreadsheet window disappears temporarily and is replaced by a settings window, which shows the current global settings of the spreadsheet environment. The submenu of the Settings command, displayed in the control panel, is

Label-Prefix Recalculation Titles Format Width Quit

The Format option is what you will use to change the default global format. You can change the default settings in the window by making selections from the menu. "The Spreadsheet Settings Window" (see box) explains how this works.

Notice the right side of the settings window, which shows that the current setting for Format is G, which stands for General. Now you will change that setting.

3. Select the Format option of the Settings menu.

This displays the following format choices:

Currency Punctuated Fixed % General Date Time Scientific Other

In Chapter 3 you used the % option to format revenue growth rates. Here you will try the Fixed option. Fixed allows you to choose exactly how many digits Symphony should display in numeric entries.

THE SPREADSHEET SETTINGS WINDOW

Each of Symphony's five environments has a Settings option that can be accessed by the MENU (F10) key. The settings window of the SHEET environment normally looks like this:

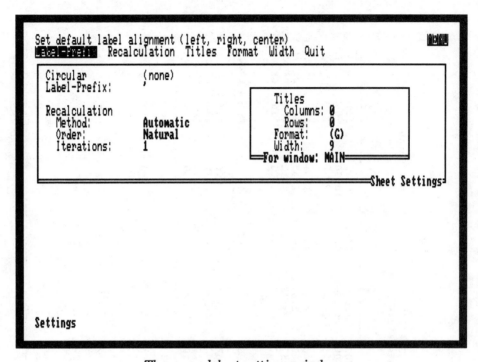

The spreadsheet settings window

You use the settings window to view or change current spreadsheet settings. Each of the selections in the control panel gives you access to a different setting in the window.

- *Label-prefix.* Sets the default alignment (left, right, or center) of labels within cells.
- *Recalculation.* Determines the method, order, and iteration count for recalculation of the spreadsheet.
- *Titles.* Fixes or clears horizontal or vertical title rows on the screen.
- *Format.* Determines the default format of numeric values on the screen.
- *Width.* Determines the default width of spreadsheet columns.
- *Quit.* Exits from the Settings menu.

One other item appears in the spreadsheet settings window but is not listed in the control panel. The "Circular" line is not actually a setting; rather it is an indicator at which Symphony lists the cell location of any circular reference (a formula that depends on its own value) appearing in the spreadsheet. Chapter 7 of the *How-To Manual* provides more information.

INCOME STATEMENT
YORICK HABERDASHERY, INC.
($ IN THOUSANDS)

	A (RATES)	B	C	D	E	F	G	H	NOTES
			0	1	2	3	4	5	
6		REVENUE	10000	12000	15600	18720	20592	22651	
7		% GROWTH OVER PREVIOUS YEAR		20.00%	30.00%	20.00%	10.00%	10.00%	
9		COST OF GOODS SOLD							
10	17.00%	MATERIALS		2040	2652	3182	3501	3851	% OF SALES
11	14.00%	WAGES		1680	2184	2621	2883	3171	% OF SALES
12	15.00%	FRINGE BENEFITS		252	328	393	432	476	% OF WAGES
13	8.00%	OTHER		100	108	117	126	136	% GROWTH RATE
15		GENERAL & ADMINISTRATIVE EXPENSE							
16	10.00%	COMPENSATION: OFFICE		1200	1320	1452	1597	1757	% GROWTH RATE
17	8.00%	COMPENSATION: SALES		960	1248	1498	1647	1812	% OF SALES
18	17.00%	FRINGE BENEFITS		367	437	501	552	607	% OF OFFICE & SALES COMP
19	2.50%	ADVERTISING & PROMOTION		300	390	468	515	566	% OF SALES
20		DEPRECIATION		20	20	20	20	20	DIRECT INPUT
21	10	MISCELLANEOUS		10	20	30	40	50	CONSTANT GROWTH
23		TOTAL OPERATING EXPENSES	6400	6929	8706	10282	11313	12446	
25		INTEREST EXPENSE	10	10	10	10	10	10	DIRECT INPUT
27		PRE-TAX INCOME	3590	5061	6884	8428	9269	10196	
29	52.00%	TAX	1867	2632	3580	4383	4820	5302	% OF PRE-TAX INCOME
31		NET INCOME	1723	2429	3304	4045	4449	4894	

Figure 5-1.   The finished income statement

4. Select the Fixed option.

The default is 2. You will opt for no decimals, however, so you can display the numbers as integers.

5. Type **0** (zero) and press RETURN.

Now take note of the settings window. The global format setting has changed from G to F0, which stands for Fixed, zero decimal places. To end the Settings command and restore the spreadsheet,

6. Select the Quit option.

Now all values except the revenue growth rates appear as integers. Bear in mind the difference between Settings format, which establishes a global format, and the spreadsheet Format command, which assigns "local" formats specific to particular cells or ranges. Cells formatted by the spreadsheet Format command are exceptions to the settings established in Settings format.

Note that the numeric cells are not internally converted to integers; they are merely displayed as such. Symphony internally stores the values with as much decimal accuracy as it can. What you see is not what you've got. Arithmetic calculations use the internally stored values, not the externally rounded integers.

Revising the Format of the Rates Column

In the process of formatting the numeric cells, what has happened to the RATES column? Most of the rates have changed to 0, or at least they appear to have changed. If you move the cell pointer to a rate cell, the control panel will show that the original input is still there. The decimal rates were not specifically formatted with the spreadsheet Format command, and so they are subject to the new default integer format. To remedy this error, apply the spreadsheet Format % command to the RATE column.

1. Move the pointer to the first cell of the RATE column (cell A6).

2. Press MENU (F10) and select Format %.

To accept Symphony's default suggestion that you display two decimal places,

3. Press RETURN.

To indicate the end of the range to be formatted,

4. Use the PG DN and down arrow keys to skip down the column to the last entry, NET INCOME, in cell A31.

5. Press RETURN.

Your display is much more consistent now. If you want to change the default global format, simply reissue the Settings Format command.

One more slight change. The rate of the MISCELLANEOUS row was supposed to represent a constant increase of $10 thousand. The spreadsheet Format command converted the 10 to 1000.00 percent. To change it back to its original General format,

6. Move to the MISCELLANEOUS rate cell (A21).

7. Press MENU (F10), select Format, then select General, and press RETURN.

Your model should now resemble Figure 5-1. To save the file,

8. Press SERVICES (F9), select File, select Save, and press RETURN to use the same file name of INC_STA (and replace the previous version of the model).

9. Select Yes to confirm the replacement.

Printing the Income Statement

As the grand finale to your work on Yorick's income statement, print a copy of the spreadsheet on a printer. Since printing is something that you would want to do from any environment, the Print command is part of the general Services command menu.

Before you can use the Print command, however, you must have provided for a printer in the Install Setup procedure, which configures Symphony for a particular set of hardware. If your Symphony Program Disk has not been set up for your printer, refer to the Symphony *Introduction* manual to customize the Setup file for your printer.

About the Print Settings Window

Before Symphony can print a report, there are several things it must be told. For one thing, Symphony needs to know what range of cells you want to print out. In your case, you want the range that encompasses the entire spreadsheet: A1..J31. You might also want to tell Symphony how to lay out the page. Do you want single, double, or triple spacing? Do you want a continuous printout or some blank lines between pages? What margins do you want to use?

You answer these questions by using a Print settings window. So far you have seen two settings windows: one for the Services menu and the other for the spreadsheet command menu. Recall that to change the spreadsheet global settings, you selected the Settings option from the menu and then specified the setting that you wanted to change. Remember too that Symphony provides default settings. Usually you only need to change a few settings to attain the results you want.

Print settings works the same way. Selecting the Services Print command brings a settings window to the screen, and selecting Settings brings a menu to the control panel that is used to change the defaults shown in the window. Take a few moments to read "The Print Settings Window" (see box) to get an idea of what settings are under your control and what the default settings are.

Most standard printers are set to print 6 lines per inch vertically and 10 characters per inch horizontally, and standard small-sized printers typically use 8 1/2- (width) by 11-inch (length) paper. Usually, then, small printers can print a maximum of 66 (11 × 6) lines per page and 85 (10 × 8.5) characters per line. That expains why the Length option defaults to 66.

The standard printer's characteristics also explain the default margins. The left, right, top, and bottom margins define a frame of white space that surrounds the printed text. The left margin is the number of spaces on the left side of this frame of white space. Thus, the default left margin of 4 means that the left side of the frame takes up four characters, so printing begins at the fifth character space of the page.

THE PRINT SETTINGS WINDOW

The Print settings window normally looks like this:

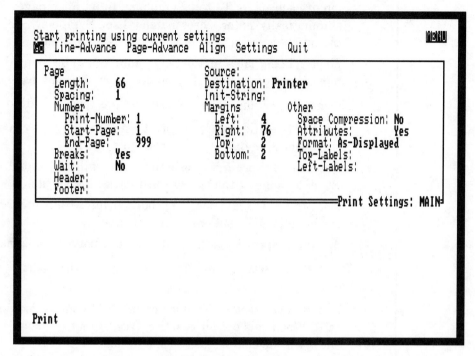

Start printing using current settings

▓▓ Line-Advance Page-Advance Align Settings Quit

```
Page                    Source:
  Length:      66        Destination: Printer
  Spacing:     1         Init-String:
  Number                 Margins        Other
    Print-Number: 1        Left:    4     Space Compression: No
    Start-Page:   1        Right:  76     Attributes:        Yes
    End-Page:   999        Top:     2     Format: As-Displayed
  Breaks:      Yes         Bottom:  2     Top-Labels:
  Wait:        No                         Left-Labels:
  Header:
  Footer:
                                         Print Settings: MAIN
```

Print

The Print settings window

There are three main parts to the window, and they are accessed by selecting the Settings option in the control panel. The left side of the window begins with page layout settings. The middle section includes settings that tell Symphony what to print, where to print it (you can send the printout to a printer, a file, or to a range of the worksheet), and what margins to use on each side of the printed material—left, right, top, and bottom. The third column of settings controls miscellaneous ("Other") options.

The Page settings are as follows:

- *Length.* The number of character spaces in a printed line. The default is 66, but Symphony can print between 20 and 100, depending on your needs and the size of your paper.

- *Spacing.* The vertical spacing of lines. You may select single, double, or triple spacing.

- *Number.* Controls page numbering. The Print-Number option tells Symphony what number to begin at if you want pages numbered in sequence. See "Header."

- *Breaks.* Turns automatic page breaks, headers, and footers on or off. The "Yes" default includes page breaks.

continued

- *Wait.* If on, printing is delayed between printed pages. The "No" default assumes continuous printing.
- *Header.* Designates text, including page numbers, to be printed on top of each page. To tell Symphony to number pages in sequence automatically, enter a crosshatch (#) and Symphony will begin with the number designated in the Print-Number line.
- *Footer.* Designates text or page numbers to be printed on the bottom of each page. See "Header" for information on page numbering.

The middle portion of the window contains several additional settings:

- *Source.* Specifies what to print. You must specify a range of a spreadsheet or database in order to print it.
- *Destination.* Specifies where the report will be printed: on a printer, on a range of the spreadsheet, or on a disk file.
- *Init-String.* A sequence of encoded printer-control characters that send special instructions to the printer.
- *Margins.* Specifies left, right, top, and bottom margins.

The "Other" settings on the right side of the spreadsheet are as follows:

- *Space Compression.* Enables or disables compression of spaces to tabs. When this option is set to "Yes," groups of spaces in a worksheet will be compressed to single tabs.
- *Attributes.* Enables or disables processing of special print attributes like **boldface** or *italics*.
- *Format.* Allows you to print worksheet cells as they are displayed or to print cell formulas.
- *Top-Labels.* Allows you to specify rows to be printed (for instance, a top border) at the top of each page.
- *Left-Labels.* Allows you to specify columns (for instance, a left border) to be printed at the left of each page.

The right margin is the position of the last printing character space on the line. A right margin of 76 means that the last printing character of a line can be in the seventy-sixth character position. With the default settings there is room for 72 (76−4) characters on a line.

If the Page Break setting is on, the top and bottom margins define the top and bottom borders (the number of blank lines on the top and bottom of the page). Thus, Page Break prevents the printer from printing continuously from one page to the next on continuous-feed paper. Top and bottom margins of 2 leave two blank lines at the top and bottom of the page. Beneath the top margin, Symphony reserves a line for the page header. If you do not ask Symphony to print the header, Symphony prints a blank line instead. Whether or not you specify a header, Symphony then prints two blank lines before it begins printing the text.

At the bottom of the page, Symphony prints two blank lines, the page footer (or a blank line, if no footer is specified) and then as many blank lines as the bottom-margin setting specifies.

Selecting Print Settings

The first step in printing is to move the pointer to the beginning of the range to be printed.

1. Press HOME to move to A1.

2. Press SERVICES (F9) and select the Print command.

This invokes the Print menu:

Go Line-Advance Page-Advance Align Settings Quit

The Go command instructs Symphony to commence printing. However, you don't want Symphony to go until you're sure it will print the spreadsheet the way you want it.

Selecting the Source Range

The first thing Symphony needs to know is the source range, the range that you want to print. To enter the source range,

1. Select the Settings option.

Notice the Settings menu in the control panel and the Source option of the menu.

2. Select the Source option.

The Source submenu is

Range Database Cancel

You will use Range to designate the source range to be printed. The Database option is used for databases, as you will see later in the book. Cancel pre-empts a previously designated source range, allowing you to enter a new one from scratch.

3. Select Range.

The settings window disappears temporarily. This allows you to point to the beginning and end of the rectangle that comprises the print source range. The highlight will be on the cell location of the cell pointer before you issued the Print command—which is convenient if you positioned the pointer at the first cell of the source range (and you already have).

4. Type a . to anchor A1 as the beginning of the range to be printed.

5. Point to the bottom right corner of the spreadsheet (cell J31). (You can do this quickly by pressing the END key and then the HOME key.)

6. Press RETURN.

Symphony commits the source range to memory and restores the Settings menu.

Are you ready to print yet? Not quite, because there is a problem with the width of the report.

Adjusting Margins

Symphony's default margins allow 74 characters to be printed on a line, but your spreadsheet needs 124 characters. You need 50 more spaces in order to print the report on one page.

If you have a wide-carriage printer with 14-inch-wide paper, there is no problem. Simply reset the left and right margins to accommodate the excess width. If you have a smaller printer and it is able to print with condensed print, you can fit more characters on a line by resetting the margins.

If your printer cannot accommodate 124 characters, you will have to live with a two-page report. You may specify part of the report as the source range (for example, A1..F31), print that range, and then specify the second part of the report (G1..J31) as the source range and print it. You can also specify the source range in its entirety (A1..J31). Symphony will print as much as it can on the first page, from left to right, and the remainder on the next page.

If your printer allows more than 124 characters in either condensed or non-condensed mode,

1. Select the Margins option of the Settings command.

Change the left margin to 0 and the right margin to 130. That will be enough space for the report.

2. Select Left, type **0**, and press RETURN.

To set the right margin,

3. Select Right, type **130**, press RETURN, and select Quit to exit from the Margins submenu.

Using Init-String to Print in Condensed Mode

If you have a wide-carriage printer that accommodates the entire spreadsheet in regular Print Mode, you're all set—you can skip the next section. If you have a small printer that has a condensed print capability, you must explicitly instruct your printer to use the condensed character set. Some printers can be put in Condensed Mode by setting the printer's switches. Others can be reset by sending special commands to the printer from the computer. Unfortunately, there are no universal commands that all printers obey. Each printer has a special code, or sequence of codes, that causes it to enter Condensed Mode. An *init-string* is a sequence of characters that you tell Symphony to send to your printer in order to give the printer special instructions. You can send an init-string to your printer by using the *Init-String command* of the Settings menu.

For example, to instruct an Epson FX-80 or FX-100 printer to use Condensed Mode, the computer must send the code number 15 to the printer. Symphony's rule for creating an init-string for a code number is to begin with a backward slash (\ ) followed by a three-digit number; so the Condensed mode init-string would be \015 for the Epson FX-80 or FX-100. The Symphony *Reference Manual* contains extensive rules for creating init strings, and your printer reference manual lists the codes specific to your printer.

If a Print command tells Symphony to send an init-string to the printer, the init-string is sent prior to printing the report, and it remains in effect until you send a different printer code that changes the Condensed Mode to another mode or until you turn the printer off. In addition, if the print settings of a worksheet include an init-string, the string is automatically sent to the printer whenever the Print Go command is issued. If you save a worksheet with an init-string print setting, the setting is saved with the worksheet, and retrieving the worksheet retrieves the saved print settings as well (including the init-string).

1. Select Init-String, and type in the string for Condensed Mode. Press RETURN.

2. Choose the Quit option to leave the Settings menu and return to the Print menu.

Printing the Spreadsheet

Now you're almost ready to print the spreadsheet. There may be one small matter to attend to, however, if you manually adjusted the paper after you turned on the printer.

When you first turn on the printer, Symphony assumes that the paper is aligned at the top of the page. It begins counting its 66 lines per page wherever the page is actually positioned. If the page is not positioned correctly, and you manually adjust it, Symphony will not notice—it will only remember the original settings and will proceed as if you had never made an adjustment.

You could remedy this by turning your printer off and on again after aligning the top of the printer paper, but Symphony provides an easier solution. The Align option of the Print menu makes Symphony reset its internal line counter to 1. Wherever the paper is when Align is executed will be considered by Symphony as the first of 66 lines of a new page. If you think that Symphony may be "confused" about the location of the top of the page, choose the Align option of the menu and then print out the report.

1. Choose the Go option.

Your report, when printed, should look like Figure 5-1. Symphony assumes that you might want to do some more printing, which is why it resumes with the Print menu on the screen instead of returning to the spreadsheet.

2. Select the Page-Advance option to advance the printer automatically to the top of the next page. (To tear out the page, you may want to select Page-Advance a second time if you are using continuous-feed paper and you want to tear the paper at the perforation.)

3. Choose the Quit option to exit the Print menu and resume your work.

Saving Print Settings

Having printed the income statement model, you have completed what you set out to do at the beginning of this chapter. Resaving the model at this point also stores the current Print command options, including all of the settings as you last left them.

1. Press SERVICES (F9), select File, select Save, press RETURN, and select Yes to resave the file and its new print settings under the name of INC_STA.

Through extensive use of the Copy command, you have developed a general model to forecast the income statement of an organization. It may take a while before you are using the Copy command fluently, but its use does become quite easy and natural with a little practice. It is well worth the effort required to master this command.

Chapter 6
Windows and What-If

The Setting Titles Command

Using Windows

Testing What-Ifs
With Windows

Using the ZOOM Key
To Enlarge a Window

The income forecast that you completed in the previous chapter included examples of the most important spreadsheet commands. There is still more that you can learn about Symphony from the income forecast; and in this chapter you will use that model to become acquainted with Symphony's windowing capabilities, as well as additional techniques that make Symphony such a powerful tool for analyzing information in a variety of ways. If you do not have the model saved on disk, you can create it by following the numbered steps in Chapters 2 through 5.

INCOME STATEMENT
YORICK HABERDASHERY, INC.
($ IN THOUSANDS)

RATES		0	1	2	3	4	5	NOTES
	REVENUE	10000	12000	15600	18720	20592	22651	
	% GROWTH OVER PREVIOUS YEAR		20.00%	30.00%	20.00%	10.00%	10.00%	
	COST OF GOODS SOLD							
17.00%	MATERIALS		2040	2652	3182	3501	3851	% OF SALES
14.00%	WAGES		1680	2184	2621	2883	3171	% OF SALES
15.00%	FRINGE BENEFITS		252	328	393	432	476	% OF WAGES
8.00%	OTHER		100	108	117	126	136	% GROWTH RATE
	GENERAL & ADMINISTRATIVE EXPENSE							
10.00%	COMPENSATION: OFFICE		1200	1320	1452	1597	1757	% GROWTH RATE
8.00%	COMPENSATION: SALES		960	1248	1498	1647	1812	% OF SALES
17.00%	FRINGE BENEFITS		367	437	501	552	607	% OF OFFICE & SALES COMP
2.50%	ADVERTISING & PROMOTION		300	390	468	515	566	% OF SALES
	DEPRECIATION		20	20	20	20	20	DIRECT INPUT
10	MISCELLANEOUS		10	20	30	40	50	CONSTANT GROWTH
	TOTAL OPERATING EXPENSES	6400	6929	8706	10282	11313	12446	
	INTEREST EXPENSE	10	10	10	10	10	10	DIRECT INPUT
	PRE-TAX INCOME	3590	5061	6884	8428	9269	10196	
52.00%	TAX	1867	2632	3580	4383	4820	5302	% OF PRE-TAX INCOME
	NET INCOME	1723	2429	3304	4045	4449	4894	

Figure 6-1. Income statement showing titles to be fixed

The Settings Titles Command

After inserting the disk in the data disk drive, load the worksheet:

1. Press SERVICES (F9), select File Retrieve, and select INC_STA as the worksheet to be retrieved.

The income statement spreadsheet, shown in Figure 6-1, is too large to fit on one screen. Horizontally, the model spans columns A through J, whereas the screen only has room for columns A through F. Vertically, the spreadsheet ends at row 31, while the screen can only show 20 rows at a time. If you wanted to look at Year 5 REVENUE, you could scroll the display by moving the pointer to H6, but then columns A and B would disappear from the screen. Similarly, to view Year 1 NET INCOME, you could scroll down to the bottom of the worksheet but lose the top rows in the process.

When the spreadsheet contains row titles (like REVENUE and MATERIALS) on the left and column titles (the year headings—0,1,2,...5) on top, it is convenient to "fix" or "lock" the row and column titles on the screen, so that they remain fixed on the screen while the rest of the display scrolls in any direction.

In the example, the row titles are in column B, and the column titles occupy rows 1 through 5 (including the row of hyphens in row 5). The Settings Titles command of the spreadsheet command menu allows you to lock in these title rows and columns so that only the cells below row 5 and to the right of column B are subject to scrolling.

Fixing Row and Column Labels

The first step in using Settings Titles, like many other Symphony commands, is to place the cell pointer in a particular position before invoking the command. For Settings Titles, the pointer should be in the top left corner of the scrollable part of the worksheet. This is cell C6 in the example, since this cell is in the first column to the right of the row titles and in the first row below the column titles.

Settings Titles will fix the rows and columns exactly as they appear on the screen before you issue the command. For this reason, it is important that the screen's first row include the first row of row titles you want to lock and the screen's first column include the first column of column titles. To make sure that this is so,

1. Press the HOME key.

Next position the pointer so that all portions of the spreadsheet to the left and above the current cell will be frozen.

2. Move the pointer to cell C6, the top left cell of the scrollable area of the display.

Now you are ready to invoke the Settings Titles command. The spreadsheet Settings command is used to control various aspects of the spreadsheet. In the previous chapter you used the spreadsheet Settings command to assign a default display format to the spreadsheet's numeric cells. Here you will use Settings to affect the spreadsheet display in a different way.

3. Press the MENU (F10) key and select Settings.

The settings window appears on the screen, replacing the worksheet. Notice the titles settings on the right side of the settings window. Currently, the column and row titles settings are zero (inactive). You will use the Titles option of the menu to change that.

4. Select Titles.

You will be locking both the column (horizontal) and row (vertical) titles by selecting Both from the menu appearing in the control panel.

5. Select Both.

It is also possible to lock just the horizontal titles or just the vertical titles and to unlock titles by using the Clear option of the Titles menu.

Notice that the titles settings in the window are no longer zero. The "2" in the column settings means that the two leftmost columns have been locked, while the "5" in the rows settings indicates that the top five rows have been locked.

6. Select Quit to exit from the Settings menu.

Let's see what happened. First, press the HOME key. When you press HOME with titles set, the pointer moves to the top left of the scrollable part of the worksheet (cell C6), instead of cell A1. Next, move to Year 5 REVENUE (cell H6). Note that the column titles remain fixed on the screen, while columns C and D have scrolled away. Now try using the left arrow key to move to the MATERIALS rate cell (A10). When you try to move left of column C, Symphony sounds a beep. You may not use the arrow keys to move into the titles area when titles are locked. Trying to move up (above row 6) yields the same result. You have been "locked out" of the titles area, so to speak. The titles area has become, for all practical purposes, an extension of Symphony's border area.

Use PG DN and the down arrow key to scroll the screen down to the NET INCOME line, row 31. Without titles settings, the top rows of the screen would have scrolled away. Instead, they remain, at the cost of some rows beneath the title rows.

What if you wanted to change the interest expense in Year 5 from 10 to 20? Without locked titles, it might have been difficult to locate Year 5 INTEREST EXPENSE, because both the row and column titles would have scrolled off the screen. Locked titles not only make it easier to interpret distant parts of the spreadsheet for viewing, but also to enter data.

7. Move to Year 5 INTEREST EXPENSE (H25) and enter the value **20**.

Year 5 NET INCOME has decreased to 4889.

Changing Data in the Titles Area

So far the titles settings have worked to your advantage. You can scroll to the farthest reaches of the spreadsheet without getting lost; the titles always tell which data line you are in.

One question may have occurred to you, though. What happens if you want to change data within the titles area?

Currently, wages have been assumed to grow by 14 percent annually. Yorick's managers would like to increase the profit earned by the firm. One way of achieving increased profit is to decrease expenses. Therefore, Yorick is considering lowering the forecast of wages from 14 percent of revenue to 7 percent.

To effect this change, you would have to position the cell pointer at the rate cell for WAGES. However, the arrow keys cannot move the pointer to the cells within the locked titles area, and the WAGES rate cell is within the area.

There are two ways to get at this rate cell. One way is to remove the lock by clearing the titles settings. The second way is to use the GOTO (F5) key to move to the desired cell (A11).

1. Press the GOTO (F5) key, type **A11**, and press RETURN.

Symphony has done something strange to the display. As you might have expected, rows 1 through 5 and columns A and B have been reserved for titles. However, as Figure 6-2 shows, Symphony displays column A again instead of displaying column C. It is in this repeat of column A that the pointer has been placed. This is a side effect of having locked titles. Even when you use GOTO, Symphony does not allow the pointer into the locked area. Instead, Symphony duplicates the column again in the unlocked area of the spreadsheet and puts the pointer in this area. This only happens when you try to use the GOTO (F5) key to access a cell in a titles area.

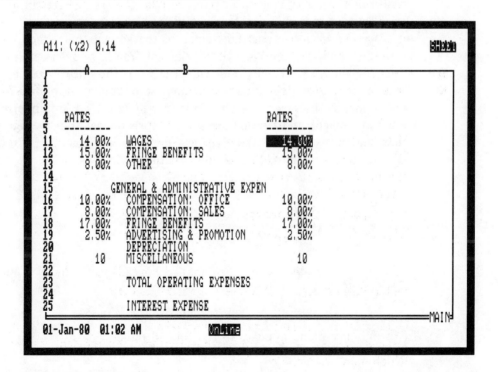

Figure 6-2. Duplicated columns as a side effect of locked titles

2. Type .07 and press RETURN to enter the new rate assumption for wages.

3. Use the arrow keys to move down to Year 1 NET INCOME (cell D31).

By moving to Year 1 net income, you return the display to normal. Decreasing wage expense from 14 to 7 percent has caused net income to increase from $2429 to $2893 thousand.

Using Windows

One of Yorick Haberdashery's goals is to increase profits (net income) by at least $1 million each year. Managers believe that your current expense forecast is essentially on target, but that revenues could be increased in order to meet the $1 million growth goal. Years 1 and 2 already show growths of more than a million dollars from the prior year. The question is, what percent growth assumptions are necessary in Years 3 through 5 to achieve the net income goal?

To find the answer, you can simply try out percentages in the % GROWTH OVER PREVIOUS YEAR cells in row 7 of the spreadsheet. You will increase the revenue growth in each year until the net income of that year is $1 million greater than the preceding year. However, if you make a change to a cell in row 7, the only way to examine the effect of that change in the NET INCOME line (row 31) is to scroll up and down the worksheet continually. The screen cannot show rows 7 and 31 simultaneously. Even titles settings do not provide any relief.

This problem is very common. There will probably be many times when you would like to view two distant parts of a large spreadsheet simultaneously. Symphony's answer to this problem is windows.

A *window* is a rectangular sector of the screen that functions as a porthole through which you can view the worksheet. You have been using a single window thus far—a SHEET window—that takes up the entire screen. Instead of one window taking up the entire screen, you can create two windows, each one occupying a part of the screen. Both windows will be SHEET windows, but they will allow you to look at different parts of the spreadsheet at once. You may remember that the first option of the Services menu is Window. This is the option that creates, alters, deletes, shapes, and positions windows.

Creating Windows
With the Window Pane Command

Let's now create two equally shaped spreadsheet windows with the Window command.

1. Press the SERVICES (F9) key and select Window.

The Window menu appears in the control panel:

Use Create Delete Layout Hide Isolate Expose Pane Settings Quit

Don't jump ahead and select Create yet. Although Create can be used to create a window of any size, there is a much easier way, provided that you are willing to split the screen exactly in half or in quarters.

Creating a screen window can be compared to installing a window. One option is to install a single sheet of glass. Another option is to "pane" the glass—that is, to use horizontal and vertical slats to divide the glass into sections. For example, by paning the glass horizontally (putting a single horizontal slat through the middle of the window), it almost looks as if you installed two windows. Or you might divide the window in half vertically. If you were to peer out of either of the two panes at the parking lot across the street, you would obtain the same view—the parking lot—no matter which pane you were looking through.

Let's see how this translates into the Pane command of the Window menu.

2. Select Pane.

This brings a new menu to the screen:

Vertical-Split Horizontal-Split Both

A vertical split makes two windows out of one by vertically dividing the original window in half. A horizontal split divides the original window in half horizontally. The Both option divides the window into four equal quarters. Since you want to be able to look at REVENUE and NET INCOME, which are horizontal rows of cells, you will select a horizontal split.

3. Select Horizontal-Split.

The screen instantaneously divides into two horizontal halves (Figure 6-3). The two windows look identical because right now they are two panes from the same glass. Each window is a porthole to the Symphony worksheet, and currently, the two portholes open up to the same view, the same portion of the worksheet. Make no mistake: you have not created two spreadsheets; you have only created, in a sense, double-vision—you are looking a single set of data through two windows.

Following a horizontal split, the cell pointer resides in the top window. You may use the pointer as you did with the single window. Press the right arrow key several times to scroll the window to the right. Notice that the top window scrolls but the bottom window does not. Press HOME. The pointer moves to cell C6 (title settings are still in effect); this doesn't yet affect the bottom window.

Look at the bottom right of the top window, where the word "MAIN" appears. "MAIN" is the name of the top window. Windows have names so that you can identify them. The name of the bottom window is "1". Symphony automatically assigned both of these names, but it is possible to change them to more meaningful ones, as you will see in a later chapter.

Two windows are not very useful if the pointer is imprisoned in one of them, but the pointer can easily be moved from window to window. For example, to transfer the pointer to the bottom window,

4. Press the WINDOW (F6) key.

The WINDOW (F6) key moves the pointer from one window to another. Pressing WINDOW (F6) again would move the pointer back to the top window. With the pointer in the bottom window, you may use the pointer keys to scroll your way around. Begin by pressing the HOME key, and note that this offspring worksheet has inherited the title settings from its parent. Since the numbers in the REVENUE and

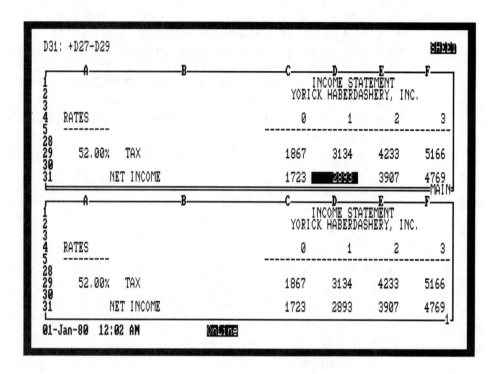

Figure 6-3. The spreadsheet showing horizontal panes

MATERIALS lines are integers, you can infer that the global format (fixed, no decimals) that you established with the Settings command in Chapter 5 is in effect in the bottom window too. In fact, everything looks the same except for the windows' names.

Now let's create some differences. With the pointer in the bottom window, move the pointer to the bottom right of the worksheet.

5. Press the END key; then press HOME.

This moves the pointer to J31 and scrolls the bottom window so that it encompasses the bottom right cell.

6. Move down once, to J32; then press the END key; and press the left arrow key.

The pointer is now in C32, and you have succeeded in scrolling the bottom window so that it shows the NET INCOME line.

As you have seen, two windows can be employed to show two parts of the same worksheet. The two parts can coincide (as when you initially created the windows with the Window Pane command), or they can be distinct, as they are at this moment.

Assigning Spreadsheet Settings To One Window

You can also assign spreadsheet settings to the bottom window that are different from the top window's settings. With the pointer still in the bottom window,

1. Press the MENU (F10) key and select Settings to fetch the spreadsheet settings window.

Here is an opportunity to look into some of the other format types.

2. Select the Format option of the Settings menu.

Try out the Currency format.

3. Select Currency.

Symphony asks how many decimals you want.

4. Type **0** and press RETURN; then select Quit.

The Currency format places a dollar sign before numeric values and displays values greater than 999 (or less than −999) with commas. Although you can't see it, the Currency format also displays negative values enclosed in parentheses, instead of preceding the negative values with minus signs. This format is often used in financial reports. Notice that the global Currency format affects the display in the bottom window but not in the top. Bear in mind, too, that the format settings of both windows only affect the display of the values. The underlying numeric data itself does not change at all as a result of formatting.

Since dollar signs clutter up this spreadsheet a bit too much, let's replace the Currency format with the Punctuated format. Punctuated format is the same as Currency but without the dollar signs.

5. Press MENU (F10) and select Settings Format.

6. Select Punctuated, type **0**, press RETURN, and select Quit.

Punctuated format looks neat and clear. Let's keep it.

Testing What-Ifs With Windows

Now you can return to the problem: finding revenue growth rates that give the company $1 million annual growth in Years 3, 4, and 5. You will use the top window to venture guesses at the growth rates and see how these estimates affect the NET INCOME line in the bottom window.

1. Press the WINDOW (F6) key to move the cursor to the top window.

2. Move to Year 3's % GROWTH OVER PREVIOUS YEAR cell (F7).

The current growth rate is 20 percent (0.2). The following steps explain how to determine Year 3's growth rate; you can apply the same steps to determine the correct growth rates for Years 4 and 5. First, use a guess of 30 percent to see if that yields a net income that clears the hurdle:

3. Enter **.3** and press RETURN.

This yields a Year 3 net income of 5241, a growth of 1334 over Year 2. Changing a value in the top window affects cells containing dependent formulas in the bottom window. Now try a lower rate to see if you can get closer to 4907, which is 1000 more than Year 2. (Remember, the spreadsheet is in thousands, so that 1 million equals 1000 on the spreadsheet.)

4. Enter .25 and press RETURN.

The new value, ~~5361~~ *5005*, is still too much.

5. Enter .22 and press RETURN.

This results in 4863, just shy of your goal of 4907. Twenty-three percent is probably the lowest whole percentage that results in a $1 million growth.

6. Enter .23 and press RETURN.

A growth of 23 percent yields 4911, which is $4 thousand above the goal.

In order to try out the percentage for Year 4 (and then for Year 5), you must scroll the top and bottom windows so that they include the Year 4 and Year 5 columns.

7. Press the right arrow key twice to scroll the window to the right.

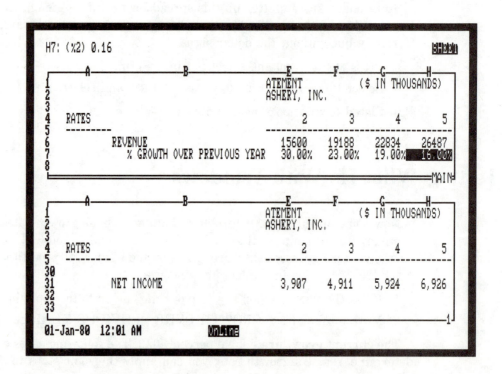

Figure 6-4. Windows showing what-if growth rate estimates

8. Press the WINDOW (F6) key to move to the lower window, and press the right arrow key until Years 4 and 5 of NET INCOME appear in the window.

9. Press the WINDOW (F6) key once more to return to the top window, and move the pointer to Year 4 % GROWTH OVER PREVIOUS YEAR (G7).

Next enter guesses at the growth rate for Year 4 and then for Year 5. The correct results are shown in Figure 6-4.

Using the ZOOM Key
To Enlarge a Window

The ZOOM key is one of the most useful keys for working with windows. Pressing the ZOOM key temporarily enlarges the window containing the pointer so that the window fills the entire screen. On an IBM PC, the ZOOM key consists of a two-key sequence: press the ALT key, and while holding the ALT key down, press (F6). Pressing the ZOOM key (ALT-F6) again restores the window to its original size.

Now that you are done with this analytical exercise, there is no more need to have the bottom window on the screen, so enlarge the top window (making sure that the pointer is in the top window first):

1. Press the ZOOM (ALT-F6) key.

Just for kicks, unzoom the window by typing ZOOM (ALT-F6) again. The two twin windows, MAIN and 1, return to the screen. Now zoom the MAIN window again with the ZOOM key.

Before saving the worksheet, you should first unlock the titles.

2. Press the MENU (F10) key and select Settings.

3. Select Titles, then Clear, and then Quit. Next press HOME to move the pointer to cell A1 again.

4. Save the worksheet under the same INC—STA file name. In Chapter 7 you will use this file as the basis for creating graphics with Symphony.

Chapter 7
Creating Graphics With Symphony

Numerical analyses are invaluable, but nothing commands attention like professional graphics. Symphony produces professional-quality graphics. In this chapter, you will see how easy it is to express spreadsheet data in graphic form. Using the INC_STA model developed in the previous chapters, you will learn how to design several graphs, specify graph settings, and view a graph on the screen. If you do not have the INC_STA worksheet on your screen, retrieve it now.

Graphing the REVENUE Row

Symphony draws six types of graphs: line graphs, bar graphs, stacked bar graphs, pie charts, high-low-close-open charts (for stock analysis), and XY graphs. This chapter introduces the first two graph types.

There is a little bit of graphics terminology to ingest before you proceed. "The Parts of a Graph" (see box) introduces you to the lingo of Symphony graphics.

THE PARTS OF A GRAPH

The following illustration shows a bar chart. Its components are similar to those of the other types of graphs that you can generate with Symphony.

A graph is mapped out by its horizontal and vertical *axes*, called the *X-axis* and *Y-axis* respectively. The Y-axis measures the values of the graphed data. The X-axis shows what the data points correspond to — in this case, the years 1982 through 1985.

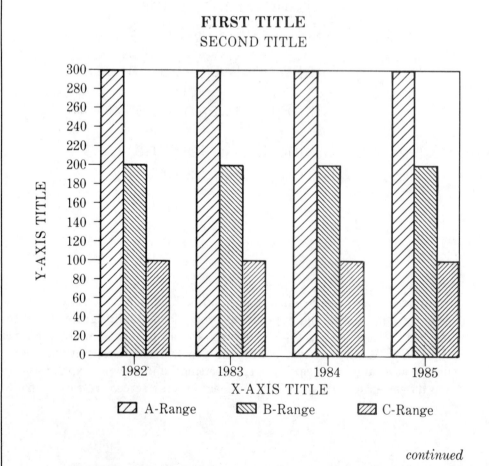

continued

> For each year the graph shows three bars that are distinguished by their shading patterns. The *legend* at the bottom of the graph tells which bar belongs to which shading pattern. The bars correspond to three *data ranges*, called the A-range, the B-range, and the C-range. Actually, Symphony allows you to graph up to six data ranges on one graph (the other three are called the D-range, E-range, and F-range). Each data range consists of values, one for each year shown on the chart. Another special range, the X-range, consists of the X-axis labels—in this case, 1982, 1983, 1984, and 1985.
>
> A graph can have up to two titles that are centered above the chart. You can also give titles to the Y-axis (such as DOLLARS) and to the X-axis (such as YEARS).

To generate a graph, you will need to provide Symphony with *graph settings*—information such as the location of the graph data on the spreadsheet (the data ranges), the titles, and the legend attributes. As you have probably guessed, there is a settings sheet for generating graphs, and you will use this settings sheet to enter the graph's settings. By now you are accustomed to the mechanics of settings. To change a setting in a settings sheet, you simply choose an option from a settings menu.

To begin a graph in the spreadsheet environment, select the *Graph command* of the spreadsheet command menu.

1. Press MENU (F10) and then select Graph.

The control panel contains the Graph menu:

Preview 1st-Settings 2nd-Settings Image-Save Quit

You will use most of these options shortly, but first you will start with the settings sheet. The settings sheet for graphs is divided into two "pages" of settings. The *1st-Settings* option invokes the first page, and *2nd-Settings* invokes the other page. "The Graph Settings Sheets" (see box) describes how each of these pages is used.

2. Select the 1st-Settings option.

Specifying the Data Range

Symphony cannot graph the entire income statement; it must be told exactly which sets of values to graph. Just as before, you need to point out a set of values to Symphony; in this case you designate a range of cells to be graphed. To specify a data range (a range of cells) for graphing, choose one of the letters A through F. Using the income statement model as an example, you could designate the range of cells containing revenue for Years 0 through 5 as the A-range.

1. Select Range to specify a data range.

To assign the A-range,

2. Select A from the menu.

The settings window temporarily disappears. Symphony brings back the spreadsheet and wants to know what range of cells to assign to the A-range. Specifying this range is like specifying any other range in Symphony. You may type the addresses of the range explicitly (for example, C6..H6), but it is probably easier to use the pointing method:

3. Move to the Year 0 REVENUE cell (C6).

4. Type a . to anchor the range.

To skip quickly to the end of the REVENUE row (cell H6),

5. Press the END key; then press the right arrow key.

As always, the range is highlighted.

6. Press RETURN.

Examine the settings window. Notice that the specified range of C6..H6 now appears beside the A-range setting. Making selections from the menus and submenus of the settings windows enters information in those windows.

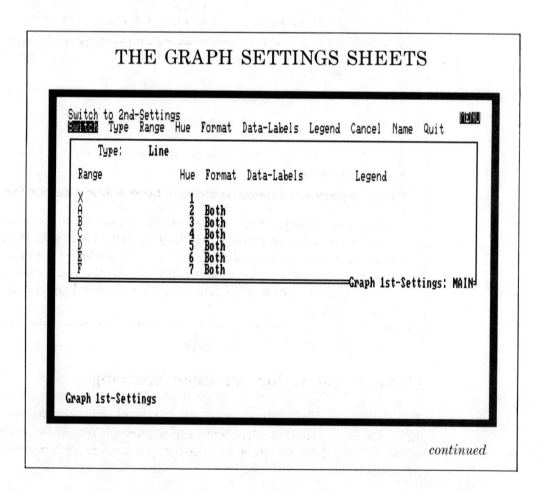

THE GRAPH SETTINGS SHEETS

continued

The 1st-Settings page, shown in the first illustration, displays a table of settings. The first item in the table is *Type*, which refers to the graph's type: line, bar, stacked bar, pie, XY, or high-low-close-open. The default graph type is "Line." The first column of this settings window is the *Range* column. It lists the range designations that are available for assigning the data to be graphed. The *Hue* setting determines shading patterns, while *Format* determines the manner in which lines are drawn in line and XY graphs. The other settings, *Data-Labels* and *Legend*, permit you to print labels beside the graphed values and to display a legend identifying the ranges being graphed. Chapter 8 of the Symphony *Reference Manual* describes these settings in detail.

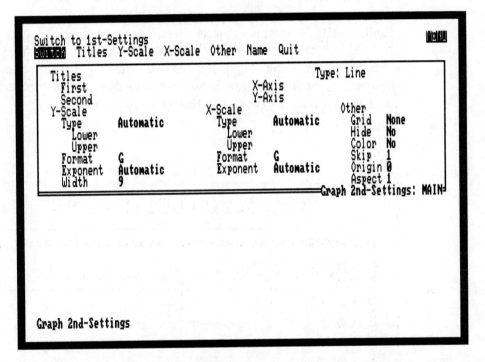

The 2nd-Settings page, shown in the second illustration, includes specifications for graph and axis titles as well as axis scaling and formatting. It also contains settings that permit you to draw a grid on the graph, turn color graphing on or off, and control certain other aspects of a graph. Chapter 8 of the *Reference Manual* also describes these settings in detail.

Using Preview for Advance Showing

You have certainly not finished setting up this graph, but Symphony already has all it needs to generate a rudimentary picture of Yorick's forecasted revenue amounts. Let's delay the other settings for a moment to get a preview of the good things to come.

1. Select Quit to exit from the Range menu; then select Quit again to exit from the 1st-Settings window.

With the Graph menu back in the control panel,

2. Select Preview to see the graph.

The Preview option replaces the spreadsheet window with the graph, which should resemble Figure 7-1. In order to create this graph, Symphony had to make several assumptions. First, because you did not explicitly specify a graph type, Symphony assumed you wanted the default and drew a line graph. Second, based on the values of the data range, Symphony figured out its own scheme for scaling the vertical (REVENUE) axis. The horizontal axis represents time, although Symphony has no idea whether the frequency of the revenue values is years, months, or weeks.

Notice also that Symphony scaled down the revenue values depicted in the graph. Year 0, for instance, was converted from 10,000 to 10. This is because Symphony automatically scales down large numbers along the Y-axis. The "(Thousands)" message along the vertical axis informs you that this has occurred. It is often very convenient to have Symphony scale down large numbers automatically. You will do your own scaling in this case, however.

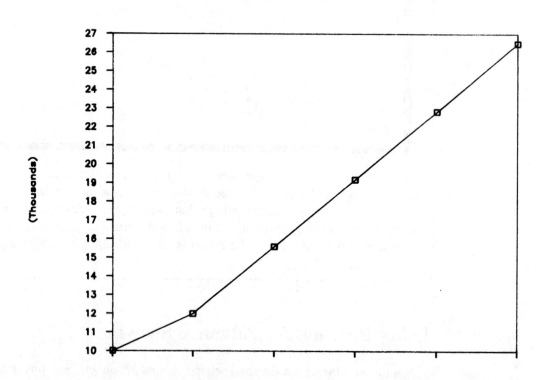

Figure 7-1. Preview graph showing revenue growth

Enhancing the Graph With Settings Options

This graph is fine, but Symphony can do better. The illustrations that appeared earlier in this chapter in "The Parts of a Graph" showed several embellishments that could make this graph much clearer. Let's see what you can do, using the options available in the 1st-Settings and 2nd-Settings windows.

Using 1st-Settings to Define X-Axis Values

The first embellishment you will make is to put labels along the tick marks of the horizontal axis to help clarify what years of data are being graphed. Assuming that somewhere in the worksheet is a range of cells containing appropriate labels or values to be used for the horizontal axis, you can choose the X option of the Graph command's 1st-Settings Range menu to assign the X-range. However, you must first rid the screen of the graph. This can be done by pressing any key.

1. Press any key to return to the Graph menu and the spreadsheet.
2. Select 1st-Settings; select Range; then select X.

The column labels, 0 through 5 in row 4, are perfect for the job.

3. Point to the 0 column label in cell C4.
4. Type a . to anchor the range.

To expand the pointer to the last column label,

5. Press END; then press the right arrow key.
6. Press RETURN; then select Quit from the Range menu and again from the 1st-Settings menu.

From the Graph menu,

7. Select Preview to view the graph.

When you are finished looking,

8. Press any key to restore the Graph menu.

Adding Graph Labels With 2nd-Settings Options

If a graph is to have an impact on the viewer, it should give an instant impression of the story it attempts to depict. Graph and axis titles go a long way toward achieving this effect. The 2nd-Settings window includes commands to incorporate these titles into the graph.

1. Select 2nd-Settings.
2. Select the Titles option.

The Titles menu includes the four types of titles available:

First Second X-axis Y-axis Quit

You may specify all, some, or none of these. *First* and *Second* refer to the main titles of the graph, which are centered over the graph. The other two titles are aligned along the respective axes.

   3. Select First.

If the "CAP" indicator does not appear in the lower-right portion of the screen, press the CAPS LOCK key to cause all typed letters to be in capitals. In response to the "First graph title:" prompt,

   4. Type **FINANCIAL FORECAST** and press RETURN.

The control panel now brings back the Titles menu because Symphony assumes you may have more titles to enter—and indeed you do. Although it isn't mandatory, enter a second title.

   5. Select Second.

   6. Type **YORICK HABERDASHERY, INC.** and press RETURN.

The Titles menu returns.

   7. Select the X-axis option, type **YEARS**, and press RETURN.

Review the results:

   8. Select Quit to exit from the Titles menu; select Quit to exit from the 2nd-Settings menu; then select Preview from the Graph menu.

As Figure 7-2 shows, this graph is certainly more illustrative than the primitive one shown in the last figure. The trend of revenue over the forecast period is quite clear from the line, and the titles describe succinctly what this graph is about. When you have finished examining the improved product,

   9. Press any key to return to the Graph menu.

Changing Scale With the Y-Scale Exponent Option

You may have noticed a problem with the graph you just viewed. The revenue data taken from the spreadsheet was originally stated in thousands (for example, the value 10,000 really represented 10 million), but Symphony has no way of knowing this. To Symphony, 10,000 means 10 thousand, not 10 million. Thus, when it scales down the data, Symphony thinks that it has converted the values to thousands when in fact it has converted them to millions.

Fortunately, you can wrest control away from Symphony's defaults and scale the Y-axis in the way you see fit or not scale it at all. In the 2nd-Settings window, an option called Y-Scale may be used to select a scaling factor, control the format of the numbers along the Y-axis, determine the amount of space reserved for Y-axis scale numbers, and determine whether or not to accept the automatic minimum and maximum Y-axis values that Symphony generates.

   1. Select 2nd-Settings; then select Y-Scale.

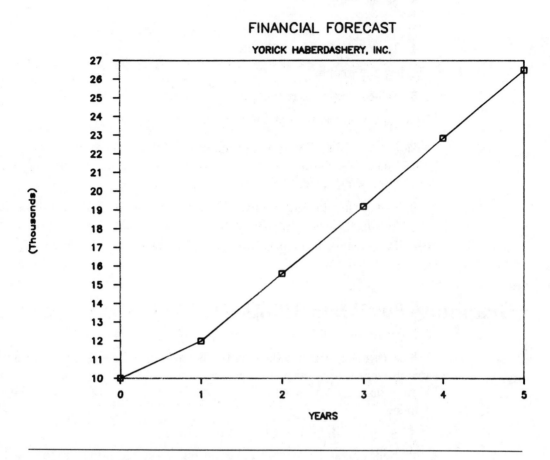

Figure 7-2. Preview graph with titles

The option that controls the scaling factor is Exponent. Strictly speaking, the exponent is the power of 10 that Symphony uses to make the number smaller. For example, using an exponent of 3, Symphony takes a value like 10,000 and converts it to 10 by dividing 10,000 by 1000 (which is 10 to the power of 3). Think of the scaling exponent as the number of zeros that Symphony removes in order to make a large number smaller. With an exponent of 3, Symphony removes three zeros from 10,000 to arrive at a scaled value of 10. Three is the exponent that Symphony presumed to use in your graph.

Suppose you told Symphony to use no exponent, which is equivalent to using an exponent of 0. In this case, Symphony would not remove any zeros at all. A number like 10,000 would remain 10,000. This is exactly what you want, except that if you portray the numbers with no scaling, you really should note somewhere in the graph that the data is expressed in thousands. Therefore, in addition to specifying an exponent of 0, you will add a Y-axis title, $ IN THOUSANDS.

2. Select Exponent.

To overrule Symphony's automatic scale factor, opt for Manual instead of Automatic.

3. Select Manual.

Next,

4. Type **0** and press RETURN.

To view the graph,

5. Select Quit to exit the Y-Scale menu.

Now, to revise the title of the vertical axis,

6. Select Titles from the 2nd-Settings menu.

7. Select the Y-axis option.

8. Type **$ IN THOUSANDS** and press RETURN.

9. Select Quit to exit from the Titles menu; select Quit again to exit from 2nd-Settings; then, select Preview to see the graph.

10. Press any key to continue.

Graphing Two Data Ranges

The revenue graph tells part of the story of Yorick's financial outlook, but a graph comparing revenue to net income would be more enlightening. This is a simple task. All you need to do is specify a second data range in the 1st-Settings window.

1. Select 1st-Settings; then select Range.

2. Select B, and move to the beginning of the second range to be graphed, Year 0 NET INCOME (cell C31).

To expand the cell pointer over the range,

3. Type a . to anchor the range.

4. Press END; then press the right arrow key to encompass the range Year 0 (C31) to Year 5 (H31); then press RETURN.

5. Select Quit from the Range menu; select Quit from the 1st-Settings menu.

6. Select Preview to see the graph.

Creating a Graph Legend

The graph looks better. There is no clear way to tell which line represents which range, however, unless you compare data points to the underlying data. If you refer back to "The Parts of a Graph" earlier in this chapter, you will see a legend on the bottom of the graph that makes the connection between the shading of the bars and their corresponding data ranges. Let's create a similar legend for the revenue and net-income graph.

1. First, press any key to return to the Graph menu.

2. Select 1st-Settings; select Legend.

The data ranges that require legends in this graph are A (REVENUE) and B (NET INCOME).

3. Select A; then type **REVENUE** and press RETURN.

4. Select B; then type **NET INCOME** and press RETURN.

5. Select Quit from the Legend menu to return to 1st-Settings.

Using Color Graphics

Now the graph looks much clearer. If your Symphony Program Disk is configured for a color system, you can go one step further by switching to the 2nd-Settings window and selecting the color option. (If you do not have the requisites for color graphics, skip this section.)

There is a Switch option in both the 1st- and 2nd-Settings menus. Selecting this option in one Settings window switches Symphony into the other Settings menu.

To use color, select Switch to invoke the 2nd-Settings window. Observe the right side of the window. Under the heading of "Other" is a Color setting that is set to "None." To change this setting,

1. Select Other from the menu; select Color; then select Yes.

2. Select Quit; then select Preview to view the graph.

Now here is a graph worth viewing! It is clear, it makes a concise statement, and it demands little interpretation on the part of the viewer.

Changing Graph Types

What more could you want? Well, perhaps one more thing. Maybe you prefer a bar chart to a line graph. No problem...simply change the Type setting to Bar.

1. First, press any key to restore the Graph menu.

2. Select 1st-Settings, select Type, select Bar, select Quit, and select Preview.

Figure 7-3 shows the final product.

Up to this point you have created three graphs: a revenue line graph, a revenue and net income line graph, and a revenue and net income bar chart. The current settings describe the last graph you generated.

Symphony creates a graph on the screen by looking at the settings sheet. Suppose you wanted to go back to the first graph. Since Symphony did not save the *picture* of the graph, you would have to change the settings sheet to re-create it. This would entail cancelling the B-range (net income) settings as well as changing the graph type.

By itself this is not a big job. But if you then wanted to review the revenue and net income bar graph, you would have to re-create its settings all over again—and lose the revenue graph.

To avoid this problem, Symphony gives you the ability to create multiple settings sheets. The Name option of the Graph Settings command allows you to assign a name to the settings sheet of a particular graph. If you have more than one graph, you would assign a unique name to each graph's settings sheet. Symphony never forgets a name. To see any particular graph, invoke it by name using the Settings Name Use command. Symphony will retrieve the settings sheet corresponding to the name you supply. In this way you can create a catalog of graphs.

If you are going to name a graph, assign its name first; then enter the graph's settings. Let's see how this is done by naming the three graphs that you have created.

To inspect the current settings sheet,

1. Press any key to restore the Graph menu.

The name MAIN appears on the bottom right of the 1st-Settings page. Symphony assigns MAIN as a default graph settings sheet name. Right now, MAIN is assigned to the revenue and net income bar graph that was just on the screen. To generate a named settings sheet for a line graph of the same data, first create a name for the new settings. There is a Name option in both the 1st- and 2nd-Settings pages. Creating a name in one settings page assigns that name to both pages at once.

2. Select 1st-Settings; then select the Name option of the menu.

The *Name command* is used to invoke a named graph, create or delete a graph name, retrieve the next or previous settings sheet in the catalog, reestablish

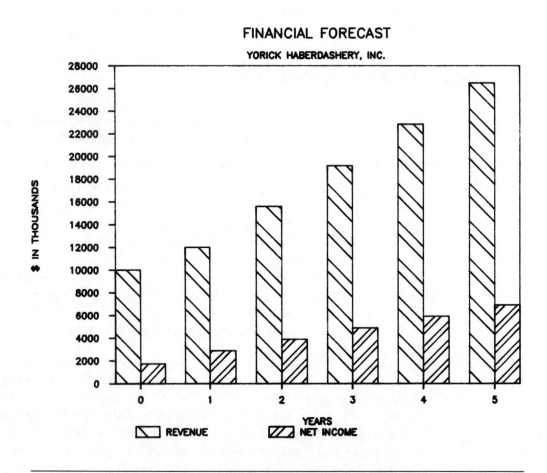

Figure 7-3. Revenue and net income shown in a bar chart

default settings, or delete (reset) all graph names at once.

3. Select Create.

The Name Create command makes a duplicate copy of the current settings sheet and assigns the name you are about to type to the duplicated settings. To make LINE_REV_NI the new name,

4. Type **LINE_REV_NI** and press RETURN.

Now you will specify the settings for the new graph. All the settings will be the same, except for Type, which must be changed to Line.

5. Select Type; then select Line.

To make sure the graph is the way you want it,

6. Select Quit, then select Preview.

Creating a Third Graph Name

Next, let's create and name the graph that you started with, the revenue line graph. First, assign the graph a name.

1. Press any key to restore the Graph menu.

2. Select 1st-Settings Name Create.

3. Type **LINE_REVENUE** and press RETURN to assign the graph name.

Now for the settings. Everything will remain the same, except that the B-range settings must be cancelled. To do so,

4. Select Cancel.

5. Select Entire-Row; then select B to delete all settings pertaining to the B-range.

To see the Graph,

6. Select Quit. Select Quit again, and then select Preview.

Viewing a Catalog of Graphs

All three graphs are now named, and you have created a graph catalog. Let's check to make sure that Symphony really can retrieve any one of the three graphs. To retrieve the revenue and net income bar graph,

1. Press any key to restore the Graph menu.

2. Select 1st-Settings Name Use.

The catalog of graph names appears in the control panel, and a pointer highlights the first graph name. To select and invoke a settings sheet, you may either type the full graph name or move the pointer to the desired name and press RETURN. Pointing is quicker, so

3. Point to LINE_REV_NI and press RETURN.

4. Select Quit; then select Preview to see the graph. When done, press any key to restore the Graph menu.

To see the next graph in the catalog,

    5. Select 1st-Settings Name Next. Then select Quit, select Quit again, and select Preview. When done, press any key to restore the Graph menu.

To see the last graph,

    6. Repeat Step 5.

    7. Select Quit to leave the Graph menu.

You now have three graphs that you can call to the screen. However, the graph names will disappear unless you save the spreadsheet file. This is an important point to remember: Symphony saves graph names and settings when you issue a File Save command. If you turn off the machine or exit Symphony without resaving the worksheet, the settings sheet that you assigned since the last File Save command will be irretrievably lost.

    8. Press SERVICES (F9), select File Save, press RETURN, and select Yes.

Now all three graph names are saved, and you will be able to retrieve them to the screen when you next retrieve the worksheet file.

Saving the Graph and Making A Hard Copy

Although naming a graph allows you to retrieve it for display on the monitor, the Graph Name command does not allow you to make a hard copy of the graph. Before you can produce a hard copy, you must go through a separate operation.

The *Image-Save command* stores the current graph in a special *graph file* that later can be used to print the graph. Image-Save is similar to the File Save command. Symphony will ask you under what file name you would like to save the graph file. A graph file name, like a worksheet file name, can be up to eight characters long, consisting of letters, numbers, or the following special characters: $ & # @ ! % ' ' ( ) - ^ ~ _ { }. No spaces are permitted. Symphony adds the extension .PIC to whatever name you type when it saves the file to disk.

For your purposes here, you will use the Image-Save command to make a graph file for the revenue line graph, which is the current graph.

    1. Press MENU (F10); then select Graph Image-Save.

    2. Type **LINE_REVENUE** as the graph file name, and press RETURN.

Notice that you can use a graph name (the name of the settings sheet) as your graph file name if you choose.

Only after you have saved the graph file can you make a hard copy of it. To make the hard copy, you must first exit the Symphony environment by pressing SERVICES (F9) and selecting Exit Yes. You must then get into the Access program and select PrintGraph. You will be asked to replace the system diskette with the PrintGraph diskette.

Because so many graphics options and hardware setups are supported by Symphony, it is not possible to provide printing instructions here. Once you have named your graph and saved both it and the worksheet, you should refer to your

Symphony documentation and follow the instructions it provides for using the particular type of graphics device you have.

This foray into graphics is completed. It is time to set aside the income statement forecast and begin a new application in the next chapter. There is a great deal more to learn about the spreadsheet environment.

Chapter 8
The @NOW Function
And Lookup Tables

Still more chapters on the spreadsheet environment? Absolutely! The spreadsheet's commands and features could fill at least an entire book. More important, the other four Symphony environments are closely related to the spreadsheet. The spreadsheet is the backbone of Symphony, and learning to use the spreadsheet is half of learning to use Symphony.

In this chapter and the next, you will discover the potency of Symphony's built-in functions and the ability to manipulate strings of characters. You will also build your first macro. *Macros* are user-designed procedures that make Symphony do your work for you quickly and accurately.

Chapter 4 introduced the @SUM function, but there are many more functions—for almost every occasion. Functions will be the foundation of the model you are about to create—a purchase order tracking system. You will not make use of all or even most of Symphony's 80-odd functions, but you will get a clear idea of how much work you can save by making clever use of them. In this chapter, you will set up the spreadsheet and learn about calendar functions, formats, and arithmetic, and about using the @VLOOKUP function to perform table lookups.

Building a Purchase Order Tracking System

Joe Doe is the Supplies Manager of Fidget Widget Manufacturing. Every few weeks, Mr. Doe takes stock of the company's office supplies and issues requisitions, called *purchase orders*, to replenish supplies of paper clips, paper pads, and other office paraphernalia. Keeping track of all the orders is a job that has gotten out of hand, and Doe needs a computerized system that tells him what items have been ordered, from whom, and whether orders have been filled or not.

Inquiring about the feasibility of developing such a system on Fidget Widget's large computer, Doe found out that the firm's Systems Development Group would charge $500,000 and six free lunches in order to complete the job. Doe has the impression that the application would be appropriate for Symphony...and that's where you come in.

The purchase order analysis that Doe (and you) will be developing is shown in Figure 8-1. Joe lists each item ordered, the date it was ordered and received, the vendor with whom the order was placed, the quantity, and the price of the order. Each purchase order is assigned a unique Purchase Order code, which helps the accounting department identify the order. The analysis also indicates whether a

	H	I	J	K	L	M	N	O	P	Q	R	S	T	U	V
1		DATE			DATE										
2		ORDERED			RECEIVED				UNIT	TOTAL		PURCHASE	ORDER	P.O.	ORDER
3	ITEM	M	D	Y	M	D	Y	QUANTITY	PRICE	PRICE	VENDOR	PREFIX	SUFFIX	CODE	STATUS
4	PENCILS	2	1	85				50	$2.50	$125.00	PENCIL PUSHER	JPEN		1	JPEN1	LATE
5	PAPER	3	27	85	3	29	85	30	$2.00	$60.00	PAPER TIGER	JPAP		2	JPAP2	CLOSED
6	CLIPS	3	6	85				100	$0.50	$50.00	YANKEE CLIPPER	JCLI		3	JCLI3	OPEN
7	STAPLES	1	3	85				75	$1.50	$112.50	STAPLETON	JSTA		4	JSTA4	LATE

Figure 8-1. Preview of Fidget Widget's supplies analysis sheet

particular order is closed (that is, whether the shipment has been received) or open (not received). For open orders, the analysis flags those that are late.

You will begin this project by putting the current date and time at the top of the spreadsheet. Before you go on, you will need to become familiar with the way Symphony handles dates and times. This is described in "A Numerical System for Date and Time" (see box).

Using the DOS Add-In
To Change the System Date

To portray the current date and time on the spreadsheet, you need to use the DOS add-in and the @NOW date function. How does Symphony know the correct date and time? More accurately, does Symphony know the correct date and time? The answer is maybe.

A NUMERICAL SYSTEM
FOR DATE AND TIME

Many reports include the current date at the top. Symphony has several date functions that not only display a date, but also perform calendar arithmetic, such as determining the number of days between two dates.

You are probably accustomed to thinking of a date as a particular month, day, and year. Symphony thinks of a date as a number; that is, it assigns a serial number to every day that has elapsed since December 31, 1899. For example, January 1, 1900, is 1; January 2, 1900, is 2; and May 15, 1985, is 31182 (because 5/15/1985 is 31,182 days after 12/31/1899). Similarly, Symphony does not think of time in terms of hours, minutes, and seconds, but in terms of a decimal number—a fractional part of a day. If midnight is 0.000 to Symphony, 1:00 A.M. is 1/24, or 0.041666, whereas 8:00 P.M. is 20/24, or 0.83333. (In other words, 83.3333 percent of a day has elapsed by 8 o'clock in the evening.)

This serialization scheme may seem cryptic to you, but it is well suited to calendar arithmetic. It is far simpler for Symphoy to figure out the difference between two dates or between two times by using a numeric system than by using customary dates or times. You might be hard pressed to figure out the number of days between May 14, 1982, and February 2, 1985, but it would be easy for you to compute 31080 minus 30085, which yields the correct answer.

Then again, unless you normally think of dates as integers (quick, what is the serial number of your birthday?), Symphony's datekeeping and timekeeping methodology would be hard to use, were it not for the Date and Time options of the Format command. *Date Format* displays a serial number in the form of a date, while *Time Format* converts the display of a serial number to actual clock time.

Remember that you answer date and time prompts when you first boot the system prior to entering the Symphony environment. If you go to the trouble of entering the real date and time, they will appear on the bottom left corner of the screen. If you press RETURN in response to the date and time prompts, an incorrect default date and time are used.

It is not too late to change the system date and time right now. In fact, since in this chapter's figures the current date used will be April 1, 1985, let's pretend that 4/1/85 actually is the current date so that your results will match those of the figures. To reset the date, you must suspend your Symphony session and enter the DOS (disk operating system) environment. After issuing the command to set the system date in DOS, you need to resume your Symphony session where you left off. This is the function of the DOS add-in program. (If you have not yet booted Symphony, simply boot the DOS disk, enter 4-01-85 as the date, and boot the program instead of performing the following steps.)

Add-ins are special programs that extend Symphony's capabilities beyond the standard program. Your Symphony package includes an add-in supplied by Lotus, the DOS add-in. It permits you to leave Symphony, perform any DOS function (such as formatting or setting the system date and time), and return to Symphony. The Symphony Help & Tutorial Disk contains the DOS add-in program.*

1. Remove the Symphony Program Disk from drive A, and replace it with the Help & Tutorial Disk.

Since attaching an add-in application is something that you might do in any environment, Lotus included an *Application Attach command* in the Services menu.

2. Press the SERVICES (F9) key and select the Application option.

3. Next, select Attach.

This causes Symphony to search the disk in drive A, list the available add-in programs of that disk in the control panel, and request which add-in you want to attach to the current session.

4. Select DOS and press RETURN.

The DOS add-in is loaded from disk to memory and is now available for use. To actually use the DOS add-in, though, you must tell Symphony you're ready.

5. Select the Invoke option from the Application menu that has returned to the control panel.

Symphony displays the add-in programs that have been attached so far and asks which of these you want. There isn't much choice, is there?

6. Press RETURN to select the DOS add-in.

Symphony is now ready to run DOS and asks you to press RETURN or enter a DOS program name. Symphony is about to search the disk for the DOS system or

---

*If you have a hard disk, you do not have to switch diskettes. Consult Chapter 4 of the Symphony *Introduction* manual for details on using the DOS add-in.

for a particular DOS program, and you must ensure that DOS is available before Symphony begins its search. Therefore, if you have a dual drive system,

7. Replace the Help & Tutorial Disk with the DOS System Disk in drive A.

8. Then press RETURN.

Symphony displays a message informing you that issuing the Exit command in your DOS session will return you to the place you left off in Symphony. Then Symphony pretends to relinquish control of the DOS system. Don't be fooled, though. Symphony still remains in RAM, and it eagerly awaits your return.

Issuing the DOS Date Command

The DOS "A>" prompt should appear on the screen. To specify a system date, issue the DOS *Date command*:

1. Type **DATE** and press RETURN.

Next, type the date that you want in *mm-dd-yy* or *mm-dd-yyyy* format:

2. Type **4-1-85** and press RETURN.

To resume Symphony,

3. Type **EXIT** and press RETURN.

The new date now appears in the lower-left corner of the screen. The next task is to put this date into the spreadsheet. The time for @NOW is now.

Using @NOW to Obtain the Current
Date and Time

The *@NOW function* is a formula that checks the calendar and clock to produce the current moment (that is, the moment that Symphony thinks is current, based on the system date and time). There are two aspects of @NOW: the current date and the current time of day. @NOW checks the calendar to count the number of days from December 31, 1899, to the current date; and it checks the clock to determine how much of the day has elapsed since midnight as of the current time. To see how @NOW works, let's store @NOW as a formula in the top left cell of the spreadsheet.

1. Press SERVICES (F9) and select New Yes to clear the screen if it isn't clear already.

2. Press HOME to move to cell A1.

3. Type **@NOW** and press RETURN.

The resulting value is a decimal number. The digits to the left of the decimal point (31138) comprise the numerical equivalent of April 1, 1985. The digits to the right of the decimal point correspond to the current time of day.

Using Format Date to Translate An Integer Date

Your immediate interest is with the date portion of the @NOW value. You will use the spreadsheet menu's Format Date command to display this value as a date.

1. Press the MENU (F10) key; select Format; then select Date.

There are several Date formats available in the Date menu appearing in the control panel. They are listed in Table 8-1 together with examples of each format. The first option displays a date separated by dashes, with two digits for the day, followed by a three-letter abbreviation of the month and then the last two digits of the year. The second option omits the year, while the third option omits the day.

Options 4 and 5 allow you to display dates in an *international format*. When you first boot Symphony, the Full International Date format is *mm/dd/yy* —the same as option 1, except that the month is displayed as a two-digit number, and slashes, instead of dashes, are used as separators. Partial International format is *mm/dd*. These formats are called international because you may change them to conform to date formats used in other countries. For example, Britain displays dates in *dd/mm/yy* format instead of *mm/dd/yy*.*

In this example, use option 1, the *dd-mmm-yy* format. Selecting a Date format is no different from selecting one of the numeric formats that you've used before.

2. Select option 1 (DD-MMM-YY).

As usual, Symphony wants to know what range of cells to format this way, and it recommends A1..A1. This is the desired range.

3. Press RETURN.

The string of asterisks that results from this format is not quite the result you expected. The problem is that the selected Date format is too wide to fit into a nine-character column. Displaying asterisks is Symphony's way of indicating this type of overflow. To solve the problem, you must widen the column. How wide must it be? You'll find out by experimenting with the spreadsheet's Width command.

4. Press the MENU (F10) key, select Width, and then select Set.
5. Press the right arrow key to widen the column. The asterisks disappear and the format is displayed correctly.
6. Press RETURN to finalize the change.

Perhaps some day, when the ultimate perfection of machines is more generally recognized, 31138 will gain greater acceptance as a date stamp for reports. For now, though, 01-Apr-85 is the more practical format.

---

*Changing the default international format requires changing Symphony's default configuration setting for International Date format. To do this, you would invoke the Services menu, select Configuration Other International, and select DD/MM/YY from a menu that includes MM/DD/YY, DD/MM/YY, DD.MM.YY, and YY-MM-DD.

Table 8-1. Date Formats

FORMAT	EXAMPLE (for April 1, 1985)
1 (DD-MMM-YY)	01-Apr-85
2 (DD-MMM)	01-Apr
3 (MMM-YY)	Apr-85
4 (Full Intn'l)	04/01/85
5 (Partial Intn'l)	04/01

The @NOW Function
Using Time Format

If you run reports several times a day, it may be important to time-stamp the spreadsheet. The @NOW function can be used for this purpose, too. Let's store another @NOW formula in the spreadsheet and use its result to display the current time of day.

1. Move the pointer to cell B1.

2. Type **@NOW** and press RETURN.

The Date Format command operates on the date-related digits of the @NOW value. To display the time-related digits in Time format, you use the Time option of the Format command.

3. Press the MENU (F10) key, select Format, and then select Time.

Table 8-2 shows the four Time formats and the results of applying them to a time of 1:15 P.M. and 30 seconds (13:15:30 on a 24-hour clock). The Symphony serial number for 13:15:30 is 0.552430. Note that International format uses a 24-hour clock.*

Let's try out option 1.

4. Select option 1 (HH:MM:SS AM/PM).

5. Press RETURN to apply this format to the range B1..B1.

Since the result is too wide to fit into the column, you will need to widen the column.

6. Press the MENU (F10) key, select Width, and then select Set.

7. Press the right arrow key to widen the column. Keep pressing the right arrow key until the asterisks disappear and the format is displayed correctly; then press RETURN to lock in the change.

---

*Using the Configuration Other International Time options of the Services menu makes three other international formats available for the Format Time command: HH:MM:SS, HH.MM.SS, and HH,MM,SS.

Table 8-2. Time Formats

FORMAT	EXAMPLE (for 1:15:30 P.M.)
1 (HH:MM:SS AM/PM)	01:15:30 PM
2 (HH:MM AM/PM)	01:15 PM
3 (Full Intn'l)	13h15m30s
4 (Partial Intn'l)	13h15m

The current time now appears in cell B1. By the way, since Symphony recalculates formulas automatically whenever you enter a new value or label, the @NOW formulas in A1 and B1 will be automatically recalculated as well. This means that the time displayed in B1 will change as time goes by and the spreadsheet is recalculated.

Developing the Analysis Sheet

Now that you have established the current date, you can proceed to the report itself. The first step is to enter a title to identify your work.

1. Press the CAPS LOCK key, if necessary, to commence all-caps typing.

2. In cell C1, enter the label **FIDGET WIDGET SUPPLIES ANALYSIS**.

The purchase order analysis will consist of two parts. The portion on the far left is a table of the supplies to be tracked. It contains the names of the supplies, their unit prices, and the vendors from whom Joe Doe obtains them. The right portion of the spreadsheet, columns H through V as shown in Figure 8-1, is the tracking system. Joe Doe, with your assistance, will record orders and receipts in this area, as well as formulas that allow him to keep track of delinquent orders and costs of supplies.

Entering the Table of Supplies

Your first task is to create a table of the supplies being tracked. The table should include columns for the name of the supply item, the price per unit of the item, and the name of the vendor from whom the supply is purchased. When Joe Doe is ready to make an order for a particular supply, such as paper, Symphony will determine the total cost of the order by multiplying the quantity ordered by the unit price stored in the table. Joe Doe can also use the table to look up the vendor that sells the item.

Place the table of supplies in the first three columns of the spreadsheet, as follows:

1. Enter the label **ITEM** in cell A4, **UNIT** in B3, **PRICE** in B4, and **VENDOR** in C4.

Figure 8-2 shows the current supplies table as it should be stored on the spreadsheet. The values in the UNIT PRICE column (column B) have been formatted in Currency format, which displays numbers with dollar signs. (Currency format also inserts commas into numbers greater than 999 and encloses negative values in parentheses).

2. In rows 5 through 8, enter the table information as shown in Figure 8-2. The currency values should be entered as decimal values.

Next, assign Currency format to the unit prices.

3. Move to cell B5, press the MENU (F10) key, and select Format Currency. Press RETURN to specify two decimal places, expand the pointer down to the last cell in the column (B8), and press RETURN.

Entering the Tracking Spreadsheet

Now you are ready to set up the tracking system itself. The column titles of the tracking system are stored in the first three rows of columns H through V of the spreadsheet. First, you should adjust the column widths to accommodate the headings you'll be entering.

1. Use the spreadsheet Width Set command to change the column widths as follows: set columns I, J, K, L, M, and N to 3; column R to 15; and T to 7. The remaining columns (H, O, P, Q, and S) should remain at the default width of 9.

2. Next, enter the headings in cells H1..V3 as they appear in Figure 8-1.

Now you are ready to enter the data and formulas necessary to track a particular purchase. Remembering from Chapters 4 and 5 that you may wish to use the same formula in several portions of the spreadsheet, you will design the formulas so they may be copied easily. In applications like this one, it pays to spend time planning each formula so that things go smoothly later on.

```
              A           B           C           D           E           F

  1  01-Apr-85 11:04:47 AM FIDGET WIDGET SUPPLIES ANALYSIS
  2
  3              UNIT
  4  ITEM        PRICE           VENDOR
  5  CLIPS              $0.50 YANKEE CLIPPER
  6  PAPER              $2.00 PAPER TIGER
  7  PENCILS            $2.50 PENCIL PUSHER
  8  STAPLES            $1.50 STAPLETON
```

Figure 8-2. The supplies table

On February 1, 1985, Joe Doe ordered 50 boxes of pencils. This is all the information you need to begin tracking the order. Begin by entering the name of the item, PENCILS, in the first row of the analysis:

3. In cell H4, enter the label **PENCILS**.

The next entry item, DATE ORDERED, consists of three fields: M (month), D (day), and Y (year). To enter a date of February 1, 1985,

4. Enter **2** in the M field (I4), **1** in the D field (J4), and **85** in the Y field (K4).

Since the pencils have not yet arrived, you should skip the DATE RECEIVED fields. This brings you to the last input field, QUANTITY. After this field is completed, all other fields can be derived from the entries in the first four fields of the analysis.

5. Enter the value **50** in the QUANTITY field (O4).

Using @VLOOKUP to Determine Unit Price

The next item in the spreadsheet, UNIT PRICE, will be derived in cell P4. This information is contained in the table of supplies that you stored in the top left corner of the spreadsheet. Symphony is able to automatically look up the item being tracked (pencils) in this table in order to retrieve information related to that item, such as its unit price.

If you were to do this lookup yourself, you might use your index finger to move down the list of items in column A and point to the item in the supplies table that matches the item you are going to track in the spreadsheet (pencils). Having located this item in the table, you would move one column to the right to determine the unit price ($2.50) or two columns to the right to determine the vendor (Pencil Pusher).

The @*VLOOKUP function* works the same way. It "looks up" an item in a table where the lookup items are stored. The function then retrieves information that has been stored in a column to the right of the lookup item. This type of lookup is called a *vertical lookup*, since the lookup table is arranged vertically—the items to be looked up are contained in the first column of the table. (Symphony also has an @*HLOOKUP function* that operates on a horizontal lookup table, in which the items to be looked up are stored horizontally in the first row of the table.)

About @VLOOKUP

The @VLOOKUP function requires three pieces of information: the item to be looked up, the range where the lookup table is stored, and the number of columns over to the right that @VLOOKUP should go in order to retrieve the information corresponding to the selected item. (This last piece of information is called the *offset*.) These three pieces of information are the *arguments* of the function. (A function argument is the information that must be supplied to a Symphony function in order for the function to operate.) The @VLOOKUP function takes the form @VLOOKUP (*item to look up, range containing vertical lookup table, offset*), as shown in Figure 8-3.

In this case, the first argument (the *item to look up*) is the item in cell H4 of the spreadsheet. The second argument required by @VLOOKUP is the *range containing the vertical lookup table*. This range consists of two conceptual parts. The first part is the column of item names (column A), which contains the items that the entries in column H of the spreadsheet will be compared to. The second part is the columns to the right of the comparative values column, which contain the values to be retrieved by the function—in this example, the UNIT PRICE and VENDOR columns. The range containing the lookup table therefore spans A5..C8. Observe that the column titles above row 5 are not included as part of the table range.

The third argument, the *offset*, tells Symphony where to find the corresponding values that must be retrieved by the function. Offset is a number representing a relative displacement from the first column of the lookup table. In this example, the offset of the UNIT PRICE column is 1, because that column is one column to the right of the ITEM column. VENDOR has an offset of 2. In another application there might be more columns to the right.

Making the Lookup Table Range Absolute

One correct way to enter the lookup formula for UNIT PRICE would be @VLOOKUP (H4,A5..C8,1). However, it is possible to develop an @VLOOKUP formula that is even more correct.

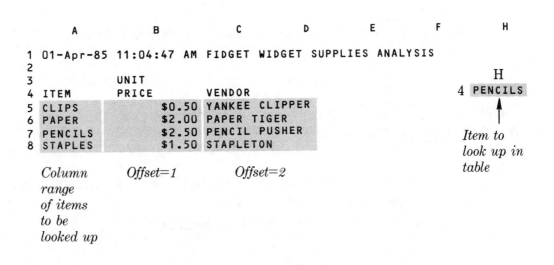

Figure 8-3. The @VLOOKUP function

Remember that you will be copying this formula down to the next line of the spreadsheet (cell P5) when you post the next order of supplies. Copying the formula @VLOOKUP(H4,A5..C8,1) relatively from P4 down to P5 would result in @VLOOKUP(H5,A6..C9,1). The item to be looked up, H5, would be appropriate for the next line, which would be in row 5. However, copying the formula relatively would move the table range from A5..C8 down to A6..C9, whereas the table is always stored in A5..C8. To ensure that the table range does not change when the formula is copied down the column, you must make the cell references to the table range absolute. The corrected formula would be @VLOOKUP(H4,$A$5..$C$8,1).

1. Move the cell pointer to P4, and begin the formula by typing **@VLOOKUP(.**
2. Point to the item in column H (cell H4).
3. Type a , to separate this argument of the function from the next one.

Begin specifying the table range.

4. Point to the top left corner of the table range (A5).

Make the range specification absolute.

5. Press the ABS (F3) key once.

The control panel now contains @VLOOKUP(H4,$A$5.

6. Type a . to anchor the range.
7. Move to the end of the table range (cell C8).

Notice that the control panel displays @VLOOKUP(H4,$A$5..$C$8. Symphony automatically inserted dollar signs into the C8 specification as a result of your pressing ABS before, so there is no need to press ABS again.

8. Type a , to separate the argument.
9. Type 1 to indicate the offset; then type) and press RETURN to end the formula.

The result, 2.5, should be formatted to indicate that it represents dollars and cents.

10. Press the MENU (F10) key, and select Format Currency.
11. Press RETURN twice.

Entering Total Price
And Vendor Formulas

Now that both QUANTITY and PRICE are available, TOTAL PRICE can be computed as the product of the two.

1. Move to the TOTAL PRICE column (Q4).
2. Type + to begin the formula entry.
3. Point to the QUANTITY cell (O4).
4. Type an * to indicate multiplication.
5. Point to the UNIT PRICE cell (P4) and press RETURN.

Format the resulting 125 using Currency format.

6. Press MENU (F10), select Format Currency, and press RETURN twice.

Determining the vendor of the pencils is simply another @VLOOKUP function; here, 2 is used as the offset. Keeping in mind that the structure of the function is @VLOOKUP (*item to look up, range containing vertical lookup table, offset*),

7. Move to the VENDOR column (R4) and type **@VLOOKUP(**.

8. Point to the item in Column H (H4).

9. Type a ,; then point to the first cell of the table range (A5); press the ABS (F3) key; type a . to anchor the range; and point to the bottom right cell of the table range (C8).

10. Type **,2)** and press RETURN to end the formula.

As you can see, @VLOOKUP may be used to retrieve alphabetic information as well as numeric information.

Saving the Worksheet

At this point, take a break and save your work.

1. Press SERVICES (F9) and select File Save.

2. Type **PURCHASE** and press RETURN.

Thus far you have created a "time-stamp" for the report using @NOW and developed a lookup table to look up price and vendor information in the purchase order tracking system. In the next chapter you will complete the spreadsheet, adding to your knowledge of calendar functions and other Symphony features in the process.

Chapter 9
Strings and Conditional Formulas

_____

_____

_____

Strings and String Functions

Conditional Formulas

Date Arithmetic
And the @DATE Function

Naming a Range

The Move Command

In this chapter, you will complete the purchase order that you began in Chapter 8. In the process, you will learn about Symphony's character-string functions and how to put them to use. You will also learn about the logical function @IF and the date function @DATE. The chapter explains how to name ranges and introduces a new command, *Move*, which allows you to rearrange the spreadsheet effortlessly.

To continue developing the model, you will need the PURCHASE file on the screen. You will also need to have the "CAP" indicator on and to set the system date to April 1, 1985 (see Chapter 8 for instructions on how to use the DOS add-in to set the system date).

Strings and String Functions

When you last left the purchase order tracking system, you had built a lookup table of supplies and vendors and created the part of the spreadsheet shown in Figure 9-1. At this point, the spreadsheet records purchasing information and looks up information in the supply lookup table.

The next few items in the spreadsheet concern the Purchase Order code, a code that identifies each order of supplies. Joe Doe, the purchasing clerk of Fidget Widget, was an encryption expert in World War II, and he has put his experience to use by establishing a coding system for purchase orders (P.O.s). The coding system not only identifies each of Fidget Widget's P.O.s, but also keeps the P.O. system secure from enemy hands. Incorporating this coding scheme into your spreadsheet will provide you with opportunities to make use of Symphony's extensive character-string manipulation functions.

Fidget's P.O. code is composed of two parts, a prefix and a suffix. The prefix is a combination of a code letter and the first three letters of the item. The code letter indicates the type of supply being purchased. Office supplies use "J" P.O. codes, while product material purchases use "Z" codes. Since the example model deals exclusively with "J" purchases, you will not work with other codes here; however, it would be easy to adapt this model to use multiple codes.

Each purchase order has a unique number that is used as the suffix of the P.O. code. The spreadsheet will automatically assign the first P.O. a value of 1, the next a value of 2, and so on.

The prefix for the current order is the letter J followed by the first three letters of the item, PEN. The prefix "JPEN" is called a *character string* and is made up of two substrings, "J" and "PEN", that are concatenated together to form a single string. A character string is a group of alphanumeric characters. Entering a character string within a cell formula permits you to use string functions or to perform string manipulations, such as combining two strings into one string.

Let's begin by experimenting with strings a bit and then proceed to deriving the P.O. code.

Combining two strings is similar to adding two numbers in a numeric formula. For example, to add 4 and 6 together you would enter the formula 4+6. As you typed the 4, Symphony would be thrown into Value Mode and expect you to enter either a number or a numeric formula. The + sign between the two numbers is an arithmetic operator indicating addition.

	H	I	J	K	L	M	N	O	P	Q	R	S	T	U	V
1			DATE			DATE									
2			ORDERED			RECEIVED			UNIT	TOTAL			PURCHASE ORDER	P.O.	ORDER
3	ITEM		M	D	Y	M	D	Y	QUANTITY	PRICE	PRICE	VENDOR	PREFIX SUFFIX	CODE	STATUS
4	PENCILS		2	1	85				50	$2.50	$125.00	PENCIL PUSHER			

Figure 9-1. The unfinished purchase order tracking spreadsheet

To combine two strings you would specify the first string, followed by a string operator, followed by the second string. The *string operator* is the & (ampersand) character, and it does to strings what the + operator does to numbers: it combines them. For example, entering the string formula +"J"&"PEN" into cell S4 would produce a result of JPEN.

There are two important things to keep in mind about the string formula entry +"J"&"PEN". First, the formula entry begins when you press the + key. A string formula is different from a label entry, because a string formula is a value—it must be entered in Value Mode. To throw Symphony into Value Mode you may type the + key, just as you would in entering a numeric formula that begins with a cell address.

Second, when you enter character strings directly into a formula, you must enclose the strings in double quotes. That is why the two strings J and PEN are entered as "J" and "PEN".

To see how Symphony handles a string formula,

1. Move to cell S4 and type + to begin a formula entry.

2. Type " (double quotes).

3. Type **J**; then type ".

4. Type **&**; then type **"PEN"**.

Make sure the control panel contains +"J"&"PEN". Then

5. Press RETURN.

Cell S4 should display the string value JPEN.

Using &, you can also combine a string with a cell containing a label, or you may combine two label cells. For example:

6. Type +**"J"&**, and then move the pointer to the ITEM cell, H4.

The control panel displays the formula +"J"&H4.

7. Press RETURN.

The result will be JPENCILS, which is quite close to the string that you are trying to derive, the P.O. prefix.

What you really want is the concatenation of "J" and the first three characters in cell H4. Symphony includes a number of string functions that are capable of extracting a subset, or *substring*, of characters from a string.

One of these functions is @LEFT, whose structure is @LEFT (*string, num*). The first argument, *string*, is the string (or the address of a cell containing a string) from which you want to extract a substring. The second argument, *num*, is the number of characters, starting from the leftmost character, that you want to extract. For example, @LEFT("BASEBALL",4) returns the string "BASE"—the leftmost four characters of BASEBALL. There is also an @RIGHT (*string, num*) function that extracts the rightmost *num* characters of a string.

Using @LEFT for the P.O. Code Prefix

In the purchase order example, the first three characters of the item in cell H4 would be derived with the formula @LEFT(H4,3). Therefore, the elusive P.O. prefix would be returned by the formula +"J"&@LEFT(H4,3).

1. You can destroy the evidence of the experiment you just performed in cell S4 by either erasing it or overwriting it. Then type the + sign to begin the formula entry.
2. Type "**J**"&@**LEFT**(.
3. Point to the ITEM cell (H4).
4. Type a ,.
5. Type **3**) and press RETURN.

The P.O. prefix is JPEN.

Using @N for the P.O. Code Suffix

The P.O. code suffix is a unique number assigned to the purchase order. The first suffix will be 1, and succeeding suffixes will increase sequentially, so that the formula for a particular suffix is the value of the previous suffix plus 1. For example, the suffix of the second purchase would be 1 plus 1 (*the value of the previous suffix*), which equals 2.

Therefore, if you are going to copy the formulas from the first record to the second record, the formula you should enter for the first suffix is 1 + *the previous cell* (or in this case, 1+T3). Right away, though, you seem to hit a snag. Instead of a numeric value, the previous cell contains a label, SUFFIX.

Try using the formula 1+T3 in cell T4: the displayed result is "ERR". As things stand, you may not add a number to a label. If only you could convert the SUFFIX label to the numeric value of 0 in the formula in T4.

Fortunately, Symphony comes to the rescue with a function called @N. The @*N function* converts a label or string to a value. The structure of the function is @N (*range*), where the argument *range* specifies a cell that contains a label or string. Using the single-cell range of T3..T3, the function @N(T3..T3) returns a value of 0. Observe that the argument of @N must be a range; it may not be a single cell address, such as @N(T3).

Thus, a working formula for the P.O. suffix is 1+@N(T3..T3). When copied down to the next cell, this formula correctly adds 1 to the numeric value of the previous cell.

1. In cell T4, begin the formula by typing **1+@N**(.
2. Move up to the previous cell (T3).
3. Type a . to anchor the range.

The control panel shows 1+@N(T3..T3 —just the range you wanted.

4. Type) and press RETURN to complete the formula.

What an elaborate way to obtain the value 1! But it works, and the effort will pay off when you enter the next purchase with the Copy command.

Using @STRING to Combine the Prefix and Suffix

The next step is to derive the P.O. code and place it in column U. The P.O. code itself is the concatenation of the prefix and suffix. This would indicate using the &

operator to combine the prefix cell, S4, with the suffix cell, T phony only permits concatenation of strings or cells containing str stores a string, "JPEN"; but the suffix contains a value, 1.

To combine the prefix and suffix into a single string, it will be ne reference the suffix as a string. You can do this by using the @STRING whose format is @STRING (num1, num2). The num1 argument is the val cell address of a value, that will be used as a string. The num2 argument specif how many decimal places should be shown in that string. Since all of the suffixes are integers, you will use a num2 argument of 0.

Note that if you use a cell reference as your num1 argument, it must be a single cell reference (such as T4), as opposed to the argument of the @N function, which had to be a range (such as T3..T3).

1. Move to cell U4.

2. Type a +; then move to the prefix in cell S4.

3. Type **&&@STRING(**.

4. Move to the suffix in cell T4; then type **,0)** and press RETURN.

The P.O. code for the first purchase order is JPEN1.

Conditional Formulas

The next item of the analysis is ORDER STATUS in column V. ORDER STATUS is the real payoff of this spreadsheet. The column will indicate which orders are still open and which have been closed. At a glance, this column tells Doe which orders to keep an eye on.

The formula for this cell will be fundamentally different from the formulas you've seen thus far. Previously, a given formula would generate a particular result. In this case, the formula may have one of two results. If the order has been received, it is closed; and the ORDER STATUS cell should display the label CLOSED. If the order is open, ORDER STATUS should display the label OPEN. The result displayed in the ORDER STATUS cell depends on whether a *condition* is satisfied: whether the order has been received or not.

What data in the worksheet indicates whether the order was received? The answer lies in the DATE RECEIVED columns (L, M, and N). If there are values in the month, day, or year columns of DATE RECEIVED, the order must be closed; otherwise, the order is open.

Symphony offers *conditional operators* that allow you to make conditional tests. These operators, and the @IF function they are used with, are described in "Conditional Operators and the @IF Function" (see box).

The @IF function for ORDER STATUS in cell V4 would be entered as @IF(N4>0,"CLOSED","OPEN"). This formula instructs Symphony to display the string "CLOSED" if N4 is greater than 0 (that is, if the result is TRUE) and to display "OPEN" otherwise. Here, *arg1* and *arg2* are strings; and in accordance with the rules of specifying strings in formulas, the characters of the string are enclosed in double quotation marks. To enter the conditional formula,

1. Move to cell V4 and begin by typing **@IF(**.

ATE RECEIVED Y field (N4).

D","**OPEN**") and press RETURN.

because the condition is FALSE.

ONDITIONAL OPERATORS
AND THE @IF FUNCTION

Among the operators (such as + or −) that may be used in formulas, Symphony includes a set of conditional operators. Conditional operators are used to perform true/false tests. For example, the condition to test whether a purchase order in cell N4 of the worksheet is closed would be N4>0. If cell N4 contains a value greater than 0, the condition is satisfied; the condition is said to be TRUE. If cell N4 is empty or contains 0, the condition fails; it is said to be FALSE. The condition N4>0 is called a conditional formula.

The conditional operators are

<	Less than
<=	Less than or equal to
>	Greater than
>=	Greater than or equal to
<>	Not equal to

also,
= Equal to

The @IF function makes full use of conditional formulas. This function provides some logic to the formula, and accordingly, it is considered a *logical function*. Using @IF, you may instruct Symphony to display a particular result if a condition is TRUE and a different result if a condition is FALSE.

The structure of the function is @IF (*condition, arg1, arg2*), where *condition* is the condition being tested, *arg1* is the result to display if the condition is TRUE, and *arg2* is the result if the condition is FALSE. *Arg1* and *arg2* may be values, formulas, or strings.

For example, suppose you stored the formula @IF(A1>B1,100,0) in cell Z55. If the contents of cell A1 were greater than the contents of B1, the condition would be true, and the value of cell Z55 would be 100 (*arg1*). Otherwise, the value would be 0 (*arg2*).

Note that conditional formulas may be used directly as cell entries. Storing the formula involves putting Symphony in Value Mode (by typing +) and entering the condition. If the condition is TRUE (satisfied), the value 1 is displayed in the cell. In the case of the pencils in row 4 of this chapter's purchase order tracking system, storing +N4>0 in some cell of the spreadsheet would return a result of 0, since there is no value in cell N4.

Nested @IF Functions

It is useful to know whether an order is open or closed, but it would be even more valuable to have a warning system that identifies orders that are truly late. For example, you might want to have three possible values for ORDER STATUS: CLOSED if the order is received, OPEN if the order is unfilled but less than 30 days old, and LATE if the order is unfilled for 31 or more days.

Such a warning system would require two @IF functions. The first @IF would test whether the order was open or closed, as before. If the order were open, the second @IF would test whether the difference between the date ordered and the current date (the date the orders are being analyzed) was greater than or equal to 31. If so, the result would be LATE; otherwise (that is, if the order were open but less than 31 days old), the status would be OPEN.

You already know that the format of the @IF function is @IF (*condition, arg1, arg2*), and you know that *arg1* and *arg2* may be values, strings, or formulas. But formulas may include functions, and @IF is a function. Therefore, you may use a second @IF function for one of the two arguments or for both. This is called "nesting @IF functions."

Now this is nirvana! Instead of the functional but simplistic logical construct

IF *there exists a DATE RECEIVED,*
THEN *display CLOSED;*
OTHERWISE *display OPEN*

nesting @IF functions allows you to use the more powerful construct

IF *there exists a DATE RECEIVED,*
THEN *display CLOSED;*
OTHERWISE
IF *the difference between the ORDER DATE and today's date is* >= 31,
THEN *display LATE;*
OTHERWISE *display OPEN*

In @IF format, this structure is expressed as

@IF (*condition1, arg1,* @IF (*condition2, arg1, arg2*))

The second @IF is actually *arg2* of the first @IF function. As long as you have the right number of arguments and the right number of parentheses, the nested functions work well. Now it is time to translate this @IF format to an actual formula entry.

Date Arithmetic and the @DATE Function

The first part of the formula, @IF (*condition1, arg1,* translates into @IF(N4>0,"CLOSED",. The second part of the formula, the nested @IF, must include a condition to test the age of the order. You can derive the age of the order by subtracting the serial number of the date ordered from the serial number of the current date. The current date is already stored in the @NOW formula at the top left corner of the spreadsheet, in cell A1. How can you derive a serial number for the date ordered?

This task will require the use of a new function, the @DATE function. @DATE converts a particular date into a Symphony serial number. The structure of the function is @DATE (*year*, *month*, *day*), where *year*, *month*, and *day* may be values, formulas, or cell addresses. In the case of DATE ORDERED, *year* is in cell K4, *month* is in I4, and *day* is in J4.

To try out the @DATE function, move to an empty cell, cell V5, and enter the formula @DATE(K4,I4,J4). The resulting serialized date is 31079. Applying a Date format to this number will yield 01-Feb-85. To compute the difference between this date and the current date, you would enter the formula @NOW—@DATE(K4,I4,J4), which equals 59 and a fraction (the fraction is the time of day that is part of the @NOW function). This order is late. Before continuing, erase cell V5 with the spreadsheet Erase command.

Calculating P.O. Status for the First Order

Now you have all of the ingredients for the nested @IF formula. The condition is @NOW—@DATE(K4,I4,J4)>=31; *arg1* is "LATE", and *arg2* is "OPEN". Enter this formula into cell V4 as follows:

1. Move to cell V4.

2. Begin the formula by typing **@IF(N4>0,"CLOSED",**.

Next enter the nested @IF function:

3. Type **@IF(@NOW—@DATE(K4,I4,J4)>=31,"LATE","OPEN").**

4. Type an additional **)** to close the first @IF function, and press RETURN to end the formula.

As shown in Figure 9-2, the ORDER STATUS for pencils should be labeled LATE. You have successfully completed tracking the first purchase order of the spreadsheet.

	H	I	J	K	L	M	N	O	P	Q	R	S	T	U	V
1		DATE				DATE									
2		ORDERED			RECEIVED				UNIT	TOTAL			PURCHASE ORDER	P.O.	ORDER
3	ITEM	M	D	Y	M	D	Y	QUANTITY	PRICE	PRICE	VENDOR	PREFIX	SUFFIX	CODE	STATUS
4	PENCILS	2	1	85				50	$2.50	$125.00	PENCIL PUSHER	JPEN		1	JPEN1	LATE

@IF(N4>0,"CLOSED",@IF(@NOW—@DATE(K4,I4,J4)>=31,"LATE","OPEN"))

Figure 9-2. Purchase order showing nested @IF formula

Entering Other Purchase Orders

Now that you've developed the formulas you need for the first purchase order, appending additional purchase orders to the analysis is a cinch. Just type in the information for ITEM, DATE ORDERED, DATE RECEIVED, and QUANTITY. Then use the Copy command to copy the formulas from the previous record to the current one.

Try entering a purchase order for 30 reams of paper ordered on March 27, 1985, and received on March 29, 1985.

1. Store the appropriate values for ITEM, DATE ORDERED, DATE RECEIVED, and QUANTITY in cells H5..O5 of the spreadsheet, as shown in Figure 9-3.

The rest of the items of information, from UNIT PRICE to ORDER STATUS, are formulas that may be replicated in a single Copy command from the previous record to the current one.

2. Move the pointer to the beginning of the FROM range, the previous record's unit price (cell P4).

3. Press MENU (F10) and select Copy.

To expand the pointer over the rest of the row of formulas to copy,

4. Press the END key; then press the right arrow key and the RETURN key to designate P4..V4 as the FROM range.

The TO range is specified by the first cell of the current record, the unit price in cell P5.

5. Point to the current record's unit price (P5) and press RETURN to complete the Copy command.

Cell V5 shows that this order is closed because it lists the date received. Also, notice that the purchase order prefix is JPAP, and the suffix has been incremented from 1 to 2.

To test whether the ORDER STATUS works properly for an order that is less than 31 days old,

6. Use row 6 to enter an order for 100 units of clips ordered on March 6, 1985, but not yet received.

H	I	J	K	L	M	N	O	P	Q	R	S	T	U	V
1	DATE			DATE										
2	ORDERED			RECEIVED				UNIT	TOTAL		PURCHASE	ORDER	P.O.	ORDER
3 ITEM	M	D	Y	M	D	Y	QUANTITY	PRICE	PRICE	VENDOR	PREFIX	SUFFIX	CODE	STATUS
4 PENCILS	2	1	85				50	$2.50	$125.00	PENCIL PUSHER	JPEN	1	JPEN1	LATE
5 PAPER	3	27	85	3	29	85	30							

Figure 9-3. The second purchase order calculation

7. Repeat steps 2 through 5, using row 5 as the previous purchase order.

Figure 9-4 shows the results. As expected, the order status is OPEN. Now that you have verified the results, you can rest assured that the Copy command functions correctly.

At this point, it is worthwhile to learn about Symphony's range-naming capability. Having a named range will affect the way you copy records. It will also give you a basis for understanding macros, which are described in Appendix A.

Naming a Range

Symphony allows you to assign a name to a range of cells. When it becomes necessary to refer to a range in a command like Copy or Erase, the range's name can be substituted for the range's beginning and ending coordinates.

In this section, you will assign a name to the range of cells, P4..V4, that contains the formulas that must be copied ever y time you add a new purchase order entry. Then, when you enter a new purchase order and perform the Copy command, you will enter the new range name as the FROM range, instead of pointing to that range.

The first step in assigning a range is to move the cursor to the first cell of the range you are about to name. You then issue the Range Name command.

1. Move the pointer to cell P4, the beginning of the range to be named.

2. Press MENU (F10) and select Range Name.

To create a new range name,

3. Select Create.

Now Symphony requests the name you would like to assign to the range. The name may contain from 1 to 15 characters or numbers. Avoid names that may be confused with cell references, such as A15 or IC256. Also, refrain from using arithmetic operator symbols like the hyphen (which Symphony translates as a minus sign). Names serve as cues, so choose a name that will help you remember

	H	I	J	K	L	M	N	O	P	Q	R	S	T	U	V
1		DATE			DATE										
2		ORDERED			RECEIVED				UNIT	TOTAL		PURCHASE	ORDER	P.O.	ORDER
3	ITEM	M	D	Y	M	D	Y	QUANTITY	PRICE	PRICE	VENDOR	PREFIX	SUFFIX	CODE	STATUS
4	PENCILS	2	1	85				50	$2.50	$125.00	PENCIL PUSHER	JPEN		1 JPEN1	LATE
5	PAPER	3	27	85	3	29	85	30	$2.00	$60.00	PAPER TIGER	JPAP		2 JPAP2	CLOSED
6	CLIPS	3	6	85				100	$0.50	$50.00	YANKEE CLIPPER	JCLI		3 JCLI3	OPEN

Figure 9-4. Results of the third purchase order calculation

what range it describes. For example, this range can be called SOURCE, since it is the source from which formulas will be copied.

4. Type **SOURCE** and press RETURN.

Note that Symphony assumes the current position of the pointer (P4) to be the beginning of the range. (That is why you moved to P4 *before* selecting the Range command.) Symphony needs to know the address of the end of the range.

If you press the RETURN key again at this point, Symphony will assign the name SOURCE to the single cell P4. Typing a . to anchor the range communicates your intention to name a multi-cell range. The last cell of the desired range is V4.

5. Type a . and then point to cell V4. (You may press END and then press the right arrow key to move there quickly.)

As usual, Symphony highlights the range for you.

6. Press the RETURN key to end the command.

Using the Range Name in the Copy Command

Cells P4..V4 now have the range name SOURCE. To see how you might use this name in a command, let's enter a new purchase order into the system.

1. Beginning in cell H7, enter the input for a purchase of 75 cases of staples ordered on January 3, 1985, but not yet received.

2. Move the cell pointer to P7, which is the beginning of the TO range in the Copy command that you are about to issue.

3. Press MENU (F10) and select Copy.

In response to the prompt for the FROM range, you will type the new range name instead of pointing to the range from a previous record.

4. Type **SOURCE** and press RETURN.

Symphony will suggest the current address of the cell pointer, P7, as the TO range. This is correct, so

5. Press RETURN to conclude the Copy.

Notice that by using the range name in the Copy command, you saved yourself quite a few keystrokes. Normally, you would have placed the pointer on the first cell of the FROM range, used arrow keys to expand the pointer over the FROM range, pressed RETURN, pointed to the TO range, and pressed RETURN. Here, however, the range name SOURCE gave Symphony all the information it needed about the FROM range, so you were able to begin the command at the TO range.

Using a range name is sometimes a matter of convenience. It can also be a matter of clarity, since using a range name in a formula can make the formula more readable. For example, suppose you had a spreadsheet in which cell A1 contained total revenues and B1 contained total expenses. If A1 were named REVENUE and B1 were named EXPENSES, you could store a formula for profit in cell C1 that could be entered as +REVENUE−EXPENSES instead of +A1−B1.

Range names can sometimes be more than a convenience: in certain instances, they can be imperative. As you will see in Appendix A, range names are required in some macros.

You will be returning to range names in the database section of this book. As you will learn, they are an important feature of Symphony.

The Move Command

The purchase order analysis is complete, but before you give the model your final blessing, let's turn to the matter of spreadsheet organization.

Figure 9-5 shows the spreadsheet's current layout. One of the problems with this organization is that the report title, current date, and time, which are supposed to appear on the analysis itself, are instead stored above the supply table in the top left corner of the spreadsheet (cells A1, B1, and C1). These three items should be moved toward the right, so that they appear on top of the spreadsheet's analysis section. However, the analysis begins in row 1 of columns H through V. There is no room to store anything on top of this area because row 1 is occupied.

What is needed is a way to move the analysis section down a few rows, and then to move the title, date, and time to the vacated area. You must also be sure that in moving cells around you do not disturb any formulas stored in the spreadsheet. This is precisely what the Move command is meant to do. "The Move Command" (see box) explains how it works.

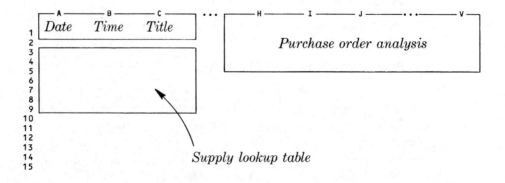

Figure 9-5. A map showing the spreadsheet's organization

Using Move to Rearrange the Spreadsheet

The first step of the reorganization is to move the entire analysis section (H1..V5) down two rows.

1. Move the cell pointer to cell H1, the beginning of the FROM range.
2. Press the MENU (F10) key and select Move.
3. Use the arrow keys to point to the end of the FROM range, cell V7. Then press RETURN.

The cell pointer returns to its original position in cell H1. To move the entire FROM range two rows downward, simply move the pointer two cells downward.

4. Press the down arrow key twice to point to cell H3, the beginning of the TO range.

Symphony already knows the shape of the FROM range. All it needs is the first cell of the TO range in order to complete the move. This is similar to copying a rectangular range to another rectangular range. Therefore, all you have to do is conclude the command.

5. Press RETURN.

The two rows above the analysis area are now blank, because the analysis area has shifted downward two rows. If you check the underlying formulas of the spreadsheet, you will find that they have been adjusted automatically.

THE MOVE COMMAND

The *Move command* transfers a range of cells from one area of the spreadsheet to another. Symphony moves a range of cells as you would slide a stack of papers from one side of your desk to another. The area where the papers originally lay is left empty. The area to which they were transferred is now occupied by the papers, and whatever used to be there has been lost. Similarly, Symphony leaves the FROM range of the Move command empty, and it overwrites any entries that were previously in the TO range, the area to which you want to move the FROM range. The Move command is doubly convenient because it automatically adjusts formulas on the spreadsheet that refer to the moved cells.

The procedure for using the Move command is similar to that for the Copy command. First, move the pointer to the beginning of the FROM range, the range of cells to be moved. Next, invoke the command by pressing the MENU (F10) key and selecting Move. Symphony will prompt you for the FROM range. You may specify the range in the usual way, by expanding the cell pointer with the pointer movement keys or by typing the address of the range. Next, Symphony prompts you for the TO range. Again, specify this range by pointing or typing. Pressing RETURN is the final step of the Move command.

Moving the Title, Date, and Time

Let's move the spreadsheet's title to cell H1, the date to cell P1, and the time to cell R1. Begin with the title.

1. Move the cell pointer to cell C1, press the MENU (F10) key, and select the Move command.

2. Press RETURN to accept C1..C1 as the FROM range.

3. Move to cell H1 and press RETURN.

To move the date,

4. Move the pointer to A1, press MENU (F10), select Move, press RETURN, point to cell P1, and press RETURN.

5. Move the pointer to cell P1.

Cell P1 contains asterisks because it is not wide enough to display the date. The Move command moves the FROM range's format settings as well as its formulas, and the Date format requires a width of ten spaces. It's easy enough to widen the column, though.

6. Press MENU (F10), select Width Set, and press the right arrow key once.

The new width is enough to display the Date format, so

7. Press RETURN.

Cell R1 is already wide enough to house the time formula, so the move presents no problems.

8. Move the pointer to cell B1.

9. Press MENU (F10), select Move, press RETURN, point to cell R1, and press RETURN.

Now that the title, date, and time are in their correct positions, you have completed the purchase order analysis. Using Symphony's date, time, character-string, and logical functions, you have developed a system that tracks purchase orders quickly and accurately. There are some additional improvements that can be made in this spreadsheet, however. It can be made even simpler by using the macro feature. To learn about this most important and powerful tool, read Appendix A, "Keystroke Macros."

Chapter 10
Introduction to Database Management

About Database
Management

Widget-Ware's
Customer File

The FORM Environment

Generating the Data Entry Form

Saving Your Work

This chapter provides an initial view of Symphony as a database management system. After you learn what database management is, you will use the FORM environment to create a simple database and use the database to develop an application that involves a variety of database management commands, features, and techniques. Symphony's database management system can operate at both a simple and sophisticated level. The applications in this chapter and Chapter 11 stick to simplicity, but they accomplish quite a lot as you will see. Chapters 12 and 13 explore the vast capabilities of Symphony's database management system in more detail, and the remainder of the book will show how database management can be integrated with Symphony's other environments.

The model developed in this chapter is a customer file. You will create an *electronic data entry form*—Symphony's counterpart to a questionnaire—to gather information about each customer and to enter information onto the form to create the database. Once the form is set up, you will begin to manage the database by editing its contents, deleting unwanted information, and sorting the information in various ways. You will also begin to add some sophistication to the data entry process by incorporating such features as *validity checking*, which establishes rules that Symphony uses to make sure that a data entry is valid, and *transformation*, which automatically transforms the information you type into something else. These exercises will also demonstrate the relationship between the database and spreadsheet environments.

About Database Management

A *database* is nothing more than a file. It is a collection of *records*, individual items of information grouped together in some meaningful way. The card catalog in your neighborhood library is an example of a database. Every card in the catalog is a record of information pertaining to a particular book.

The individual records of a database are further broken down into *fields* of information. On a library catalog card such as those shown in the illustration, the fields include the catalog number, the name of the author, and the title of the book.

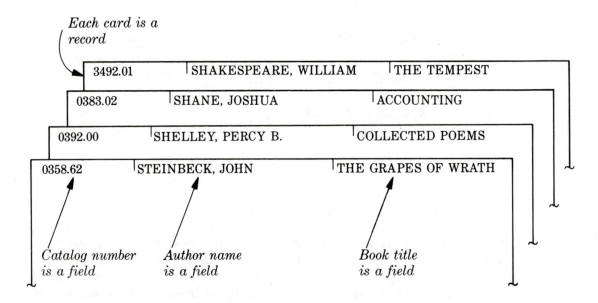

One way to conceptualize a database is to view it as a collection of forms. A *form* is a document containing a single record of data. A single card from the library catalog is a form that lists the items pertaining to a particular book. A library catalog uses a *forms-oriented approach*: you flip through the database (the catalog) of library books one card, or one filled-out form, at a time.

Another way to view a database is as a *table of information*, a collection of data organized into rows and columns. As shown in the next illustration, a database may be organized into rows and columns. Instead of a collection of cards, the library's book collection could be portrayed on paper (or on a computer's screen) in tabular format. Each row of the table is a record of a book, and the columns are the fields: title, author, and catalog number. In tabular format you look at the data all at once, not record by record as in the forms-oriented approach.

```
            LIBRARY CATALOG DATABASE

AUTHOR                   TITLE              CATALOG NUMBER
------------------       --------------     --------------
Shakespeare, William     The Tempest        3492.01
Shane, Joshua            Accounting         0383.02
Shelley, Percy B.        Collected Poems    0392.00
Steinbeck, John          The Grapes of Wrath 0358.62
```

You have been creating and using databases like the library catalog for most of your life. Your telephone directory is a database. The forms approach to the phone directory is a file box of index cards, one card for each person whose phone number you want to keep track of. The tabular approach is the phone book you get from the telephone company, with the names, addresses, and phone numbers listed down the page. Invoices of credit-card purchases, checkbook registers, baseball statistics, stock portfolios—these are but a few of the databases that you use every day.

But if databases have been around since Noah, why have they received so much attention in recent years? The reason for all the fuss is database management, not the database itself.

Database management is the manipulation of information contained in a file: updating the file, deleting old records, reorganizing the file's structure, and printing the file in a particular format.

Sorting information is an essential function of database management. Sorting is one of the most tedious tasks of manual file maintenance. One wonders whether Noah would have escaped the flood if he had been required to alphabetize his passenger list or list his passengers by date of birth. With Symphony, Noah could have sorted thousands of records in a matter of seconds.

Another facet of database management is data retrieval, the ability to search for and select particular items of the data file. Data retrieval, or *querying*, involves several tasks. The database query might consist merely of finding a particular record—exactly what you do when you look up a book in a library's catalog to determine whether the library owns it or to find out the author's name.

A database query also might consist of extracting records—choosing particular records from a file and putting them in another place. In a library, for example, you might write down on scratch paper the titles and catalog numbers of the books you want to borrow. In doing so, you are extracting records from the card-catalog database.

The rules that dictate which records should be located or extracted from the file are called *criteria*. A criterion can be a simple *match*, which is what occurs when you select the library catalog card that contains a book title that coincides with the one you want to borrow. A criterion can also be a *condition*, such as "Select all records that have catalog numbers greater than 500."

Symphony has the capacity for all of these database management functions and more. Each will be illustrated in the next few chapters. The Symphony database is capable of managing up to 8191 records and up to 256 fields per record. However, your computer will not have enough memory to utilize the complete potential database of 8191 records by 256 fields. Nevertheless, even the minimum RAM requirement of 320K will accommodate a wide variety of applications, including the one that you will develop next.

Widget-Ware

The p_____ _____ _____ _____ _____ lget Manufacturing, maker of those _____ _____ _____ _____ ings of the world's machinery. On _____ _____ _____ _____ established a subsidiary to vend W_____ _____ software _____ _____ _____ nd end users. The new venture, W_____ W_____ began _____ _____ product _____ etWorksheet, WidgetWord, and Wid_____ Window _____ _____ _____ these packages, they send a registra_____ _____ _____ W_____ _____ _____ _____ _____ _____ g, they validate their warranty, p_____ the _____ _____ _____ _____ _____ ome eligible for discounts toward f_____ W_____ _____ products and _____ _____

The co_____ _____ _____ keep _____ these cards _____ _____ lex file, but the resounding applause _____ _____ W_____ Ware ha_____ _____ in the _____ place has caused a flood of orders. T_____ _____ _____ _____ _____ so that _____ _____ are can keep track of registered cus_____, especially since the company will be sending out a mailing in the near future. Because the clerks in charge of recordkeeping are accustomed to dealing with registration cards, it makes sense to use Symphony's forms-oriented database management to establish an electronic filing system.

The system will store the customer's name and address as well as such warranty-related data as the product purchased and the date of registration (the beginning of the one-year warranty period). You will eventually be using the system to determine some marketing statistics about the firm's software sales and to print form letters to be sent to registered owners of Widget-Ware products.

Three Characteristics of a Data Field

The first step in designing a database is to decide what items you want to store (the fields of the record) and how you want to store them. There are three characteristics of a data field: the field's *name*, its *type*, and its *length*. Symphony will need to know all three characteristics for each field in the form.

In this example, the field names will be LAST NAME, FIRST NAME, STREET, CITY, STATE, ZIP CODE, DATE OF REGISTRATION, PRODUCT, and a final item, WARRANTY STATUS. The warranty status is an item that states whether the warranty is currently in effect ("alive") or expired ("dead"). This item is not contained on the registration card submitted by the purchaser, but it is useful for recordkeeping, since it shows at a glance whether a purchaser is still under warranty. As long as you're automating this system, let's do it up right.

Table 10-1. Symphony Database Field-type Codes

CODE	FIELD TYPE
L	Label field
N	Number field
D	Date
T	Time
C	Computed field

The second characteristic Symphony needs to know is the nature of the data you are storing in each field. The valid field types, which are designated by one-letter codes, are listed in Table 10-1.

The field type is important because Symphony uses it to check whether you entered data correctly. For example, if you tell Symphony that the registration date is a date entry (the code would be D), it will only allow valid dates to be entered into that field. An item defined as numeric (code N) will be permitted to store only numeric data entries. Field types are also significant in that they determine how you can treat data. Numerical fields can be used in numeric calculations and functions, and date fields can be used in date arithmetic and formatted with Date formats.

There is a special field type called a *computed field.* A computed field is an item that Symphony calculates for you; you do not enter any data into this field yourself. You will be using a computed field as you develop your application.

The last piece of information Symphony needs to know is the maximum field length, for Symphony must allocate space for each field. Thus, the field storing the customer's last name might be assigned a maximum field length of 20, which would mean that names up to 20 characters long could be entered in this field.*

Entering Field Names
And Descriptions

To implement the form, you begin by entering the field descriptions in a continuous column or row of label cells in an empty area of the spreadsheet. (You will move to the FORM environment shortly.) If you begin in cell A1, you enter the first field description in cell A1, the second in A2, and so forth. The entries must

---

*It is sometimes sufficient to give Symphony only the field names and let it assign a default type and length to all of the fields. However, this is only convenient if most of the fields are the same type and length. In most cases, as in this example, it is simpler to specify all three field items—name, type, and length—for all fields before generating the form.

be in consecutive cells; you may not leave any blank cells between field descriptions.

The field description that will be stored in each of these label cells consists of the field name followed by a colon, a field-type code, another colon, and the field length. The appropriate field descriptions for this example are shown in Table 10-2.

1. Boot DOS (or use the DOS add-in program described in Chapter 8), set today's date at 4-01-85, and load Symphony.

You will start out in the spreadsheet environment of a new worksheet. As usual, make sure that the "CAP" indicator is on.

2. Beginning in cell A1 and continuing downward in column A, enter the field description labels shown in the right-hand column of Table 10-2.

You now have everything you need to generate a data form.

The FORM Environment

To generate a data entry form, it is necessary to switch from the spreadsheet into the FORM environment. Until now you have been doing all of your work in a single environment, the spreadsheet. More precisely, you have been looking at the data through a spreadsheet-type window. Now you are going to see a different view—you are going to view the data through a form-type window.

The indicator on the top right of the screen currently says SHEET. To switch to a different window, you issue the combination of keys that comprise the *Type command*, which changes the window type from one work environment to another.

1. Press the TYPE key sequence (hold down ALT and press F10).

Table 10-2. Field Names and Descriptions for Widget-Ware Database

FIELD NAME	TYPE	LENGTH	FIELD DESCRIPTION TO ENTER IN COLUMN A
LAST NAME	L (Label)	20	LAST NAME:L:20
FIRST NAME	L (Label)	20	FIRST NAME:L:20
STREET	L (Label)	30	STREET:L:30
CITY	L (Label)	20	CITY:L:20
STATE	L (Label)	15	STATE:L:15
ZIP CODE	N (Number)	5	ZIP CODE:N:5
PRODUCT	N (Number)	15	PRODUCT:N:15
DATE OF REGISTRATION	D (Date)	13	DATE OF REGISTRATION:D:13
WARRANTY STATUS	C (Computed)	5	WARRANTY STATUS:C:5

A menu containing the five window types appears in the control panel:

SHEET DOC GRAPH FORM COMM

To change the window type,

2. Select FORM.

The window's appearance instantly changes. First of all, the borders of the window no longer indicate spreadsheet rows and columns. Moreover, the field descriptions have disappeared. The indicator on the top right has changed to FORM, and a strange message appears in the control panel: "(No Definition range defined)." Where has Symphony put you? What has it done with your input?

Don't fidget; the field descriptions are still where they were, and you can prove it to yourself. Issue the Type command again (ALT-F10) to revert to a SHEET window; then return again to the FORM environment.

You are now looking at a blank FORM screen that is not really representative of anything stored in the worksheet. It is an *overlay*, a screen that will be used to house a data entry form. Later, when you enter data into the form, you will see how it relates to the actual data storage of the worksheet.

Take a look at the FORM environment's command menu. Recall that when you were in the SHEET environment, pressing the MENU key (F10) would invoke a menu of spreadsheet-specific commands. The MENU key has the same function in the current window: it invokes a command menu that is specific to the FORM environment.

3. Press the MENU (F10) key.

The FORM menu has the following options:

Attach Criteria Initialize Record-Sort Generate Settings

Instead of learning about each of these options now, let's go right to the command that you will use to create your form: the *Generate command*.

Generating the Data Entry Form

The Generate command tells Symphony to create a data entry form based on the field definition labels that you stored in the spreadsheet. The form that Symphony generates will be used to enter data into the database. Later you will see that Generate does more than just create a data entry form; it does all of the startup tasks that are necessary to create a new database.

1. Select Generate.

Symphony asks you to designate a default field type. This would be useful if you had entered field descriptions that consisted of field names but did not include information about field type. Since you included the field type in all of your descriptions, a default type doesn't really matter. By accepting Symphony's recommendation, you can tell Symphony to use its default type only if no other type is designated.

2. Press RETURN to select a default field type of Label.

Next Symphony wants to assign a default field length to any descriptions that do not have a specified field length. Again, you can simply accept Symphony's recommended default of 9, since the lengths are already specified.

3. Press RETURN.

Like the spreadsheet and the graph, the database has certain settings that are stored in a database settings sheet. The Generate command creates the FORM settings sheet, and you will see it in the next chapter. Symphony identifies your database and its settings sheet with a name. You could specify a name of your choice, using up to 15 characters, or you could use the name that Symphony suggests, MAIN. Let's use the name WARRANTY.

4. Type **WARRANTY** and press RETURN.

The next and last thing Symphony needs is the range of cells containing the field descriptions. Since you will need to specify this range either by pointing or

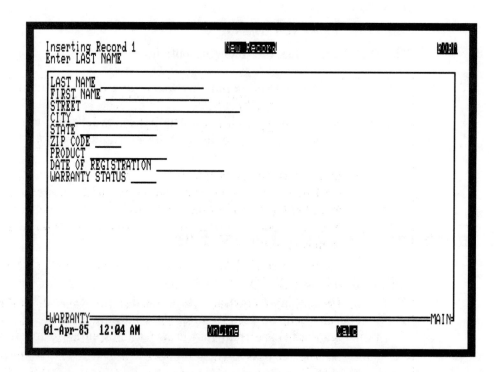

Figure 10-1. Data entry form for the WARRANTY database

using cell addresses, Symphony temporarily changes the window into a SHEET window, displaying the entries that you stored initially. You specify a range in the usual way, by typing or pointing.

5. If the pointer is not on A1, press the HOME key.

6. Type a . to anchor the range.

7. Press the END key and then the down arrow key to expand the range to the last label cell, A9.

8. Press RETURN to complete the range entry and the Generate command.

The resulting entry form, duplicated in Figure 10-1, includes all of the field names you entered. Each field name is followed by a line delineating the length of the field. For instance, LAST NAME has a line of 20 underscores, and ZIP CODE has 5.

Actually, Symphony has not only generated an input form, it has also assumed that you created this form for a purpose—to enter data. It is now waiting for you to fill in the blanks of the first record of the database. You know this because of the NEW RECORD indicator centered on the top line of the control panel. The top left of the control panel indicates that whatever is entered onto this form will be stored as Record 1 of the database, and the second line of the control panel contains a prompt for the first data field, LAST NAME.

After you have gone through the process once or twice, creating an input form is a breeze. It takes only a couple of minutes to run through the steps summarized in "Steps for Creating a Data Entry Form" (see box).

STEPS FOR CREATING
A DATA ENTRY FORM

1. In a spreadsheet window, move to an unused section of the worksheet and enter the database's field descriptions in the form *field name: field type code: field length*. These descriptions must be label entries stored in consecutive cells down a column or across a row.

2. Switch to a FORM window by pressing TYPE (ALT-F10) and selecting FORM.

3. Press the MENU (F10) key and select the Generate option from the menu of FORM commands. In response to the prompts, select a default field type and field length, and specify a name for the database. Then indicate the range in the spreadsheet containing the field descriptions, and press RETURN.

4. You're ready to enter data into the entry form.

Saving Your Work

With the entry form generated, Symphony is ready for you to enter data. In fact, it assumes that the first thing you want to do after generating a form is to enter your first record. You will continue with data entry in the next chapter, but you should save your work first.

The form that you have created is an integral part of the worksheet. When you save the worksheet with the File Save command, Symphony saves all of the work that you have stored in the spreadsheet, including the data entry form. Thus, there is no separate command for saving an entry form or a database; just save the file as usual. In this case, name the file WARRANTY.

1. Press SERVICES (F9), select File Save, type **WARRANTY**, and then press RETURN.

When you next retrieve the WARRANTY file, you'll be able to resume exactly where you left off when you saved the worksheet. The FORM window automatically appears on the screen, and you will be able to enter data directly.

Chapter 11
Entering, Editing, And Sorting Data

Entering Data
Into an Entry Form

Storing the Form
In the Database

Moving From Form to Form
In a Database

Changing Data
In a Data Record

Sorting the Database

Saving the Database

In Chapter 10 you took the first steps in creating a database. In the FORM environment, you created a data entry form to store customer warranty information for Widget-Ware. Now you will begin to use this form to enter data into the database. This chapter covers data entry and editing, viewing the contents of the database, and sorting the database.

Entering Data Into an Entry Form

Before you begin, you should use the DOS Date command to set the current date at April 1, 1985; then load Symphony and retrieve the WARRANTY file that you saved in the previous chapter. When you retrieve the file, the data entry form will appear, because that portion of your file was displayed on your monitor when you saved the file in the previous chapter.

You will be filling out the data entry form with data records. Each filled-out form will constitute a database record. When you're in the FORM environment, think of the database as the collection of filled-out data-entry forms. A filled-out form is equivalent to a database record, and in fact, the words *form* and *record* will sometimes be used interchangeably.

Notice the inverse-video cursor beneath the first character space of the LAST NAME field. Symphony is waiting for your entry. In a moment you will enter the first data record. As you might guess, all you have to do is type the entry and press RETURN. Pressing RETURN moves the cursor to the next entry, FIRST NAME, and causes the control panel to display the prompt for the next field.

You may press either RETURN or the down arrow key to move to the next field. The up arrow key moves to the previous field. You will enter five records to give yourself something to play with. The first filled-out form is shown in Figure 11-1.

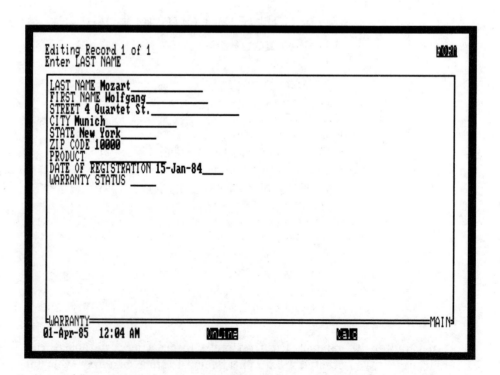

Figure 11-1. Record 1 in the data entry form

You will go through the steps of editing in detail. Then you will enter the other four forms on your own.

Before you proceed, it is worthwhile to acknowledge the possibility of errors. Although you may be renowned as an expert typist, even you might make a mistake. "What to Do About Data Entry Errors" (see box) describes the various types

---

WHAT TO DO
ABOUT DATA ENTRY ERRORS

As you enter data into your database, you may make a typing error. Here are steps you can take to fix it.

1. *If you have not yet pressed RETURN to end the entry:*
   a. You may press the BACKSPACE key to get back to the character(s) you want to correct. Each press of BACKSPACE erases the character to the left of the cursor and moves the cursor one space to the left.
   b. You may use the arrow keys to move the cursor through the entry without erasing characters, just as you would to edit a cell entry in the spreadsheet's Edit Mode. Then type characters to make insertions in the entry; the characters you type will be added at the position of the cursor, pushing all characters above and after the cursor toward the right.
   c. You may use the DEL key to delete characters from the entry at the position of the cursor.
   d. You may press ESC to remove the typed entry altogether and begin the entry from scratch. The cursor will go back to the first space in the entry. Be careful, because if you press ESC a second time, all entries of the form will be cleared.

2. *If you have already pressed RETURN:* Use the up and down arrow keys to move the pointer to the field that you want to correct. Then do one of the following:
   a. To redo the entire entry, simply begin typing the new entry. As soon as you type the first key, the old entry will disappear. You may also press the BACKSPACE key to erase the old entry before making the new one.
   b. To change just part of the entry, press the EDIT (F2) key. Then use the left and right arrow keys to move within the entry and make corrections as in 1b.
   c. You may use the ESC key to clear all entries on the data entry form. If you position the pointer at an existing entry and then press ESC, all of the form's entries will be cleared. The form becomes just an empty new form waiting to be filled. (Be careful, because once you have pressed ESC, there is no way to get back the original entries unless you previously saved them.) Pressing ESC a second time cancels entry of the current form entirely and moves you back to the previous record.

of entry errors you might make and how you can correct them. Keep in mind that the ESC key usually helps in undoing problems.

The field names are in capital letters. In order to differentiate the entries, you should type them in upper- and lowercase. Make sure the "CAP" indicator is off. Then

1. With the cursor on the LAST NAME field, type **Mozart** and press RETURN.

This puts the cursor on FIRST NAME.

2. Type **Wolfgang** and press RETURN.

3. Enter the following fields:

FIELD	ENTRY
STREET	**4 Quartet St.**
CITY	**Munich**
STATE	**New York**
ZIP CODE	**10000**

The next field is PRODUCT. In Chapter 12 you will learn how to avoid the inconvenience of typing the entire product name, which may be long and tedious to type. You will assign one-digit code numbers to the products and enter these code numbers instead of the names. Then you will resort to a clever way of displaying the product name, by magically transforming the code number into the name. For now, however, let's skip the PRODUCT field entirely. You'll return to it in the next chapter.

4. With the cursor on the PRODUCT field, press RETURN to leave the field blank and skip to the next field.

Because DATE OF REGISTRATION is a date field, you must make a special type of entry. Don't worry—Symphony doesn't want you to enter the date serial number. Instead you enter the date in standard *mm/dd/yy* Date format (the month, day, and year numbers separated by slashes), such as 1/15/84 for January 15, 1984. You may also make the entry in *dd-mmm-yy* format, such as 15-Jan-84. Either way, the result is displayed as 15-Jan-84.*

5. Type **1/15/84** and press RETURN.

As soon as you press RETURN, the cursor jumps to the top of the form instead of proceeding to the next field, WARRANTY STATUS. Try pressing the down arrow or RETURN key to move the cursor to the WARRANTY STATUS field. You can't. The reason is not that you made a mistake. Remember from Chapter 10 that you defined this field with a C (computed field) type, and that Symphony won't let you input data into a computed field. These fields are automatically entered by Symphony, or at least they will be when you get around to telling Symphony how to compute the warranty status.

---

*There are several additional Date formats available. See the Symphony *How-To Manual*, Chapter 7, "Calculating With Dates and Times."

Storing the Form in the Database

For the meantime, you will ignore the WARRANTY STATUS field and store the form in the database as is. It is important to note that even though you have filled out the form, it has not been stored as a database record yet.

To store a new record in the database, you must press the INS (Insert) key on the bottom right of the keyboard. Pressing INS stores the form's contents, clears the fields, and readies Symphony for entry of the next form. First check to make sure that the form's fields have been entered correctly.

1. Press the INS key to store the record and continue data entry.

Now the next form appears on the screen. You already know how to fill out forms (type in the entries and press INS when done), so

2. Fill out the remaining four forms, using the entries shown in Table 11-1. Remember to press INS after each form is completed.

Now that you have added some flesh to your database's skeleton, it is time to see what else you can do with the database. At present, Symphony should be waiting to receive the sixth form. Instead of entering another form, let's see how to browse through the forms that you've already stored.

Moving From Form to Form in a Database

In the SHEET environment, you moved through a spreadsheet by scrolling. You move through the FORM environment differently. You can't simply move left, right, up, and down to see everything you've entered, because the records aren't next to each other. They are more like pages of a book: you can look up and down on a single page and flip through the pages. At any given moment, your perspective is a single form. You cannot view several records simultaneously in the FORM environment.

Table 11-1. Data for Entry Records 2 Through 5

	RECORD 2	RECORD 3	RECORD 4	RECORD 5
LAST NAME	Beethoven	Gershwin	Gershwin	Bach
FIRST NAME	Ludwig	Ira	George	J.S.
STREET	1812 Overture St.	4 Rhapsody Lane	10 Tenth Street	7 Surprise Street
CITY	Reno	Xanadu	Miami	Dallas
STATE	Nevada	Ohio	Florida	Texas
ZIP CODE	33333	44444	99999	66666
PRODUCT	*(blank)*	*(blank)*	*(blank)*	*(blank)*
DATE OF REGISTRATION	2/11/85	5/1/85	3/22/85	1/25/85

The most important keys for browsing through a database are PG UP and PG DN. The PG UP key displays the previous record on the screen. PG DN moves to the next record. If you are currently viewing the last record (or the empty form after the last record), you cannot move farther down with PG DN. Similarly, if you were viewing the first record, you would not be able to use PG UP.

1. Press the PG UP key to move to the previous (last) form.

The fields pertaining to J.S. Bach appear on the form. The control panel reminds you that this is the fifth record out of a total of five, so that you know exactly where you are in the file. It also tells you that Symphony is editing this record. This means that if you want, you may change or update the data on this form. Instead, though,

2. Press the PG UP key once more.

This brings the fourth record to the screen. As it happens, the fourth record is just where you want to be, because one of the fields of this record needs to be updated.

Changing Data in a Data Record

When George Gershwin mailed in his registration card, it listed his address as 10 Tenth St. This morning, Mr. Gershwin called to inform you that he has moved to 3 Porgy Place. You'll need to update his record.

1. Use the down arrow key to move the cursor to the **STREET** field.
2. Type **3 Porgy Place** and press RETURN.

To store the update in the database, you could press INS as you did when you completed a new form. However, it is also permissible to press PG DN or PG UP, which not only stores the updated form, but also moves to a different form.

3. Press PG UP.

Record 3 also needs to be corrected. Ira Gershwin's DATE OF REGISTRATION is listed as 01-May-85, but it's still only April. The correct month should be March, not May.

4. Use the down arrow or RETURN to move the cursor to DATE OF REGIS-TRATION.

In order to alter part of the entry without having to retype the whole thing,

5. Press the EDIT (F2) key.

This permits you to use the arrow keys to move through the field and make insertions.

6. Press the right arrow key until the cursor is underneath the letter y of May.
7. Type r̶c̶h̶ to change the entry to 01-March-85.
8. Press the DEL key to delete the y, changing the entry to 01-March-85.
9. Press RETURN.
10. Press PG UP to move to the previous record.

In addition to PG UP and PG DN, there are two other handy keys that provide quick movement through the forms. The HOME key moves directly to the first form of the database, and the END key moves to the last record. Try them out.

There are seemingly countless ways to edit records. You have learned the ones that are most often used, but for completeness you may wish to study Table 11-2. It is a virtual database of form-related keystrokes used on the IBM PC keyboard.

Table 11-2. Special Keys Used in the FORM Environment

Key	Entering New Data And Criterion Records	Editing Data And Criterion Records	Moving Among Records
↑	Moves cursor to previous field	Moves cursor to previous field	
↓	Moves cursor to next field	Moves cursor to next field	
→	Moves cursor to next field	Moves cursor to next field	
←	Moves cursor to previous field	Moves cursor to next field	
TAB	Moves cursor to next field	Moves cursor to next field	
INS	Adds current record to database and displays a new form, allowing you to enter another record	Adds current record to database, leaving record in form; moves cursor to first field	
PG UP	Adds current record to database and displays previous record	Adds current record to database and displays previous record	Displays previous record
PG DN		Adds current record to database and displays next record or a new, blank record	Displays next record
CTRL-RIGHT	Moves cursor to last field	Moves cursor to last entry field	
CTRL-LEFT	Moves cursor to first field	Moves cursor to first entry field	
HOME or END	Adds current record to database and displays first or last record	Adds current record to database and displays first or last record	Displays first or last record
RETURN	Moves cursor to next field	Moves cursor to next field	
EDIT (F2)	Puts you in Edit Mode, allowing you to change individual characters in the field	Puts you in Edit Mode, allowing you to change individual characters in the field	

continued

Table 11-2. Special Keys Used in the FORM Environment (*continued*)

Key	Entering New Data And Criterion Records	Editing Data And Criterion Records	Moving Among Records
ESC	*Once:* clears current field (only if field is active)	*Once:* clears current field (only if field is active)	
	Twice: ~~clears all fields and~~ restores default values	*Twice:* restores field to its current value in database	
	Three times: ~~cancels new record entry and~~ returns to last existing record	*Three times:* restores all fields to their current values in database	
BACKSPACE	Clears current field (only if field is not active)	Clears current field (only if field is not active)	
DEL		Deletes current record (confirmation required)	

[Handwritten annotations:] Book's 3 times should read 4 times; of current field Clears all fields but defaults; 4 times cancels; Takes cursor to 1st field of current data/record; 3 times = Clears all fields but defaults

With permission copyright 1984 Lotus Development Corporation.

Sorting the Database

Widget-Ware's database is now up to date. You have seen that Symphony can create a set of forms and allow you to browse through these forms, which are stored in the order that you entered them. Symphony also allows you to edit data stored in the forms. Another function of database management is reordering the file's records. For example, you might want to sort a database alphabetically to be able to find particular customers more easily. Since sorting is a little more sophisticated use of a database than data entry, you might expect it to take longer to learn and use. In fact, sorting a database requires only a few keystrokes.

This brings you to the settings sheet of the FORM environment, shown in Figure 11-2. The FORM settings sheet contains settings that pertain to the database, including settings that affect database sorting and reporting. To examine the settings sheet for the WARRANTY form,

1. Press the MENU (F10) key, and select Settings.

Most of the settings and menu selections have no relevance for you yet, except for the Sort setting area in the last three rows of the settings window. This section is empty now, but you will soon be entering sort keys into it.

About Sorting

When you sort a database, you sort based on a field. For example, you might sort the forms by last name, in ascending alphabetical order (from A to Z). The field that you use to perform the sort is called a *sort key*.

It is not always sufficient to perform a sort on just one key. In the WARRANTY file, for instance, there are two Gershwins, Ira and George. You might want to sort using two keys, LAST NAME and FIRST NAME, so that records containing the same last name (such as Gershwin) will be further alphabetized by first name (George would come first, then Ira). The second key is used as a "tie-breaker" to sort out records that have identical first-key entries. You can even specify three sort keys in Symphony. The second key breaks ties in the first key, and the third key breaks ties in the second key.

Sorting can be performed in any order, ascending or descending, using either numeric or label fields as sort keys. The secret to sorting, then, is to tell Symphony what fields to use as sort keys and what sort order to apply to each key field. You do this with the Sort-Keys option of the settings sheet.

Sorting by 1st-Key and 2nd-Key

You will assign the sort keys necessary to sort the Widget-Ware database according to last name and first name. To assign a sort key,

1. Select Sort-Keys.

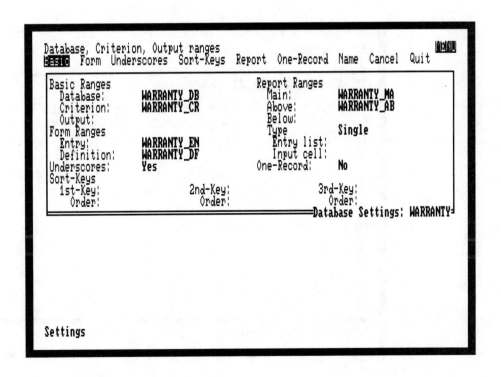

Figure 11-2. The FORM settings sheet

You may now elect to specify a 1st-Key, 2nd-Key, or 3rd-Key. When you select one of the three options of the Sort-Key menu, Symphony will temporarily bring up a spreadsheet window and ask you to show it which field you want to assign as one of the three keys. You have probably guessed that Symphony will give you a chance to point to this field. But if this is your first experience with the database management system, you are about to uncover a big secret that has been hidden from you up to now.

2. Select 1st-Key.

Symphony reverts to a spreadsheet window where, quite unexpectedly, all of your records have been placed in a table of rows and columns. On your screen, and in Figure 11-3, you are looking at the left side of a wide table that begins in row 40 of the spreadsheet. The rows of the table contain the forms, with one form stored in each row. Use the right arrow key to explore the right-hand side of this table. The columns of the table contain the fields. Symphony has taken each of the forms that you entered and stored it as a separate row in the spreadsheet.

Notice that Symphony used the field names as column headings in the table. You can designate one of them as the 1st-Key by pointing to any cell in that field's column and pressing RETURN. Alternatively, you may type the address of any cell in that column.

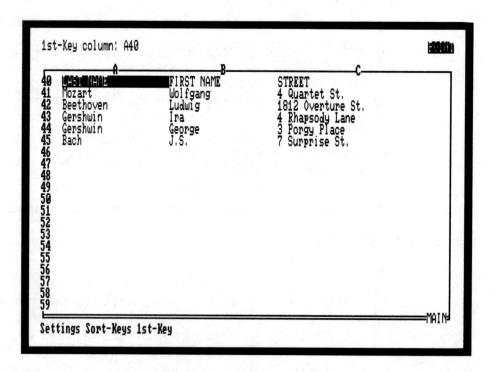

Figure 11-3. The database in table form

3. Move the cell pointer to a cell in the LAST NAME column (use cell A40), and press RETURN.

The settings sheet returns to the screen, and Symphony prompts for the sort order, with a recommendation of A (Ascending). Since an alphabetic sort is in ascending order of the alphabet,

4. Press RETURN to accept Ascending sort order.

This puts the correct entries into the settings sheet. The 1st-Key is set to the range A40..A40, which is the single cell in the LAST NAME column that you pointed to. The order for this key is set to Ascending. To assign the 2nd-Key,

5. Select Sort-Keys; then select 2nd-Key.

6. Move the cell pointer to the FIRST NAME column.

7. Press RETURN.

8. Press RETURN again to select Ascending order.

This completes the settings assignments, so

9. Select Quit.

To actually implement the sort,

10. Press the MENU (F10) key and select Record-Sort from the FORM command menu.

The menu offers two options, Unique and All. The *Unique option* sorts the records, but it also deletes those that are exact duplicates. If you accidentally entered a form twice, Unique is a good way to correct the mistake. The *All option* performs the sort without deleting the duplicates.

11. Select All.

Faster than you can say "Moussorgsky," Symphony reorders the forms. To check them, press HOME to display the first form, and press PG DN to browse through the rest. Note that whereas Ira Gershwin preceded George in the original file, these two records have now changed places, thanks to the 2nd-Key sort.

You can sort the file in a different order simply by changing the sort keys in the settings sheet and reissuing the Record-Sort command. Or you can leave the settings the way they are, enter any number of new records in any order, and reorder the file by selecting Record-Sort.

Saving the Database

Sorting is only the beginning of database management. You still have some loose ends to tie up, such as the warranty status, and there is a lot more that you can do with forms before proceeding to the tabular approach to database management. But you have accomplished quite a bit with the simple procedures that you've learned thus far.

You will need this database in the next chapter, so make sure you save it now.

1. Press SERVICES (F9), and select File Save.

Symphony will suggest saving the file under the original file name WARRANTY.

To update the original file,

2. Press RETURN and select Yes when asked whether you want to replace the original file.

In the next chapters, you will master a powerful collection of database management procedures that require a much higher level of sophistication and experience. If that sounds difficult, just make a mental note of how easy it has been to generate an input form, create database records, and sort a file.

Chapter 12
The Database From the SHEET Perspective

The Spreadsheet Version
Of the Database

The Definition Range

Establishing a Computed
Field

Entering a New Record
With a Computed Field

The Database Range

You have accomplished quite a bit with the database that you created in the previous chapter, but there is much more to database management than you have seen so far. In this chapter and the next you will explore the greater potential of the forms management system, examining the relationship between forms management and the spreadsheet environment. You will learn how to

- Incorporate automatically computed fields into the form
- Transform an entered input into a totally different value
- Make default values appear on the form
- Perform tailor-made validity checks on entered information
- Customize prompts for data input fields.

One cannot study Symphony's FORM environment without the spreadsheet. The two environments are tightly integrated; they share the same data and perform complementary functions. You will move back and forth between the spreadsheet and database environments as you proceed through this chapter.

You will need the WARRANTY file that you designed in Chapter 11. You will also need to specify a system date of 4-1-85 (April 1, 1985) before booting Symphony, so that you obtain the same results as those presented in this chapter's figures. If you have already booted Symphony, use the DOS add-in program to suspend the session and issue the DOS Date command as described in Chapter 8.

The Spreadsheet Version of the Database

When you last left the Widget-Ware application, you sorted the warranty registration forms and, in the process of designating the sort keys, caught a glimpse of the spreadsheet. This glimpse disclosed the fact that Symphony stored the records in tabular format. To find out exactly what Symphony did with the data, you can change the type of window we are using from FORM to SHEET. Instead of showing a single record at a time, the SHEET window shows the database of records stored in the spreadsheet.

To change the window type, issue the TYPE key sequence:

1. Press the TYPE (ALT-F10) key; then select SHEET. Press the HOME key to move to the top left corner of the spreadsheet.

The window border changes to identify the columns and rows of the spreadsheet, and the indicator on the top right of the screen is labeled "SHEET," as depicted in Figure 12-1.

What is this stuff, and who put it there? Part of it—the top part—is your own doing. The top nine rows are the field description labels that you entered as the first step when you created the data entry form in Chapter 10.

Cells A11 through A19 were put there by Symphony itself, and they should look familiar to you. They are label cells that Symphony used to produce the input form. By issuing the Generate command of the FORM command menu, you instructed Symphony to examine the field descriptions and then create the data entry form that was displayed in Figure 10-1. As you are about to find out, the Generate command instructs Symphony to do much more than that.

2. Press the PG DN key once.

Figure 12-2 portrays the screen as you see it. Symphony has done quite a bit of work, and you still haven't seen all of it.

3. Hold down the CTRL key and press the right arrow key to move the pointer one window to the right.

In a moment, you will clear up the mystery behind these seemingly haphazard spreadsheet entries, but first let's explore the spreadsheet some more. To move

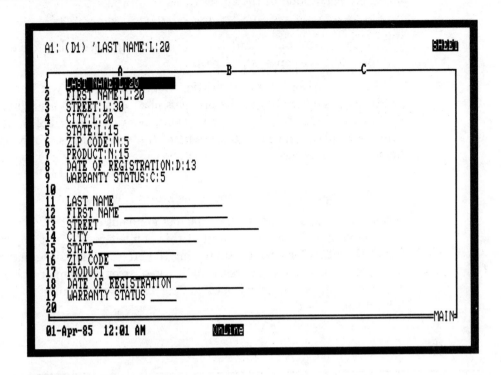

Figure 12-1. A SHEET-type view of the entry form

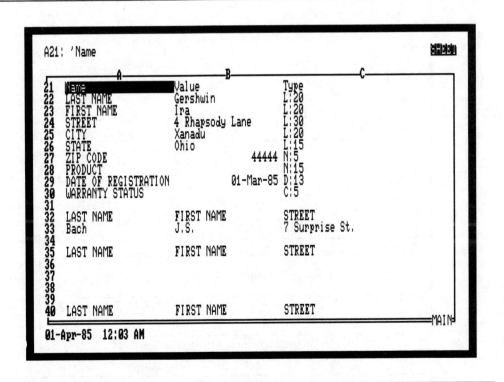

Figure 12-2. More of the database seen in the SHEET window

back to the left side of the sheet,

4. Hold down the CTRL key and press the left arrow key.

5. Press PG DN once, and then press the up arrow key once, so that row 40 occupies the top of the screen.

Now you are looking at the portion of the screen that you saw when you issued the Sort-Keys command in the previous chapter. Row 40 contains the field names of the database, and each subsequent row contains a record of the database. This is where Symphony stored the contents of the entry forms. You will find the other fields of the database records if you use the right arrow key to scroll the window toward the right.

6. Press the HOME key to move back to A1.

Don't worry; your spreadsheet has not gone out of control. The structure of this will be explained thoroughly, but at this point it really isn't important. After all, you've lived this long without knowing the effect of database management on the spreadsheet; and you've successfully worked through form creation, entry, editing, and sorting procedures without having to know anything about what went on behind the scenes.

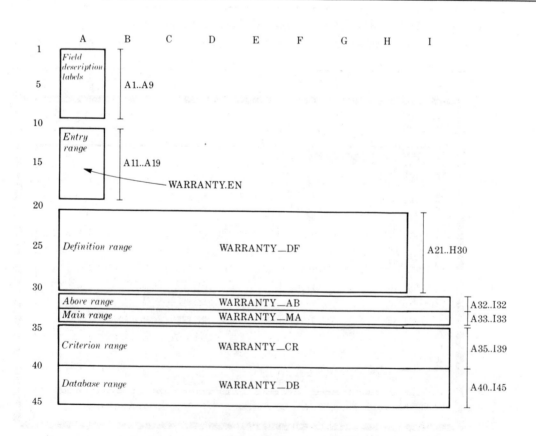

Figure 12-3. A map of the database's spreadsheet ranges

The fact is, you could go even a little farther without knowing much more about the spreadsheet. However, to use more sophisticated data management procedures, you do have to understand how Symphony stores the database in the spreadsheet.

A map of the spreadsheet is shown in Figure 12-3. With the exception of the field description labels in cells A1..A9, all of these ranges were created by Symphony in response to the Generate command. Symphony uses these ranges for various aspects of database management, such as reporting, record selection, and data calculation. The field description labels and Entry ranges have already been explained. Of the other ranges—the Definition range, the Above range, the Main range, the Criterion range, and the Database range—you will only work with the Definition and Database ranges here. You will make use of the other ranges later in the book.

The Definition Range

The *Definition range* is a table that describes every characteristic of the fields that comprise the data entry form (and therefore, the database itself). When you first issued the Generate command, Symphony took whatever it knew about the fields and put this information into its standard database Definition range table, shown in Figure 12-4.

Starting from the left, the first column of the Definition range is the *Name column*, the familiar list of field names that you entered in the field description labels range. The next column, the *Value column*, contains the data entries for one of the records of the database, the one you last used in the FORM environment. Figure 12-4 indicates that the Ira Gershwin record was the last record used. If you had used a different record, that record would be shown on your screen.

When you are in the FORM environment and you invoke an existing record (as you would do by pressing PG UP), Symphony temporarily stores the data entries of that record in the Value column of the Definition range. Also, when you enter a brand-new record into the database by filling out a form and pressing INS, the entries of that record are not only stored in the database, but also put into this temporary area of the Definition range.

The third column of the Definition range is the *Type column*. Symphony has examined the field types and lengths that you specified in the field descriptions and has inserted these two items into the Type column. Thus, you may look up any field in the database in the first (Name) column of the Definition range, move over two columns, and determine the type and length of the field.

The *Default column* comes next. Symphony looks here to see if you have specified that a particular field should have a default value. For example, if Symphony found the label "Ohio" stored in the Default cell corresponding to the STATE field, then whenever you bring up a blank form to make a new record entry into the database, Symphony will automatically place "Ohio" into the STATE field of the input form. The advantage of an entry default is the convenience of having Symphony fill in a field for you when that entry has the same value for most records. Thus, if most of Widget-Ware's registered customers lived in Ohio, it would make sense to designate Ohio as the default entry for STATE. Naturally, you can override the default by typing over it in the data entry form.

	A	B	C	D	E	F G	H I
	Name	Value	Type	Default	Formula	ValidInput	Prompt
21	Name	Value	Type	Default	Formula	ValidInput	Prompt
22	LAST NAME	Gershwin	L:20			ValidName	Enter LAST NAME
23	FIRST NAME	Ira	L:20				Enter FIRST NAME
24	STREET	4 Rhapsody Lane	L:30				Enter STREET
25	CITY	Xanadu	L:20				Enter CITY
26	STATE	Ohio	L:15				Enter STATE
27	ZIP CODE	44444	N:5				Enter ZIP CODE
28	PRODUCT	3	N:15				Enter PRODUCT
29	DATE OF REGISTRATION	C1-March-85	D:13				Enter DATE OF REGISTRATION
30	WARRANTY STATUS		C:5				Enter WARRANTY STATUS

Figure 12-4. The Definition range

By now you can see that the Definition range has a twofold purpose. It is there for Symphony's use as a temporary work area, but the more important use you will have for the Definition range is to establish rules about how Symphony should treat your entry form. Making an entry in the Default column is one method by which you can control the way that Symphony handles your data.

Another feature available for your use is computed fields. In the WARRANTY form you designated the WARRANTY STATUS field as a computed field. To create this computed field, you will be entering a formula into the next column of the Definition range, the *Formula* column. Symphony will use that formula to calculate, based on the date of registration, whether a particular warranty is still in effect (that is, less than a year old) or has expired. There is a dual purpose for the Formula column, just as there is for the Definition range. Symphony uses it to check a formula (if one is present) against the record currently being accessed in the form, and you use it to enter such a calculation if you so choose.

The *Validity* column (the heading is truncated to "Validi" on your screen) works in a similar fashion. This column stores a formula that checks the validity of data entered in the associated field. For example, in order to be certain that only product codes 1, 2, or 3 are entered into the PRODUCT field, you may enter a formula into the Validity field that Symphony will use to ensure that only the appropriate values are entered as input. Incorrect values will be rejected.

Next is the *Input* column. It is a temporary storage area for a record as it is being entered into the form. The Input column on your screen will appear blank. You should never make an entry directly into the Input column of the spreadsheet; instead, data is entered through the FORM data-entry record.

The last column in the Definition range is the *Prompt* column. As its name implies, this column is used to designate the prompt that is displayed in the control panel as you move to a particular field in the form to make an entry. The Generate command initially assigns a default prompt to all entries: the word "Enter" followed by the field name (for instance, "Enter LAST NAME").

Usually the default prompt is fine. However, there are instances where customized prompts save a lot of trouble. Consider the PRODUCT field. The application is designed so that the user enters a product code of 1, 2, or 3. It would be helpful to have a prompt that stated up front that a code number, rather than a product name, should be entered; the user would probably appreciate a prompt that stated which code corresponds to which product. You will be making this modification later in the chapter.

The point to all of the optional modifications and enhancements available through the Definition range is control. The ability to change Definition attributes puts a lot more power into your hands—it begins to make database management more than merely simple filing. Control is the difference between database management and an unmanageable database.

Establishing a Computed Field

Let's put theory into practice by implementing the computed field for WARRANTY STATUS. Recall that you originally entered the field definition of WARRANTY STATUS:C:5, designating this field as a computed field. Because of this, Symphony did not allow you to make any entries in this field. However, Symphony didn't make an entry in this field either—and for a good reason: it did not have the formula to make the necessary computation. Whatever that formula may be, it is your responsibility to supply it to Symphony. You do this by entering it into the Formula column of the Definition range.

First, it is necessary to decide what form this formula must take. If the registration is less than a year old, the warranty is "alive"; if a year has elapsed, the warranty is "dead." Thus, the WARRANTY STATUS field can take on one of two values—"alive" or "dead"—a situation that calls for a logical function like @IF, which you used in Chapter 9.

The format of the @IF function is @IF (*condition, arg1, arg2*), where *arg1* is the resulting value of the cell if the condition is satisfied (it's "alive") and *arg2* the result if the condition fails (it's "dead"). The *condition* itself is a logical formula, a test that is either passed or failed. The test is whether "today's date" (the date that this application is being run, which can be derived from the @NOW function) is less than a year after the date of registration. Thus, the *condition* can be expressed as *today's date* — DATE OF REGISTRATION < 365.

The formula should be stored in the cell of the Formula column corresponding to WARRANTY STATUS. You must position the cell pointer on this cell. Because the Definition range is too wide to display the Name column and Formula column on the screen simultaneously, it would be helpful to lock in the column titles row (row 21) and the Name column using the spreadsheet's Settings Titles Both command, so that the names and column titles don't scroll off the screen.

Locking Titles With the Settings Titles Command

The first step in locking titles is to position the screen so that the title rows and columns appear on the top and left of the window. Then move to the first cell that you want to be able to scroll and issue the Titles command.

You can use a trick to make sure that the correct titles appear on the top and left of the display. Determine the top left cell of the area that you want to fix, in this case cell A21. Scroll the screen away from that cell so that the cell is not displayed on the spreadsheet. If you do this, using the GOTO key to move back to the desired cell will position the window so that the cell occupies the top left corner of the display.

1. Press HOME to move to a distant area of the spreadsheet.
2. Press the GOTO (F5) key; then type **A21** and press RETURN.

The screen should now show A21 as the top left cell of the window. To lock the titles,

3. Press the right arrow key; then press the down arrow key to move to cell B22, the first cell to be scrollable.
4. Press the MENU (F10) key; then select Settings Titles Both.
5. Select Quit.

Next,

6. Use the arrow keys to move the pointer to the Formula cell for WARRANTY STATUS (cell E30).

Entering the Formula for the Computed Field

When you enter a formula for a computed field, the cells referred to in that formula should be in the Value column (column B). If the condition of the formula is *today's date* − DATE OF REGISTRATION < 365, the cell you use to describe the DATE OF REGISTRATION should be the corresponding cell of the Value column, which is cell B29. To get the current date, you use the @NOW function, which was introduced in Chapter 8. More precisely, since @NOW returns a value that includes a fractional representation of the time of day, which you don't want, you use @INT(@NOW). *@INT* is a function you haven't met before. Its job is to strip off the decimal portion of the @NOW result, making the number an integer.

Therefore, the condition is @INT(@NOW)−B29<365, and the logical formula takes the form @IF(@INT(@NOW)−B29<365,"alive","dead"). If the warranty is less than 365 days old, the string "alive" will be displayed in the form; otherwise, death sets in. It would be fair to say that on the 365th day, the warranty's life "hangs by a string," so to speak.

You can use pointer movement to help enter the formula.

1. Type @if(@int(@now).
2. Type a − (minus).
3. Move the pointer to the cell of the Value column corresponding to DATE OF REGISTRATION (cell B29).
4. Type <365,"alive","dead".
5. Type the) key and press RETURN.

In Figure 12-5, the record for Ira Gershwin is contained in the Value column. Gershwin's registration date is one month old, so his warranty is alive and well, as shown by the result of the @IF formula in cell E30.

Entering a New Record With A Computed Field

Now that the formula is in its place in the Definition range, how does it affect the data entry form? To find out, you must return to the FORM environment.

1. Press TYPE (ALT-F10), select FORM, and press RETURN.
2. Press END to move to the last form of the database, the form for Wolfgang Mozart.
3. Press PG DN to move to the next record, which is blank.

Symphony is now ready to accept the next record of the database, Record 6. Notice that the warranty status is "dead," even though the data for this form has yet to be entered. No, Symphony is not assuming that a warranty is dead until proven alive; rather, it is performing its calculation as normal; but when it finds no entry in the DATE OF REGISTRATION field, it substitutes 0 for the registration date in the computed field formula. Subtracting 0 from the result of @NOW in the formula that determines the age of this registration makes this a very old

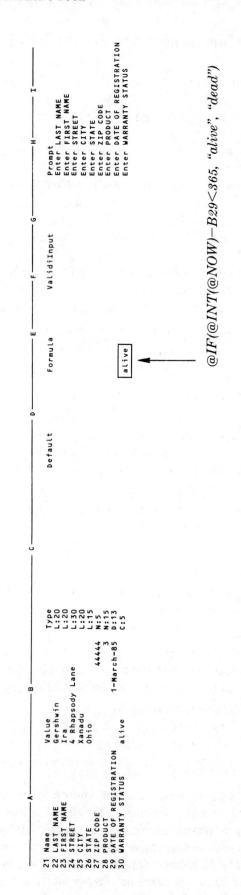

$$@IF(@INT(@NOW)-B29<365, \text{``alive''}, \text{``dead''})$$

Figure 12-5. WARRANTY STATUS and underlying @IF formula

form indeed. To Symphony, the warranty is quite dead. Now you can bring it back to life, by filling out the form.

4. Fill out the form with the entries shown in the column on the right:

LAST NAME	Mozart
FIRST NAME	Susan
STREET	22 22nd St.
CITY	Munich
STATE	New York
ZIP CODE	10000
PRODUCT	1
DATE OF REGISTRATION	1/20/85

As soon as you finish entering the DATE OF REGISTRATION, the WARRANTY STATUS changes to "alive." Remember that the form is not stored in the database until you insert it:

5. Press the INS key to insert the record and move to the next form.

To get a clearer picture of what happened, let's return to the spreadsheet environment.

6. Press the TYPE (ALT-F10) key and select SHEET.

The Definition range returns to the screen, and the data entries of Susan Mozart's record appear in the Value column. The first five data entries are left-justified in the column because they are label entries; the next three (numeric) entries are right-justified; and the last entry—the string result of the computed field formula—is left-justified.

The Database Range

What about the database itself? You have been pressing INS to store the form in a database. That database is stored in the Database range of the spreadsheet. To see it,

1. Press HOME; then press the PG DN key. (Note that row 21 does not scroll with the rest of the screen because it has been fixed with the Titles command.)

The database records are arrayed in tabular format in the range beginning in row 40. Susan Mozart's record has been appended to the end of the database. Whenever you insert a new record into the database, that record is placed in the next available row of the Database range. If you edit an existing record, pressing INS, PG UP, or PG DN replaces the old version of the record with the updated version in the same location.

An interesting feature of the Database range, and of the entire spreadsheet, is that the column widths have been changed from the default of nine characters. Symphony has used the field lengths that you specified in the field definitions to assign column widths to the spreadsheet. These column widths are one space wider than those specified in the field descriptions. For example, the LAST NAME field was given a length of 20, so the corresponding LAST NAME column of the Database range (column A) has a length of 21.

2. Press the right arrow key several times so that column F, the ZIP CODE column, scrolls into the display.

The column is six characters wide, one more than the field length of ZIP CODE. This is not wide enough to show the entire field name, ZIP CODE, that is stored on top of this column in the Database range (cell F40). You would see the entire ZIP CODE label if you widened column F, but you must be careful not to disturb the column widths just yet—they are important for database reporting purposes.

3. Use the arrow keys to scroll the screen over to the DATE OF REGISTRA-TION (column H) and the WARRANTY STATUS (column I).

Curiously, Symphony has stored the registration dates in its own serial-number format (31072, 31089, and so on). Yet when you viewed the records in the FORM window, the dates looked like normal dates. The reason is that Symphony reformats the date on a record-by-record basis. When you use a particular record in a form, the data from that record resides temporarily in the Definition range (and in the Database range if the record existed before). Only then is the date changed, temporarily, to normal Date format.

As long as you are using entry forms to view the database, there is no need to worry about how Symphony stores dates. However, if you want to change the format of the dates in the Database range, you may do so by applying the spreadsheet Format Date command to the column of dates.

Another curiosity of the Database range is the WARRANTY STATUS column. Only two records in the Database range show a WARRANTY STATUS: the Ira Gershwin record and the Susan Mozart record that you just entered. The other records don't have an entry for this field because they were stored in the database before the formula for the computed field was stored in the Definition range. In order to evaluate the WARRANTY STATUS formula for the older records, it is necessary to edit those records and to press a recalculation key to instruct Symphony to perform the formula calculation for each record.

To see how this works, you will need to return to the FORM environment. A greater familiarity with windows will make it easier to go back and forth between the SHEET and the FORM environments, so the next chapter will introduce the Window Create command.

Before going on, save your work.

4. Press SERVICES (F9), select File Save, press RETURN, and select Yes to replace the old version of the WARRANTY file.

Chapter 13
More on Windows And Database Features

Using a Window to Change
Environments

Calculating Computed
Fields in Existing Records

Using the Definition Range
To Transform Data Entries

Getting Back Into FORM

The previous chapter concluded by explaining how to create a computed field for the WARRANTY database's WARRANTY STATUS field. After exploring Symphony's windowing capabilities, this chapter will continue where Chapter 12 left off, expanding the features of your database even further. You will learn about the Window Create command. You will also learn how to perform data entry transformations, change entry prompts, establish default data entry values, and perform value checking on the data entered into the form.

You will need the WARRANTY file that you saved in Chapter 12, and the "CAP" indicator should be off.

Using a Window to Change Environments

You are going to do a lot of switching between the FORM and the SHEET environment in this chapter. So far, you have been pressing three keys each time you change environment: the ALT key, the F10 key, and the first letter of the environment type (such as F for FORM). This requires a good deal of effort, relatively speaking. It is also confusing to look through a single window that keeps changing its characteristics. You can avoid this confusion by creating separate windows for the database and the spreadsheet. That way, the differing aspects of your application will be distinct, but you will be able to move between environments with a single keystroke.

Two Commands: Window Pane Versus Window Create

This is not the first time you have used windows. Recall that in Chapter 6 you created two equal windows with the Window Pane Horizontal-Split command of the Services menu. Both windows were SHEET windows that acted as ports looking onto the spreadsheet. The difference between them was that they displayed different areas of the spreadsheet; they enabled you to see two distant windowfuls of information that would not otherwise have fit on the same screen.

In this chapter, your requirements are somewhat different. Here you want two windows that may well be used to view identical information—the database—but in different work environments. One window will show the SHEET environment, where the database is actually stored. The other window shows the FORM environment, which displays the database one record at a time through data entry forms. These windows will provide two ways of looking at the same data.

If you wanted to have a split screen of two windows devoted to different environments, you could use the Window Pane command. However, since there is so much information on the spreadsheet, it would be more convenient to let the SHEET window occupy the entire screen by itself, without having to give up a portion of the screen to another window. Window Pane only creates two or four windows of equal dimensions on the screen; it cannot create full-screen windows. On the other hand, the *Window Create command* gives you much more control over window design.

Using Window Create

The default name of the current window is MAIN, as indicated in the bottom right corner of the screen.*

---

*Recall that whenever you begin work in Symphony, the window you are working in is given the default name, MAIN, unless you specifically change the name of the window. This default name can be changed with the *Configuration command* of the Services menu.

The MAIN window is currently a SHEET window. You will create a second window, called WARRANTYFORM (window names may be anything you like, up to 15 characters long). As its name suggests, WARRANTYFORM will be a FORM window. MAIN will be the window you use for spreadsheet purposes, while WARRANTYFORM will be the window for forms management.

To invoke the Window command,

1. Press the SERVICES (F9) key and select Window.

2. Select Create.

Symphony's initial response is to prompt you for the window name. It also lists any current window names in the control panel. If you wanted to change the characteristics of a current window, you would select an existing name. To create a new window, however, you must type a new name.

3. Type **WARRANTYFORM** and press RETURN.

Next, Symphony requests the window type—the environment that the window will be assigned to.

4. Select FORM.

The size and location of the window are now highlighted on the screen. It is possible to change the size and location, but you don't have to at this point. For now, Symphony's suggestion is acceptable.

5. Press RETURN to accept the size and location of the window.

A window settings sheet appears, allowing you to assign or change certain characteristics of the window, such as its name and type. Since everything is satisfactory at this point,

6. Select Quit.

Presto!—the same FORM environment appears. The window displays the entry form that was last in use, the Susan Mozart form. Notice that the window name in the lower-right corner of the border is "WARRANTYFORM."

You might recall from Chapter 6 that moving from window to window is accomplished with the WINDOW (F6) key. To switch to the spreadsheet window,

7. Press the WINDOW (F6) key.

The SHEET window now occupies the screen. Its window name, "MAIN," is displayed in the bottom right corner, and the mode indicator in the top right corner is labeled "SHEET." Instead of pressing three keys to switch environments, you pressed only one. To switch back to the FORM environment,

8. Press WINDOW (F6) again.

Calculating Computed Fields
In Existing Records

Now that you know how to move easily between the SHEET and FORM environments, you are ready to take care of the problem that arose at the end of Chapter 12. You'll recall that with the exception of Ira Gershwin and Susan Mozart,

Symphony had not calculated the WARRANTY STATUS line for any of the records in the database. The @IF formula stored in the Formula column of the Definition range did not operate retroactively on the original records. How can you determine their warranty status?

Fortunately, it is very easy to rectify the original records. Simply retrieve a record and then instruct Symphony to recalculate all computed fields for the record. This can be done by pressing the CALC (F8) key.

1. Press HOME to move to the first record.

2. Press the CALC (F8) key.

J.S. Bach's warranty is alive. To store the updated record in the database and move to the next record,

3. Press the PG DN key.

Again, the record must be recalculated.

4. Press the CALC (F8) key.

To update the other records,

5. Repeat steps 3 and 4 for the third, fourth, and fifth forms of the file. When done, press END to retrieve the last record of the file.

The only instance in which you have to use this recalculation procedure is when you make a change in the Definition range after you have created some database records. Any records entered after a change to the Definition range will automatically reflect the change.

Using the Definition Range
To Transform Data Entries

Chapter 12 introduced the Definition range and explained how to use the Formula column to calculate warranty status. This is a good start, but you have only scratched the surface of Symphony's ability to control and manipulate data entries.

The Definition range makes several other enhancements possible. The next several pages will explore these enhancements and the way in which they affect the entry form.

A computed field uses a formula to make an automatic entry. A *transformation* also involves a formula, but that formula causes the data entry itself to be transformed into something else. In a transformation, you make an entry yourself, and Symphony uses a formula to change the entry automatically. This differs from a computed field, because you do not make an entry into a computed field; Symphony does it for you.

How would a transformation be useful in the WARRANTY database? Up to now, for example, you have avoided entering product names because they would take too long to type. You used one-digit product codes instead. But product codes are cryptic; they force you to memorize the meanings of the code. A transformation formula would allow the user to type a code of 1, 2, or 3, leaving it up to Symphony to transform the code into a product name. The codes used for this application are 1=WidgetWorksheet, 2=WidgetWord, 3=WidgetWindow. Thus, if you typed 1, the transformed string "WidgetWorksheet" would be displayed in the form and stored in the database.

Using @CHOOSE to Transform Product Codes

Like a computed field, an entry transformation requires that the transformation formula reside in the Formula column of the Definition range. You could use the @IF function to perform the transformation, but its form would be rather complicated and cumbersome: if the entry is 1, use the string "WidgetWorksheet"; if the entry is 2, use the string "WidgetWord"; if the entry is 3, use the string "Widget-Window"; if the entry is not 1, 2, or 3, don't use any string—it is an erroneous entry.

A much neater and more compact formula can be used for transforming the entry. It requires a new function: the *@CHOOSE function*. This function selects an argument from among a series of arguments, based on the value of a selector number. Its format is @CHOOSE (*selector-number, arg0, arg1,...*), where *selector-number* is an integer value such as 0 or 1. Depending on the value of the selector number, Symphony chooses the argument corresponding to that value. If the selector number is 0, Symphony finds *arg0* and uses it as the result of the function. If the selector number is 1, *arg1* is the result.

For example, a formula with the general form of @CHOOSE(*selector-number*, "ERR","WidgetWorksheet","WidgetWord", "WidgetWindow") will return a value of "ERR" if *selector-number* is 0, "WidgetWorksheet" if *selector-number* is 1, "WidgetWord" if *selector-number* is 2, and "WidgetWindow" if *selector-number* is 3. If *selector-number* is greater than 3 or less than 0, the @CHOOSE function will also return an error.

The selector number can be a numeric value, or it can be the address of a cell that contains a numeric value. The formula that you are going to store in the Definition range will include a selector number referring to the value that is input for the PRODUCT field; that is, the value stored in the Input column of the Definition range.

Entering the Transformation Formula

To make a change in the Definition range, switch to the spreadsheet window.

1. Press the WINDOW (F6) key.
2. Press HOME.
3. Move down to the row of the Definition range that corresponds to PRODUCT (row 28); then move across to the Formula column (column E).

With the pointer on cell E28, you will begin to enter the transformation formula. The *selector-number* of the @CHOOSE function must refer to the PRODUCT cell in row 28 of the Input column (cell G28), for this is where product codes will be entered into new records. In general, transformation formulas that depend upon data entries of the form should refer to cells in the Input column (as opposed to formulas for computed fields, which must make reference to cells in the Value column). This particular transformation formula will be @choose(G28,"err", "WidgetWorksheet","WidgetWord","WidgetWindow").

4. Type **@choose(** to begin the formula.

5. Point to the Input entry for PRODUCT, cell G28.

6. Type the , key.

7. Type the rest of the formula:

   "err","WidgetWorksheet","WidgetWord","WidgetWindow")

8. Press RETURN to store the formula.

The Input column is totally blank. Cell G28 is considered to be 0 in the formula, so the @CHOOSE function returns *arg0*, which is "err". When you enter a new record (or recalculate an old one), the correct transformation will occur. But before testing the transformation, you can make some other modifications to the Definition range.

This returns ∅

Changing Entry Prompts

The last column of the Definition range includes the prompts that appear in the control panel as you prepare to make entries in the form. The default prompt is "Enter" followed by the field name. Now that the PRODUCT field is defined to be a transformation of input value 0, 1, 2, or 3, it would be helpful to have a prompt that said, "Enter PRODUCT code (1=WidgetWorksheet, 2=WidgetWord, 3= WidgetWindow)". To change the prompt, all you need to do is change the appropriate prompt entry in the Definition range.

1. Move the pointer to the prompt for PRODUCT (cell H28).

The prompt already includes the words "Enter PRODUCT." Instead of typing the whole prompt from scratch, you can enter the spreadsheet Edit Mode and add the rest of the customized prompt, as follows:

2. Press the EDIT (F2) key.

3. Press the space bar once.

4. Type the remainder of the prompt:

   code (1=WidgetWorksheet, 2=WidgetWord, 3=WidgetWindow)

5. Press RETURN to store the prompt label.

While you're at it, you might also want to improve upon the DATE OF REGISTRATION prompt. You have been entering the date in *mm/dd/yy* format. To guide the user, it will be helpful to change the entry prompt from "Enter DATE OF REGISTRATION" to "Enter DATE OF REGISTRATION as mm/dd/yy."

6. Move the cell pointer to the DATE OF REGISTRATION prompt (cell H29).
7. Press the EDIT (F2) key.
8. Press the space bar once.
9. Type the following: **as mm/dd/yy**.
10. Press RETURN.

Formatting a Field in the Entry Form

Another use for the Definition range is to tell Symphony to assign a particular format to a field in the entry form.

As a rule, Symphony uses the General format to display numeric fields (no commas, $ signs, or parentheses, and as many decimal places as will fit in the cell). Label fields are left-justified, date fields are displayed in *dd-mmm-yy* format (for instance, 20-Jan-85), and time fields are displayed in *hh:mm:ss* A.M./P.M. format (such as 01:55:20 P.M.).

It is possible to specify any one of the many numeric, calendar, and time formats available through the spreadsheet Format command, or to change the default adjustment of label entries with the Range Label-Alignment command. All you have to do is assign the desired format to the appropriate cell of the Value column.

In the WARRANTY form, the date of registration is entered in *mm/dd/yy* format, yet the field is displayed in the default *dd-mmm-yy* format. To make things consistent, use the Format command to change the format of the corresponding cell in the Value column to *mm/dd/yy* format.

1. Move to the Value cell for DATE OF REGISTRATION (cell B29).
2. Press the MENU (F10) key and select Format Date.
3. Choose the fourth option of the Format menu, Full-Intn'l.
4. Press RETURN to apply this format to the single cell B29.

When you return to the FORM environment, the registration date will be displayed in the new format.

Setting a Default Value

As was mentioned in Chapter 12, defaults are useful when an entry field usually assumes a particular value. Using the Default column of the Definition range, for example, you can have Symphony automatically place the string "New York" in the STATE field for new records. Using a default value is a real advantage in this case, for most of Widget-Ware's customers are New Yorkers. If a customer is not a New Yorker, you can cancel the default simply by typing a different STATE entry; otherwise, Symphony will enter New York for you.

To set up a default, all you have to do is store the default value in the Default column of the appropriate field. In the spreadsheet window,

1. Move to the cell in the Default column that corresponds to STATE (cell D26).
2. Type **New York** and press RETURN.

The default is now in effect.

Value Checking

Before returning to the FORM environment, you can put the Definition range to one more use: refining Symphony's error-checking procedures. By assigning a particular field type to a field, you have already instructed Symphony to check that an entry of the correct type is entered into that field. Thus, typing a label into a numeric field produces an error signal (a beep), as does typing a date into a numeric field or a number into a date field. Symphony does not even accept the entry. This provides some measure of built-in error checking.

You can go further, however, by using the Validity column of the Definition range. A *value check* allows you to apply customized error checking to any field you like. One candidate for a value check is the DATE OF REGISTRATION. Since Widget-Ware began selling its products on January 1, 1984, some errors could be avoided by making sure that all entries are dated after 1/1/84.

To make Symphony perform a value check, you enter a logical formula in the Validity column. This logical formula must make reference to the Value column. Thus, to check the DATE OF REGISTRATION, the logical formula would refer to cell B29, the Value cell of the field. To make sure that B29 is greater than 1/1/84, Symphony must use calendar arithmetic, comparing the serial value of the registration date to the serial value of 1/1/84. Symphony already stores date entries in serial value, so there is no need to perform a conversion. To convert 1/1/84 to a serial value, you can use the @DATE function, whose form is @DATE(*yy,mm,dd*). The appropriate logical formula is therefore +B29>=@DATE(84,1,1).

1. Move the cell pointer to the Validity cell of the DATE OF REGISTRATION field (cell F29).
2. Type + to begin the formula.
3. Point to the Value cell of DATE OF REGISTRATION (cell B29).
4. Type **>=@date(84,1,1)** and press RETURN.

The result of a logical formula is either 1 (TRUE) or 0 (FALSE). For Susan Mozart's entry, the result is 1 (TRUE), because January 20, 1985 is later than January 1, 1984.

Getting Back Into FORM

Now that you have whipped this entry form into shape, let's see how useful it really is.

1. Press the WINDOW (F6) key to switch to the WARRANTYFORM window.
2. Press the PG DN key to move to a new entry form (Record 7).

Notice the default entry, "New York," in the STATE field, and the "dead" WARRANTY STATUS. Now fill out four more entry forms. For those that have a STATE field of New York, simply press RETURN or the down arrow key to accept the default value. Otherwise, type an entry into STATE; "New York" will be overwritten by the new entry.

Remember to watch for the transformation and the Date format to see if they are working, and try entering an invalid date (for example, January 1, 1960) to verify the value check on the date field.

3. Fill out four forms with the data shown in Figure 13-1.

When you're done, you may want to switch to the SHEET window and see how Symphony has stored your records in the Database range.

```
LAST NAME Bach_____
FIRST NAME Jim_____
STREET 5 5th St._____
CITY Brooklyn_____
STATE New York_____
ZIP CODE 11111
PRODUCT 2_____
DATE OF REGISTRATION 1/20/85_____


LAST NAME Bernstein_____
FIRST NAME Leonard_____
STREET West Side Ave._____
CITY Ithaca_____
STATE New York_____
ZIP CODE 12222
PRODUCT 3_____
DATE OF REGISTRATION 2/10/84_____


LAST NAME Dvorak_____
FIRST NAME Anton_____
STREET 1 New World St._____
CITY Chicago_____
STATE Illinois_____
ZIP CODE 60609
PRODUCT 2_____
DATE OF REGISTRATION 2/3/84_____


LAST NAME Liszt_____
FIRST NAME Franz_____
STREET 4 Piano Place_____
CITY Boise_____
STATE Idaho_____
ZIP CODE 55555
PRODUCT 2_____
DATE OF REGISTRATION 11/10/84____
```

Figure 13-1. Entries for Records 7 through 10

Now is a good time to save your worksheet. To replace the old version of the WARRANTY file with the new one,

4. Press SERVICES (F9) and select File Save.

5. Press RETURN to replace the old worksheet file with the updated version.

The records you have just entered have increased the size of the database. This provides a nice assortment of records for the next two chapters, which deal with database querying, extraction, and special functions.

In this chapter you learned how to harness the features of the Definition range to design a form that does a considerable amount of work for you. The WAR-RANTY form now incorporates such sophisticated capabilities as computed fields, transformations, value checks, special formats, defaults, and custom prompts. You also learned a new function, @CHOOSE.

The Window Create command, which you used to create the two windows, has more features than were discussed in this chapter. As you proceed through the book, you will be revisiting this command several times.

Chapter 14
Criteria Selection, Database Queries, And Database Functions

Types of Database Queries

Using Criterion Records
In the FORM Environment

Using Wildcards
For Label Matches

Formula Criteria

Using Strings
In Formula Criteria:
The @FIND Function

Using Compound
Conditional Formulas

Now that you've perfected the method for entering and maintaining information in a file, the next step in database management is to use the database to answer questions about the information it contains. A good database management system like Symphony will allow you to ask complicated questions about the database, and it will report the answers easily and effectively.

This process is called *database querying*. A database query can be detailed or general in nature. An example of a *detail-oriented query* would be "What are the names of the customers whose warranties have expired?" In contrast, *general queries* are summaries of information: "How many customers have expired warranties?"

Symphony encompasses a wealth of capabilities that permit you to manipulate a database almost any way you want and to use querying techniques as sophisticated as your imagination allows. In this chapter, you will learn how to perform database queries; formulate and implement selection rules to focus attention on the information that pertains to your query; and locate records that conform to your selection rules. More will come in the following chapter. By the end of that chapter, you will be able to find a needle in a haystack.

You will, of course, need a database to query. For this you will use the WARRANTY database that has been developed over the last four chapters. Before continuing, set the system date to April, 1, 1985, and then load Symphony and retrieve the WARRANTY file. The database has only ten records, but these will be enough to demonstrate a great deal about criteria selection and database querying. The same rules and techniques apply equally to 8000 records as to 10.

Types of Database Queries

The questions you might ask about the Fidget Widget Widget-Ware database are typical of the queries that might be addressed to any database. Some examples are

- What records have LAST NAME fields beginning with the letter B?
- Who are the registered customers from New York?
- Which customers' warranties will expire within 60 days?
- How many people are registered purchasers of WidgetWorksheet?

Answering these questions requires going through the database and identifying records that specifically relate to the query. This involves instructing Symphony to apply one or more criteria to the database records. A *criterion* is a rule for selecting records. Those records that pass the selection criteria are used to answer the query.

The simplest selection criteria (and probably the most frequent) involve *matching*: selecting records if one or more fields match particular values. A selection of records whose LAST NAME matches the string "Mozart" is a *label match*, since the selection involves comparing two labels. A criterion that selects records whose ZIP CODE field is 10000 is called a *number match*, since ZIP CODE and 10000 are numbers. There are also criteria to match dates and times.

You can specify criteria in two ways. One is in the spreadsheet environment, the other in the FORM environment. You will use the FORM environment in this chapter and the next.

Using Criterion Records
In the FORM Environment

Specifying selection criteria in the FORM environment is similar to entering data: you fill out a form with the criteria you want. In fact, the form you fill out is the same one that you use for data entry—a form you design yourself. However, instead of entering data, you enter criteria. A filled-out form is called a *Criterion record*. For simple label and number matches, all you need to do is enter the matching string or value into the form.

Once the Criterion record is completed, you can store it by pressing the PG UP or PG DN key. (You may also press the INS key to store the record and keep it on the screen.) In a sense, Symphony treats the completed Criterion records just as it treats data entry forms; it stores them as records of a small database of criteria in a special area of the spreadsheet called the *Criterion range* (see Figure 12-3's schematic map). You may use as many as four Criterion records to design a single selection rule.

Let's take a look at a Criterion record. You invoke the Criterion record form from the command menu of the FORM environment.

1. If you are not in the FORM environment, press the WINDOW (F6) key.

2. Press the MENU (F10) key from within the FORM environment.

3. Select the Criteria option.

The Criteria menu permits you to enter new criteria (using the Edit option) and to use or ignore existing criteria.

4. Select Edit to prepare to enter a new criterion.

The *Criteria Edit command* brings the blank Criterion record to the screen. The field names, field lengths, and the prompts for entries are all the same as those for the data entry form. The procedure for moving the entry cursor through the form is the same, too: use the RETURN, down arrow, right arrow, or TAB keys to move to the next field; use the up arrow key to back up to the previous field.

Entering a Label-Match Criterion

The WARRANTY database contains information about the registered customers of Widget-Ware products. With only ten records in the database, it would not be very difficult to get information about a particular customer. But when the database grows to several thousand records, you need a speedy way to locate the specific information you want. Selection criteria provide a quick way to find the records you need.

Suppose that Widget-Ware's Director of Marketing, Bridgeotte Fidget, would like to send a letter to Wolfgang Mozart in response to a telephone complaint. Ms. Fidget needs to know Mozart's address and registration information. In order to locate the record containing this data, you can use a label-match criterion, matching the LAST NAME field with the string "Mozart." All you have to do is enter the string into the LAST NAME field of the Criterion record, store the Criterion record, and then use it to locate the desired information. These steps are outlined in "Using Criterion Records for Database Queries" (see box).

The entry cursor is already stationed on LAST NAME (unless you moved it, in which case you should press HOME). It does not matter whether you type the name in uppercase letters (MOZART), in all lowercase letters (mozart), or with an initial capital letter (Mozart)—Symphony's matching facility treats all three strings the same way.

1. Type **Mozart** and press RETURN.

The form should now look like Figure 14-1.

2. Press the PG UP key to store the Criterion record and return to the FORM environment.

Symphony returns you to the FORM environment, just where you were before invoking the Criteria Edit command.

The selection criterion has not yet been put into effect. This will not happen until you specifically instruct Symphony to use the criterion. To perform the selection, you must issue the Criteria Use command.

USING CRITERION RECORDS FOR DATABASE QUERIES

Criterion records are used to query a database—to find out specific or general information about the records stored in the database. The steps for using Criterion records are as follows:

1. In the FORM environment, select the Criteria command; then select Edit.

2. Enter criteria into the first Criterion record.

3. If you are creating only one Criterion record, press PG UP to store the record and return to the form, or press PG DN to store the record and advance to the second Criterion record form.

After creating a second, third, or fourth Criterion record, you can store it either by pressing PG UP (which also moves to the previous Criterion record) or by pressing INS (which stores the Criterion record and advances to the next Criterion record). Note that for the first Criterion record, you press PG DN to store the Criterion record and advance to the next one, whereas for the other Criterion records, you press INS to store the Criterion record and advance to the next one.

If you have created multiple Criterion records, you conclude Criterion editing by pressing PG UP until you get to the first record, and then press PG UP one more time to return to the database.

4. To activate the criteria selection, press MENU (F10) and select Criteria Use.

3. Press the MENU (F10) key.

4. Select Criteria; then select Use.

Symphony instantly displays the record of Wolfgang Mozart. You have succeeded in locating the specific information you wanted by using a simple label-match query.

Examine the top line of the control panel, which says "Editing record 5 of 10 (Match 1 of 2)." Not only does Symphony retrieve the Mozart record; it also tells you exactly where in the file this form is stored and how many records in the file have "Mozart" as the LAST NAME field.

You were lucky enough to find the Mozart you wanted: Wolfgang. However, there is another Mozart registered with Widget-Ware. To see what other records passed the label-match criterion, use the standard FORM environment movement keys. PG DN will advance to the next matched record, and PG UP will move to the previous matched record.

5. Press the PG DN key.

Symphony rushes to retrieve the next matching record, that of Susan Mozart. The control panel tells you that this is the second of two matching records. Thus, Susan and Wolfgang are the only Mozarts in the file.

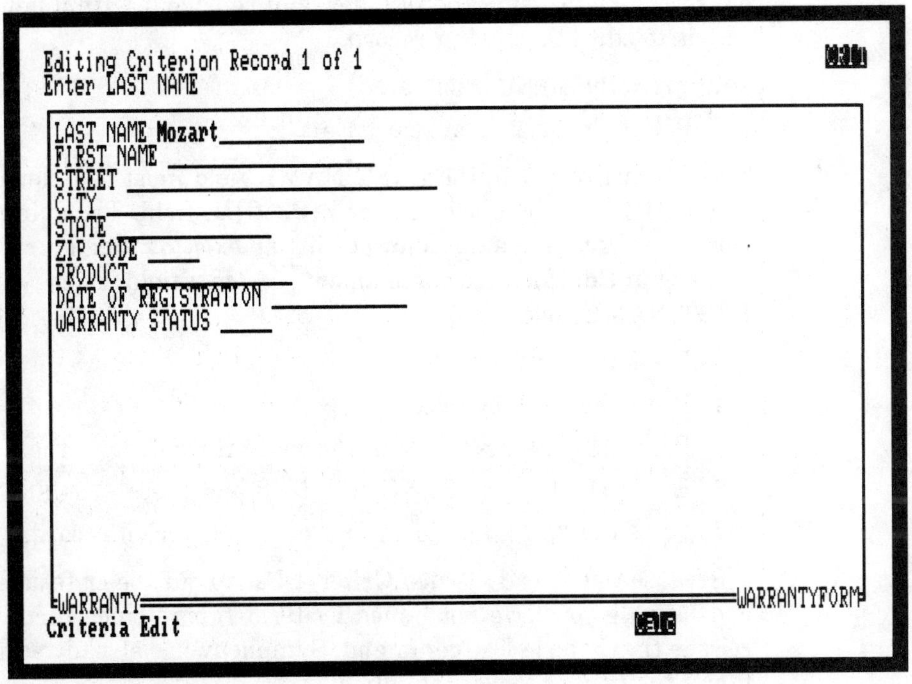

```
Editing Criterion Record 1 of 1                              READY
Enter LAST NAME

 LAST NAME Mozart_____
 FIRST NAME _____
 STREET _____
 CITY_____
 STATE_____
 ZIP CODE ____
 PRODUCT _____
 DATE OF REGISTRATION _____
 WARRANTY STATUS ____




 WARRANTY                                               WARRANTYFORM
Criteria Edit                                 Calc
```

Figure 14-1. The Criterion record showing the first entry

If you tried to press PG DN again, Symphony would emit a polite but firm beep. There are no more matching records after the second match. If you pressed HOME to jump to the first matching record and then pressed PG UP to try to move to the previous record, Symphony would beep again. When criteria have been implemented with the Criteria Use command, you may not retrieve any records other than the ones that pass the criteria.

The Criteria Use command creates a subsidiary database from the original full set of forms. You may browse through that subsidiary database or edit records within it; but you are restricted to the data records that conform to the criteria. To release this restriction, you would have to issue the Criteria Ignore command from the FORM command menu. Do not issue Ignore just yet, though; there are more criterion selection procedures to try out first.

Entering a Number-Match Criterion

Number matches are essentially the same as label matches, except that the criterion tests for numeric instead of alphabetic equivalence. ZIP CODE is the only field defined with an N (numeric) field type. To locate and select records having the ZIP code 11111, you will create a Criterion record with the desired ZIP code stored in the ZIP CODE field.

You have already filled out one Criterion record. To change the criterion from the previous label match to the current number match, it is necessary to replace the old Criterion record with the new one. There are two ways to do this. One way is to retrieve the Criterion record (using the Criteria Edit command), delete the old record by pressing the DEL key, and replace it with a new record. The easier way is to edit the existing record.

1. Press the MENU (F10) key.
2. Select Criteria; then select Edit.

The "Mozart" entry in the LAST NAME field must be deleted, and the ZIP code value 11111 must be placed in the ZIP CODE field. The rules for editing a Criterion record are the same as for editing an existing data entry form. First, use the ESC key in Edit Mode to erase an entry from a field. Then, with the cursor in the LAST NAME field,

3. Press the EDIT (F2) key.
4. Press the ESC key once.
5. Press RETURN several times to move the cursor to the ZIP CODE field.
6. Enter **11111** in the ZIP CODE field and press RETURN.
7. Press the PG UP key to store the new Criterion record.

Because you already issued Criteria Use to put the criteria selection into effect, and because you have not issued Criteria Ignore since then, there is no need to reissue the Criteria Use command. Symphony has already assumed that you want to put the new criterion into effect.

As indicated in the control panel, the new Criterion record yields a single match. Jim Bach is the only customer with a ZIP code of 11111.

Entering a Date-Match Criterion

Clark Clerk, the data entry clerk for Widget-Ware, has not been sleeping well. In his dreams, he imagines that on March 22, 1985, he made a typing error in a form he entered. However, he has no idea which form it was. He would like to retrieve all forms with that registration date.

By now you already know how you can help Clark Clerk: issue Criteria Edit, change the Criterion record so that it reflects a match for March 22, 1985 in the DATE OF REGISTRATION field, store the record, and return to the FORM window. The only difference here is that the criterion is a date match. It differs from the label and number matches only in that the matching values must be valid dates. Try implementing the criterion yourself. Then check your work against the following steps:

1. Press the MENU (F10) key.
2. Select Criteria; then select Edit.
3. Move the cursor down to the ZIP CODE field.
4. Press the EDIT (F2) key to enter Edit Mode; then press ESC to delete the current entry in ZIP CODE.
5. Press the RETURN key twice until the cursor points to DATE OF REGISTRATION.

Because this is a date field, the entry you make must be in Date format, such as 3/22/85 or 22-Mar-85.

6. Type **3/22/85** and press RETURN.
7. Press PG UP to store the Criterion record and return to the FORM window.

Luckily, Clark Clerk entered only one record on March 22. However, everything seems in order in this record (unless you made an error when you entered it yourself). False alarms are one of many Clark Clerk quirks.

So far, you have used three types of selection criteria to query the WARRANTY database: label matches, number matches, and date matches. "Spelling and Spaces in Label Matches" (see box) reviews some of the rules that apply in matching strings to criteria. Knowing these rules may help you avoid future mistakes or trace them more easily if they occur.

Using Wildcards for Label Matches

Symphony offers ways to relax the strict rules of label matching. One of these is the use of *wildcard characters*, which are placed in label criteria to make them more general. A wildcard is a character that can be used in a string to represent one or more characters. Symphony recognizes two wildcards in selection criteria, the asterisk (*) and the question mark (?). Both wildcards can only be used for label matches.

SPELLING AND SPACES IN LABEL MATCHES

Symphony treats uppercase and lowercase letters as equivalent when it searches for a string in a label match. MOZART, mozart, and Mozart are all the same for the purposes of record selection—which is good, for in some cases (such as WidgetWord), you might forget which letters are uppercase.

While Symphony is not concerned with case, it is extremely particular about what characters comprise the matching string and about the sequence of these characters.

A misspelled string cannot be matched correctly. Spaces are another source of problems. A character string preceded or followed by one or more spaces is different from a character string with no spaces. For example, using " Mozart" (space-Mozart) instead of "Mozart" (no space before the M) would return no matches in the WARRANTY database. "Mozart " (Mozart-space) would also malfunction. In short, spaces count. Since there is no way to relax the preciseness that Symphony requires in an exact label match, you must be extremely careful not only in specifying criteria, but also in making entries into the data record. An accidental space at the end of a data entry may be invisible, but it can cause a record to fail a criterion that should have been passed.

The Asterisk (*) Wildcard Character

The *asterisk (*) wildcard character* can be used in a selection criterion to represent any character or group of characters in a label-match criterion so long as those characters are contiguous. The * character must be the final character in a label-match criterion.

For example, entering "Moz*" in the LAST NAME field of a Criterion record selects all customers whose last name begins with the letters Moz (and ends with anything). The Moz* criterion would select the Mozart records of Wolfgang and Susan. It would also select records of George Mozambique, Eleanor Mozer, or Joe Moz if they were in the database. Not only does the * wildcard character increase flexibility and save typing; it also eliminates the problem of hidden, trailing spaces at the end of field entries. The * tells Symphony to match the record even if it contains trailing blanks, as long as the characters preceding the * cause a match.

Clark Clerk has just remembered where the data entry problem was—almost. He can't recall the exact date of the record containing the error, but he does remember that the customer's name begins with the letter B. Use the * wildcard character to retrieve those records that have a LAST NAME beginning with the letter B.

1. Prepare to edit the Criterion record by pressing MENU (F10) and selecting Criteria Edit.

Instead of erasing the DATE OF REGISTRATION field to edit the old criterion, delete the old Criterion record altogether.

2. Press the DEL key to delete the Criterion record.

Symphony wants to make sure that your delete command is intentional, so it prompts, "Are you sure you want to delete this record?"

3. Select Yes to delete the record.

Now you are ready to begin a new Criterion record. With the cursor pointing to LAST NAME, enter the label-match string.

4. Type **B*** and press RETURN.

5. Press PG UP to implement the criterion.

Four records have LAST NAMEs beginning with B. Browse through the selected records to verify that they conform to the criterion.

The Question Mark (?) Wildcard Character

The wildcard database query you just completed came up with four matches in a ten-record database. A database of thousands would yield many more, making it more difficult to find the record that will help Clerk find the elusive data entry error. Fortunately, Clerk has one more clue that you can use to narrow the search. Not only does the last name begin with B, but it also contains exactly four letters. He has no idea which four letters: the name could be Burr, Bubb, or Beam. Still, this extra information should reduce the number of records that survive the search, if you can translate the selection rule into a label-match criterion.

The asterisk only takes you part of the way, for it will select names with any number of letters. You need a way of specifying a field that begins with B but is followed by only three other characters. The *question mark (?) wildcard character* may be used for this purpose.

Each ? character replaces exactly one character in a string. A selection criterion "B???" for LAST NAME instructs Symphony to select records that begin with B and contain any three characters in the places occupied by the question marks. Because there are a total of four characters in the B??? criterion, Symphony will only select records having exactly four characters in the last name. (Careful—trailing blanks in a data field might not match up with a selection criterion that uses ?s. For example, a form for "Burr ", with one trailing blank, would not be selected by B???.)

To put this selection criterion into effect,

1. Press the MENU (F10) key, select Criteria, and then select Edit.

With the cursor on the LAST NAME field, replace the old criterion by simply entering the new one.

2. Type **B???** and press RETURN.

3. Press PG UP to exit from Criteria Edit.

Two records have been selected, those for J.S. Bach and Jim Bach. It turns out that Jim's record contains an error. The registration date contains the wrong year; it should be 1984 instead of 1985. To make the correction,

4. Retrieve the Jim Bach record (if you haven't already done so) by pressing PG DN.

5. Press the down arrow key until the cursor points to DATE OF REGISTRATION.

6. Press the EDIT (F2) key to initiate Edit Mode.

7. Press the END key to move the cursor to the end of the entry.

The edit cursor is stationed on the space after the last character of the field, the 5 of January 20, 1985. To change the 5 to a 4,

8. Press the BACKSPACE key; then type **4** and press RETURN.

The WARRANTY STATUS automatically changes from alive to dead, because the registration date is more than a year before the April 1, 1985 system date.

9. Press INS to insert the revised record into the database.

Observe that criteria selection allows you to do more than just look at the records that pass the match-up. You can also edit the records that Symphony retrieves for you.

Formula Criteria

Simple matching criteria are not always sufficient for answering questions about the information contained in a database. For instance, the * and ? wildcard characters wouldn't help you find the customers who purchased software after January 1, 1985. That kind of database query requires a selection criterion that can compare two dates—the date of registration and January 1, 1985. Unlike the criteria that you have used so far, this query involves a condition rather than a match. To use a condition in a database query, you need a different kind of selection criterion: a *formula criterion.*

You have used conditional formulas on several occasions in this book. You were introduced to conditional formulas in Chapter 9, and in Chapter 12 you used a conditional formula to design a computed field for the WARRANTY STATUS of the data entry form. Here, a conditional formula will be used as an entry in a field of the Criterion record.

The form of the condition is DATE OF REGISTRATION>@DATE(85,1,1). This formula uses calendar arithmetic to compare two dates, so both dates must be in Symphony's serial-number format. The DATE OF REGISTRATION field is already stored in the database as a serial number. You use the @DATE function to convert January 1, 1985 to a serial date. If the DATE OF REGISTRATION of a particular record is after January 1, 1985, the condition will be satisfied (TRUE), and that record will be selected. If the condition fails, the record will be ignored.

The rules for entering a formula criterion differ slightly from those for simple matches. As before, you issue Criteria Edit and move the cursor to the field that will be involved in the condition—in this case, DATE OF REGISTRATION. The next step is to stipulate the condition: *the current field*>@DATE(85,1,1). In place of *the current field*, you substitute a ? (question mark).

Symphony will understand that the question mark represents the field in which you entered the condition: the DATE OF REGISTRATION field. In general, a condition relating to a particular field of the Criterion record should be entered into that field, and any reference to that field in the conditional formula should be replaced by a question mark. Thus, the criterion you will enter in the DATE OF REGISTRATION field is ?>@DATE(85,1,1), which means *the current field* contains a date that is later than January 1, 1985.

Entering the Formula Criterion

Now you are ready to enter the formula. But there is a problem: since ?>@DATE(85,1,1) is a formula like those you would enter in a spreadsheet, you must begin the formula with a character that Symphony interprets as a value, not a label. Unfortunately, Symphony considers the question mark to be the beginning of a label. By starting the formula entry with a question mark, you will be telling Symphony to accept your entry as a label-match criterion. This is not your intention.

The problem is the same one you encountered in the spreadsheet when you attempted to enter a formula such as A1+6. To force Symphony into Value Mode in those situations, you began the formula by typing a plus sign (+). You do the same here. The actual formula entry will therefore be +?>@DATE(85,1,1).

To try out this formula criterion,

1. Press the MENU (F10) key, and select Criteria Edit.
2. Press the DEL key and select Yes to delete the previous Criterion record.
3. Press RETURN until the cursor points to DATE OF REGISTRATION.
4. Type **+?>@date(85,1,1)** and press RETURN to establish the condition that *the current field* is greater than the serial number of January 1, 1985.

The formula is longer than the field length of DATE OF REGISTRATION, but that doesn't matter. Symphony accepts the entire formula and shows as much of the formula in the field as it can, scrolling the rest off the screen.

Once you press RETURN, Symphony substitutes the question mark that you typed with something that appears to be the field name. The resulting entry is +DATE OF REGISTRATION>@DATE(85,1,1). In reality, Symphony has substituted a range name that it created from the question mark. If you were to switch to the spreadsheet and enter the Range Name Create command (introduced in Chapter 9), and then specify DATE OF REGISTRATION as the range name, you would find that the name is assigned to the first DATE OF REGISTRATION field in the first record of the spreadsheet's Database range. The reason for this will become clear later in this chapter. For now, it suffices to know that Symphony has accepted the criterion as a valid one.

To see how the criterion took effect,

5. Press the PG UP key to exit from Criteria Edit.

Five records passed the test. You may use the PG DN key to verify that the criterion worked properly.

Using Formula Criteria
For Character Strings

Formula criteria do not have to be number-oriented. You may use any valid conditional formula that you like, including those that reference character strings. For example, you can look for customers whose last names begin with a letter from the lower half of the alphabet, using the criterion LAST NAME greater than or equal to the string "L".

1. Issue the Criteria Edit command and delete the previous criteria using steps 1 and 2 of the previous section.

With the cursor on LAST NAME,

2. Type + to begin formula entry.

3. Enter the formula ?>="l" and press RETURN.

Again, Symphony substitutes the ? in the entry with a range name equivalent to the field name, LAST NAME.

4. Press PG UP to exit Criteria Edit.

The formula criterion chose three records: the two Mozarts and Liszt.

Using Strings in Formula Criteria:
The @FIND Function

The string functions add greater flexibility to criteria selection. You have already seen several string functions in Chapter 9, among them @LEFT and @STRING. Another string function is @FIND.

Bridgeotte Fidget needs to contact a customer whose name she cannot recall. The only thing she remembers is that the letter V appears somewhere in the last name. There is no guarantee that the last name begins with V, so a label match of V* would not be appropriate. The ? wildcard character would not be of any help either, since Ms. Fidget has no idea how many characters the last name contains. There is no easy way to obtain the information with simple matches.

However, the formula criterion gives you the flexibility of using a string function to check whether a particular character or set of characters is contained within a character string (for instance, if "h" is contained in "Mahler"). That function is @FIND.

The @FIND function determines where a substring may be found within a string. The syntax of the function is @FIND (str1, str2, num). The str1 argument is the substring you want to locate in another string. The str2 argument is the string that potentially contains str1 somewhere within it. The num argument specifies where in str2 Symphony should begin looking for str1, with 0 designating a search beginning at the first character, 1 designating the second character, and so forth. When you want to begin searching from the beginning of the string, use a num of 0. The result of @FIND("h","Mahler",0) would be 3. Of course, you may specify a cell address or range name in place of strings for either str1 or str2. Thus, if cell J1 contained "h" and cell J2 contained "Mahler", then @FIND(J1,J2,0) would be a valid equivalent of @FIND("h","Mahler",0).

The @FIND function tells where to find *str1* in *str2*, but how do you determine whether *str1* is contained in *str2* in the first place? Simple: just use the @FIND function as if you knew for sure that *str1* is in *str2*. If Symphony cannot find *str1*, the result will be ERR; otherwise, the function returns a number. That number will be the number of characters to the right of the beginning of the *str2* at which *str1* appears.

When Symphony evaluates a formula and finds that the result is a nonzero number, it considers this result TRUE. If it finds a result of 0 or ERR, it considers this result FALSE. Therefore, if @FIND locates the desired substring, it results in a positive value (the location of the substring), which is TRUE in logical terms. If the substring cannot be found, the result is ERR, which is FALSE in logical terms. And since only TRUE logical conditions are chosen by formula criteria, records will be selected if the @FIND function succeeds in its search. In this way, @FIND may be used to determine whether or not a substring is contained in another string.

[handwritten margin note: not true Ø is good for @FIND]

Translating Ms. Fidget's criterion into a formula is now a straightforward task. Simply use @FIND, with "v" as *str1* (the substring), the LAST NAME field as *str2* (substitute ? for the reference to LAST NAME, since that is the current field), and 0 as the *num* argument.

1. Issue Criteria Edit and delete the previous Criterion record.

With the cursor on LAST NAME,

2. Type **@find("v",?,0)** and press RETURN to locate the letter v in this field.

3. Press the PG UP key to exit from Criteria Edit.

Two customer names contain a "v": Beethoven and Dvorak. Now if only Bridgeotte could remember which customer she needs to contact.

Using Compound
Conditional Formulas

The conditional formulas you have used so far have involved a single condition, such as DATE OF REGISTRATION>@DATE(85,1,1) or LAST NAME>="L". As discussed in Chapter 9, the condition performs a comparison of two values based on an operator such as =, >, <, <>, >=, or <=.

It is also possible to construct a *compound conditional formula* that specifies more than one condition. You may structure the formula so that all conditions must be satisfied in order to evaluate the formula as TRUE, or you may stipulate that only one of several conditions needs to be satisfied in order to produce a TRUE result. Such compound conditional formulas may be used as criteria to create multiple selection rules.

Two special logical operators are used to create compound conditions: *#AND#* and *#OR#*. Like the other operators you have used, #AND# and #OR# are placed between two items. The two items are conditions. Two conditions that are joined by the #AND# operator must both be satisfied in order for the entire formula to be TRUE. When two conditions are connected by #OR#, the entire formula will be TRUE if either one (or both) conditions are TRUE.

A Compound Formula Criterion
Using #AND#

Suppose Widget-Ware wanted to send a mailing to all customers who purchased their software between October 1, 1984 and March 1, 1985. To obtain the names and addresses of these people, you could select records from the WARRANTY database with a compound formula. The first condition is that the registration date is on or after October 1, 1984. The records passing this first test must also pass an additional test—namely, that the registration date is on or before March 1, 1985. Since there are two conditions and both must be satisfied, the formula is a compound logical formula using the #AND# operator.

The syntax of such a compound formula is *condition1 #AND# condition2*. You enter each of the conditions the same way that you have been entering formula criteria all along. Thus, to retrieve the records for the mailing, you would create a Criterion record with a formula criterion in the DATE OF REGISTRATION field. Remembering to substitute ? for any reference to DATE OF REGISTRATION, you would enter the following formula:

$$+?>=@date(84,10,1)\#and\#?<=@date(85,3,1)$$

1. Issue the Criteria Edit command and delete the previous Criterion record.
2. Move the cursor to DATE OF REGISTRATION.
3. Type **+?>=@date(84,10,1)#and#?<=@date(85,3,1)** and press RETURN.
4. Press PG UP to exit from Criteria Edit.

Five records pass the test. Four of them are 1985 dates, while the last is in 1984.

The #OR# and #NOT# Operators

Suppose Widget-Ware wanted to send a WidgetWord brochure to the customers of its two other packages. One selection rule would be to choose records whose PRODUCT field contains either WidgetWorksheet or WidgetWindow. This would be an #OR# condition, since it is satisfied if either product is stored in the field. You would enter the formula in the PRODUCT field of the Criterion record, and it would look like this:

$$+?="WidgetWorksheet"\#or\#?="WidgetWindow"$$

There is another way to express this condition. Instead of testing whether the product is Worksheet or Window, you can instruct Symphony to select records whose product is not WidgetWord (the one being advertised). This negative condition involves a new operator, *#NOT#*. This operator's syntax is *#NOT#condition*. Notice that this is not a compound formula, since only one condition has to be met: the product must not be WidgetWord. Thus, the formula that you would store in PRODUCT is

$$\#NOT\#?="WidgetWord"$$

The steps for implementing this selection are essentially the same as those used for the previous #AND# formula, except that the criterion field and formula are different. Try out the formulas on your own—you should obtain five records that satisfy the criterion.

Chapter 15
Using the Spreadsheet
For Multiple Criteria

Using Multiple Criteria

Using the Spreadsheet for
Database Management

The Output Range

The previous chapter discussed several ways of using criteria to select records from a database, including how to apply more than one selection criterion to the database by using the #AND# and #OR# operators. In this chapter you will learn a simpler way of entering AND and OR criteria that can be used in many types of situations.

You will also learn to use the spreadsheet for database management. So far, you have manipulated the database entirely within the FORM environment, but you can also use the SHEET environment for many operations. In this chapter you will be using the spreadsheet to extract records and store them in a special range of the spreadsheet.

You will need to retrieve the WARRANTY file that you have been developing over the last several chapters. Once the file is on the screen, make sure you are in the FORM window. If not, press the WINDOW (F6) key until the FORM window appears.

Using Multiple Criteria

Until now, you have used only one criterion record at a time, entering criteria in only a single field within that record. It is also possible to use more than one criterion in a single Criterion record by placing additional criteria in other fields of the form. In addition, it is possible to use more than one Criterion record; Symphony handles as many as four at a time.

Using One Criterion Record
For an AND Condition

If you enter criteria into more than one field on a single Criterion record, then all criteria on the form must be satisfied in order for a record to be selected. In other words, placing multiple criteria on a single Criterion record produces an AND condition equivalent to joining multiple conditions with the #AND# operator in a logical formula.

but #AND# is entered in one field, but may refer to diff... ones

Suppose you wanted to select all WidgetWindow customers from New York. This is an AND condition, so you may choose to enter the two conditions as two label matches in the Criterion record.

1. Issue Criteria Edit and delete the previous Criterion record.

Now establish the first condition of the AND criterion, a label match for the STATE field.

2. Move the cursor to the STATE field and type **New York**; then press RETURN.

The second condition is a label match for the PRODUCT field. Remember that you set up PRODUCT as a transformation; you enter the product code number, and Symphony transforms your entry into a label based on the code you enter.

3. Move the cursor to the PRODUCT field and type **3**, the product code for WidgetWindow; then press RETURN.

4. Press PG UP to exit from Criteria Edit.

The selected data record should be a WidgetWindow customer from the great state of New York.

Using Several Criterion Records
For an OR Condition

Entering multiple criteria in a single Criterion record is an easy way to produce an AND condition. How can you duplicate an OR condition without entering a long formula?

An OR condition (in which a match is selected if any of the criteria are met) can be produced by filling out more than one Criterion record. If you choose to fill out more than one record, the records are combined into a single OR-condition selection criterion. If a data record cannot pass all of the criteria specified in the first Criterion record, Symphony examines the next Criterion record to see if the data record satisfies all of its conditions. If the data record can pass all of the criteria on any one of the Criterion records, that data record is selected.

It is important to know the difference between multiple criteria in a single record and multiple Criterion records. Within a given record, all criteria are joined by an AND; they must all be satisfied in order for a data record to pass that particular Criterion record. Among several Criterion records, a data record passes selection if it satisfies the conditions of any single Criterion record.

Let's try it out. Bridgeotte Fidget wants to obtain the records of Ira Gershwin, Wolfgang Mozart, and Jim Bach. For this task, you would want to use an OR condition, asking Symphony to select records with a last name containing Gershwin, Mozart, or Bach. However, since there is more than one Gershwin, Mozart, and Bach in the database, you must be a bit more specific. You want records that have (a) a last name of Gershwin AND a first name of Ira; OR (b) a last name of Mozart AND a first name of Wolfgang; OR (c) a last name of Bach AND a first name of Jim. There are three sets of OR conditions here: if a record passes any one of conditions (a), (b), or (c), it should be chosen. However, within each of the three sets of conditions is an AND condition: both last name and first name must match in order for the record to be a selection candidate.

The criterion sounds complicated, and it would be if you tried to encapsulate it into a logical formula. Instead, you can use three Criterion records that make the criteria simpler to design and simpler to understand.

To do this, you will take each last name and first name set and enter it on a separate Criterion record. Storing an entry for both last name and first name on a single record forces Symphony to match both items in an AND relationship. Storing each of the three sets of names on different Criterion records tells Symphony not to give up if a data record doesn't pass the first criterion; it should continue searching the other Criterion records. This gives the selection rule an OR relationship.

Begin by erasing the last Criterion record.

1. Return to the Criterion record by issuing the Criteria Edit command, and delete the Criterion record.

2. With the cursor on LAST NAME, type **Gershwin** and press RETURN.

3. With the cursor on FIRST NAME, type **Ira** and press RETURN.

The first Criterion record is now complete. To continue using Criteria Edit and advance to the second Criterion record,

4. Press the PG DN key. (Do not press PG UP, which would return you to the database.)

5. Enter **Mozart** for LAST NAME and **Wolfgang** for FIRST NAME.

6. Press INS to store the second record and advance to the third.

7. Enter **Bach** for LAST NAME and **Jim** for FIRST NAME.

8. Press PG UP three times to return to the database, or you may press ESC to back up to the Criteria menu and then select Use.

You should have obtained the three records you were looking for. If you didn't, you probably misspelled a name, or you might have embedded blanks in either the data record or the Criterion record. If the latter is the case, you may wish to go back to the Criterion records and use the * wildcard character after each name to guard against hidden spaces.

Compound Formulas Versus Multiple Criterion Records

You now know three ways of using multiple criteria: in compound formulas, in multiple Criterion records, and in a single Criterion record. Are the three methods interchangeable, or is one preferable to the others? In many cases, the methods produce the same results, so you can select whichever one you wish (although using multiple Criterion records or making multiple matches within a Criterion record is usually clearer and easier than entering a long formula).

However, there is one particular instance in which multiple Criterion records will not suffice. That is when you have to specify two or more conditions that relate to a single field in an AND condition. For example, if you wanted to select records whose registration date was after November 2, 1984, AND before March 1, 1985, you would have to use a compound formula, because there is no way to separate the two conditions into two separate Criterion records.

Using the Spreadsheet For Database Management

Criteria selection in the FORM environment is useful when you want to focus on one or two records in the database. When you want to use criteria to select more than a few records, however, the FORM environment's "one record at a time" operation loses its usefulness. From the SHEET environment, you can see all of the database, in tabular form, as a group of rows and columns. It has been stored in a range of the spreadsheet called the Database range, which was introduced in Chapter 12.

Having the information in tabular format allows you to go to a SHEET window and manipulate the data as a spreadsheet, using all of the commands and functions available to you in that environment. Some database management functions that you have used in the FORM environment can also be performed within the SHEET environment. You can sort a spreadsheet and locate records based on criteria. In addition, a number of database management commands are available exclusively through the spreadsheet. The most useful of these is the *Data Query Extract command.*

The Data Query Extract Command

As you may recall, the FORM environment's Criteria Edit command allows you to browse through the data records that satisfy the selection criteria. It does not collect the records for you, however, so that you can compare them easily at a glance. The Data Query Extract command takes advantage of the SHEET environment, permitting you to store the selected records in a range of the spreadsheet. In effect, Data Query Extract creates a second database in the spreadsheet, composed of the records that conform to the criteria you apply to the database.

If you have already created a database with the FORM Generate command, it is an easy matter to extract records from the database and store the information in an unused portion of the spreadsheet. Let's give it a try.

Suppose that you want a listing of the records of all WidgetWord customers. Instead of viewing these records one by one, you would like to see a table with one row for each customer and with columns that store the information pertaining to each customer.

There are three pieces of information that Symphony needs to know in order to extract the data. First, where in the spreadsheet is the database stored? Second, what records should be extracted? And third, where in the spreadsheet should Symphony store the selected records?

A Closer Look at the Database Range

Because you used the Generate command to create the WARRANTY database, Symphony already knows where the database is located in the spreadsheet. Remember that as you filled out the forms of the file, Symphony copied each one into the Database range.

Symphony also assigned a range name to the rectangular range encompassing the data records. The name that Symphony assigned is composed of the database name (which you designated as WARRANTY when you executed the Generate command) followed by the characters _DB. DB stands for database. The Database range of the WARRANTY file is therefore called WARRANTY_DB.

To get a concrete impression of what WARRANTY_DB is, invoke the spreadsheet window.

1. Press the WINDOW (F6) key.

Recall from Chapter 9 that the Range Name Create command assigns a range name to a range of cells. You may also use it to get a quick idea of what range a name has been assigned to. (Another command, *Range Name Table*, can also be used to do this.) By issuing Range Name Create and selecting the name of an existing range, you cause Symphony to highlight the range.

2. Press MENU (F10) and select Range Name Create.

A list of existing names is then displayed in the control panel. There are quite a few of them, assigned by Symphony as a result of the Generate command. It would be helpful to see a full-screen listing of the range names at this point.

3. Again press MENU (F10) to get a full listing of range names on the screen.

4. Select WARRANTY_DB by pointing with the arrow keys or by typing **WARRANTY_DB** yourself.

Symphony highlights as much of the Database range as will fit on the screen and shows you the coordinates in the right corner of the control panel: A40..I50. If you wanted to change this range, you would be able to do so now; but since you don't want to, just

5. Press RETURN.

When you used the spreadsheet in Chapter 12, you locked in titles to make it easier to examine the Definition range. Before proceeding, let's unlock the titles.

6. Press MENU (F10); then select Settings Titles Clear.

7. Select Quit.

Now take a look at the spreadsheet version of the database.

8. Press HOME, press the GOTO (F5) key, type **A40**, and press RETURN.

The first row of the Database range consists of the field names of the database. If you move across the spreadsheet, you will find that every field is represented in the table. The rows beneath the first row of the range represent the data records. There are ten records with nine fields each, which is why WARRANTY—DB extends from A40 to I50. Make a mental note that Symphony includes the row of field names (row 40) as part of the Database range, in addition to the data itself.

An immediate benefit of the spreadsheet's Database format is that you can see many records at a time. It is also easy to print the whole database by using the Print command of the Services menu as if you were printing a standard spreadsheet, designating the Database range as the range that you want to print.

Symphony has stored the date values of the DATE OF REGISTRATION as serial numbers. Although it displays these numbers as standard dates in the data entry form, it stores the dates without formats in the spreadsheet. Thus, you might use the spreadsheet's Format Date command to make the Database range more presentable in printed reports.

Applying Selection Criteria To a Database Extraction

To return to the task at hand, recall that Symphony needs to know the location of the database in the spreadsheet, the records to be extracted, and the location where these records should be stored. Since Symphony knows where the Database range is, you don't need to worry about the first of these three pieces of information. The second thing Symphony needs to know is the selection criteria.

There are two ways to specify criteria in Symphony. You already know one way: filling out Criterion records in the FORM environment. The other way is by storing criteria in cells directly in the spreadsheet, from within the spreadsheet environment. For now, let's stick with the familiar method. It is usually as flexible as the spreadsheet method, and it is also easier and less susceptible to error.

To select WidgetWord customers,

1. Press the WINDOW (F6) key to switch to the FORM window.

2. Press MENU (F10); then select Criteria Edit.

The last time you were in Criteria Edit, you created three Criterion records. These must be deleted before you continue.

3. Press the DEL key and select Yes to delete the first Criterion record.

4. Repeat step 3 two more times to delete the other two Criterion records.

5. Move the cursor to the PRODUCT field; type 2 (the code for WidgetWord) and press RETURN.

6. Press PG UP to exit from Criteria Edit.

The control panel tells you that there were seven matching records. When you perform the extraction, you would expect seven rows to be extracted from the Database range.

7. Switch back to the spreadsheet by pressing the WINDOW (F6) key.

Incidentally, Symphony stored the criterion entry in a range of the spreadsheet called the Criterion range and assigned this range a name: WARRANTY_CR. This name is assigned to the range A35..I39, which can be verified with the Range Name Create command. If you are curious to see how Symphony stores the criterion in the spreadsheet, you may scroll to this range. (Figure 12-3 can serve as a broad topographical guide, for it shows the Criterion range's comparative location.)

The Output Range

Now that you have established where to find the data and how to select it, you must tell Symphony where to put the extracted data. This destination is called the *Output range*. The Data Query Extract command causes Symphony to examine the database, identify the records that conform to the selection criteria, and copy these records to the Output range.

As Figure 15-1 shows, the Output range is a rectangle of cells. It may be divided into two conceptual parts. The top row of the Output range contains the names of fields that will be copied for the selected records. You may copy entire records by specifying all of the field names in the top row of the Output range. If you want to extract only particular fields of the database, you can do this by including only the desired fields in the top row of the range. Symphony will extract only the fields included in the top row.

The Output range's field names need not be in the same order as they appear in the Database range. But whatever field names you use, they must be spelled and entered exactly as they appear in the Database range. The surest way of duplicating field names accurately is to use the Copy command when you are preparing the Output range.

The second component of the Output range is a block of rows beneath the field names. This area will contain the extracted records. There must be at least as many rows in your Output range as there are selected records. Otherwise, the Extract operation will not be completed.

With a large database, it is often hard to know how many records you will be extracting. For this situation, there is a way to tell Symphony to make the Output range a "bottomless pit." If you designate only one row —the row of field names— as the Output range, Symphony will use as much space as it needs to put the extracted records into the Output range.

You should be careful in using this "bottomless pit" method. If entries are stored below the Output range's field names before the Extract command is issued, these entries will be erased, even if the extracted records do not extend to the row in which these entries are stored. Therefore, always make sure that no important entries are stored anywhere in the columns below the Output-range field names.

Setting Up the Output Range

The map of spreadsheet ranges that was shown in Figure 12-3 does not contain an Output range, and for a good reason. The Output range is one of the few ranges

	A	B	C	D	E	F	G
	LAST NAME	FIRST NAME	STREET	CITY	STATE	ZIP	COPRODUCT
100							
101							
102							
103							
104							
105							
106							
107							
108							
109							
110							

Figure 15-1. The Output range

that Symphony cannot set up for you automatically. That is because you must choose where you want to put extracted records and exactly which fields you want to include. However, creating the Output range manually is not very difficult. The most important thing is to select a location on the spreadsheet that does not interfere with other important data, especially if you are going to use the "bottomless pit" method.

You create the Output range in two steps. First, store the top row of field names somewhere in the spreadsheet. Second, let Symphony know where the Output range is located.

In the WARRANTY database, there is room for the Output range to the right of the used portion of the spreadsheet. There is also plenty of room below the database. If you put the Output range below the database, however, you must be sure to leave enough room above it to allow for growth in the length of the Database range, since you will be adding records to the database.

Placing the Output range on the right side of the spreadsheet raises other considerations. One is available space. The columns on the right of the spreadsheet have the default width of nine characters. Some of the fields of the database, such as LAST NAME and FIRST NAME, are too wide to be displayed within these widths. Thus, if you place the Output range there, you will have to revise the widths of several columns.

Another issue is memory, a limited resource on your computer. Symphony reserves memory based on the size of the rectangle of cells required to contain the rightmost column and the bottom row of the utilized portion of the spreadsheet. If a database occupies many rows, adding a number of columns for an Output range causes Symphony to allocate memory for a very large rectangle, even if the Output range only stores a few extracted records. For these reasons, you should position the Output range below the Database range.

To determine the bottom row of the utilized portion of the spreadsheet,

1. Press the END key; then press the HOME key to move the pointer to the bottom right cell of the used portion of the spreadsheet (cell I50), the last row of the Database range.

The Output range should be below row 50. Since the market for Widget-related software is rather limited, the database range will not grow by more than 30 records in a year's time. Therefore, it should be safe to begin the Output range in row 100. (If the database eventually grows larger than expected, you can always use the Move command, introduced in Chapter 9, to move the Output range to an area that is out of the way.)

If you needed all of the fields of the selected records, you would copy all of the field names to the row of cells beginning with cell A100. However, since you are only interested in the first seven fields for this particular extraction, you only need to copy those field names from the Database range.

2. Use the GOTO (F5) key to move the cell pointer to A40, the beginning of the range from which you will copy the field names.

3. Press MENU (F10) and select Copy.

4. Type a . to anchor the beginning of the range.

5. Move to the right until the FROM range encompasses cell G40, the PRODUCT field name.

6. Press RETURN; then type **A100** (the TO range) and press RETURN.

7. Use the GOTO (F5) key to move to cell A100.

Using Query Settings
For the Output Range

The last step is to tell Symphony where to find the Output range. Since the location of the Output range is a database-related setting, it stands to reason that you would designate the addresses of the Output range through a settings sheet. The database settings sheet may be accessed through either the SHEET or the FORM environment. From the spreadsheet, you would use the Query Settings command.

1. Press MENU (F10); then select Query.

The menu of the Query command includes Settings. (It also includes the Extract command, which you are working your way toward.)

2. Select Settings.

As in all settings sheets, you may enter or alter a setting by making a selection from the Settings menu. Notice the top left corner of the settings sheet. Under the heading "Basic Ranges," Symphony displays the names of three of the most important database-related ranges. Symphony has already filled in the settings of the Database and Criterion ranges, supplying the range names representing addresses of the ranges created by the FORM Generate command. The third Basic range is the Output range.

The reason Symphony does not supply the Output range automatically is that it does not know where you wish to locate the Output range. Symphony cannot make that decision for you. Still, designating the range yourself is a simple matter.

3. Select Basic to enter a Basic range setting.

4. Select Output to assign the Output range.

Symphony switches to the spreadsheet, waiting for you to point out the location of the range. Conveniently, Symphony returns you to the place in the spreadsheet that you just left and recommends that cell—A100—as the beginning of the range.

5. Type a . to anchor the range.

To expand the pointer to the right side of the range,

6. Press the END key; then press the right arrow key.

If you were to press RETURN at this point, you would have designated a "bottomless pit" range. Although nothing is below the Output range at this point, you may want to put something there at some later date. Creating a bottomless pit now would preclude this possibility, since Symphony erases everything below the field names row when you execute the extraction. To be safe, assign a rectangular Output range instead of the bottomless pit. Space for ten extracted records will be sufficient for this example.

7. Press the down arrow key ten times to expand the range to cell G110.

8. Press RETURN; then select Quit.

9. Select Quit again to return to the Query menu.

Issuing the Extract Command

With the three requisite Basic range settings in place, you are now within one keystroke of performing the extraction. All you have to do now is issue the Extract command.

1. Select Extract.

Seven records are copied from the Database range. To verify that they are all WidgetWord customers,

2. Select Quit and then scroll over to column G, the PRODUCT column.

The Query Extract command is a quick way of selecting and grouping records from a database. Using label matches, number matches, formula criteria, and multiple criteria, you can query the database in thousands of ways. To extract, all you have to do is make sure that Symphony knows the Database range, the Criterion range, and the Output range. And if you used the FORM Generate command to create the database, Symphony does most of the work for you.

Although this chapter has introduced Query Extract in the context of database management, it is also possible to apply the same command to a spreadsheet. For example, if you had a spreadsheet analysis of the monthly sales performance of 500 salespeople, you might want to extract groups of rows from the spreadsheet (for example, the rows relating to salespeople who sold over 110 percent of their sales quota in the month of February). To do so, you would have to use the Query settings sheet to designate the Database range, Criterion range, and Output range. You would also have to create criteria from within the spreadsheet environment.

The spreadsheet's Query command has some other interesting options. *Query Find* locates a record in a Database range based on user-defined criteria. *Query Record-Sort* performs a sort on a range of the spreadsheet. Query Delete allows you to delete groups of records based on user-defined criteria.

The WARRANTY example demonstrates the close relationship between the FORM and SHEET environments. By sharing data, the two environments complement each other and increase the number of ways and the sophistication with which you can approach database management. However, there are other aspects of database management that have not yet been introduced. Word processing and database reporting constitute an entirely different facet of information management, and they will be covered in the remaining three chapters.

Chapter 16
Database Reporting

Two Options
For Database Reporting

Using the Spreadsheet
Print Command

Using the Print Command's
Database Option

Printing the Database

The last few chapters described how to create, maintain, and query a database. This chapter shows how to generate and print database reports. It also discusses the relationship between criteria selection and database reporting.

You will use the database in the WARRANTY file for the examples in this chapter, so retrieve it now if you have not done so already. You should also establish April 1, 1985, as the system date.

Two Options for Database Reporting

Symphony can perform many tasks in more than one way. *Database reporting* is one of these tasks. You can print a simple database report the same way you print a spreadsheet report: use the Print command in the spreadsheet environment to print a range of the spreadsheet that contains the database. Symphony also offers report generation capabilities that are unique to database management. Sophisticated database reporting is more complicated than the simple use of the Print command, but it is also more powerful.

Database reporting allows you to print selected records of the database. It also enables you to print special types of database reports, such as mailing labels, form letters, and reports with subtotals. For example, you can generate a personalized form letter addressed to each customer in the WARRANTY database. Using selection criteria, you can also select a particular group of customers to send this form letter to, such as those customers who live in New York.

You will begin this chapter by producing a plain printout of the database, using the Print command as you have used it before. Then you will learn to use an option of the Print command that is specific to databases. This option can be used to produce the same type of report, but it also provides much more flexibility. In fact, the same concepts of database reporting presented in this chapter will provide the basis for a form-letter report that you will produce in Chapter 18.

Using the Spreadsheet
Print Command

The simplest way to print the contents of a database is to use the Services menu's Print command, specifying the Database range as the Source range (the range to be printed). Because you created the WARRANTY database with the FORM Generate command, Symphony automatically created and maintained the Database range for you and assigned the name WARRANTY_DB to the range. To print the database, you move the pointer to the beginning of the range, issue the Print command, provide the range name as the Source range, and print.

Before you print a database, however, there is one important consideration to bear in mind. If you were to tally the column widths of the fields that comprise the database, you would arrive at a total of 143. But when Symphony creates the database with the Generate command, it makes the column widths of the Database range one character wider than those specified in the Definition range. The actual total width of the reported fields would then be 151 characters, because the Print command uses the widths of the columns in the Source range.

The margins of the printout must therefore accommodate 151 spaces. As you saw in Chapter 5, many printers accept commands from Symphony to condense the print size, so that the printer can fit most oversized reports on a page. Printers that do not offer condensed print or that cannot accommodate the required report width must split up the report into parts.

To begin the report, you must move the pointer to the first cell of the Source range. You may do this with the GOTO (F5) key, specifying the range name as the destination; Symphony transfers the pointer to the top left cell of the range represented by the name. In the SHEET window,

1. Press the GOTO (F5) key and type **WARRANTY_DB**. Press RETURN.
2. Press the SERVICES (F9) key and select Print.
3. Select Settings; then select Source.
4. Select Range (do not select Database).
5. Type **WARRANTY_DB** and press RETURN.

Next, set the margins.

6. Select Margins.

With initial defaults of 4 and 76 for the left and right margins, you would need to expand the right margin to 160 in order to leave enough space for a 151-character line.

7. Select Right and type **160**. Press RETURN.
8. Select Quit to exit from the Margins menu.

If your printer has a Condensed Mode that prints at least 160 characters per line, the next step is to send an init-string to the printer that instructs it to print in Condensed Mode. As mentioned in Chapter 5, the specific init-string you send depends on your printer. Consult your printer manual or the Lotus *Reference Manual* for details. For an Epson FX-model printer, you would enter the init-string \015.

9. Select the Init-String option and enter the init-string that tells your printer to print in Condensed Mode. Press RETURN.

With all the settings now in place,

10. Select Quit to return to the main menu.
11. Select Go to print the report. Then select Quit to exit from the Print command.

The printout of the database is shown in Figure 16-1. It is essentially a snapshot of the Database range as it appears on screen. Notice that the DATE OF REGISTRATION column does not appear in Date format. That is because the dates are stored in their serial-number form in the spreadsheet, and the report duplicates the contents of the spreadsheet exactly. You can obtain formatted dates by applying the Format Date command to the DATE OF REGISTRATION column of the Database range. As you will soon discover, however, there is no need to worry about Date format when you use the database printing capabilities.

Using the Print Command's Database Option

The printout in Figure 16-1 was generated with the Range option of the Print Settings Source command. The other Print Settings Source option, the Database selection, provides capabilities particular to database reporting.

LAST NAME	FIRST NAME	STREET	CITY	STATE	ZIP CO	PRODUCT	DATE OF REGIST	WARRANTY STATUS
Bach	J.S.	7 Surprise St.	Dallas	Texas	66666	WidgetWorksheet	31072	alive
Beethoven	Ludwig	1812 Overture St.	Reno	Nevada	33333	WidgetWindow	31089	alive
Gershwin	George	3 Porgy Place	Miami	Florida	99999	WidgetWord	31128	alive
Gershwin	Ira	4 Rhapsody Lane	Xanadu	Ohio	44444	WidgetWord	31107	alive
Mozart	Wolfgang	4 Quartet St.	Munich	New York	10000	WidgetWord	30696	dead
Mozart	Susan	22 22nd St.	Munich	New York	10000	WidgetWord	31067	alive
Bach	Jim	5 5th St.	Brooklyn	New York	11111	WidgetWord	30701	dead
Bernstein	Leonard	West Side Ave.	Ithaca	New York	12222	WidgetWindow	30722	dead
Dvorak	Anton	1 New World St.	Chicago	Illinois	60609	WidgetWord	30715	dead
Liszt	Franz	4 Piano Place	Boise	Idaho	55555	WidgetWord	30996	alive

Figure 16-1. Printout of the database

The Database option causes Symphony to divide a database report into three sections. The first section consists of headings that you designate to be printed once at the top of the report. This section is called the *Above range*. The second section, called the *Main range*, consists of the database information itself. The third section of the report, the *Below range*, is printed after the Main range at the bottom of the report. The Below range might consist of a message or some summary database statistics. The Above and Below ranges are optional, but the Main range is mandatory. (After all, why would you choose the Database option unless you wanted to print information from the database?)

When Symphony prints a database with the Database option, it first prints the Above range, assuming there is one. Typically, the Above range consists of the database field names. Next, Symphony prints the first record and proceeds one by one through the other records of the database. Finally, after the last record has been printed, Symphony prints the Below range if there is one.

Actually, the Above range and the Main range were shown earlier in this book, in Figure 12-3. These two ranges are among those automatically assigned by Symphony as a result of the FORM Generate command. Let's take a look once more, in Figure 16-2, at the schematic diagram of the ranges created and assigned by the FORM Generate command.

The Above range, which extends from cell A32 to I32, consists of the field names of the database. When you use the Generate command, Symphony assumes that some day you may want to print a database report with the field names on top. Therefore, Symphony automatically creates a range of cells, located below the Definition range, that includes the field names. The range is named WARRANTY_AB.

Immediately below this range, in row 33, is the Main range. The contents of the Main range change as Symphony processes the database report. Initially, the Main range contains references to the fields of the first record of the Database range, which is the record in row 41 of the spreadsheet. Printing of the Above range is followed by the current contents of the Main range, which is the first record of the database.

As a result of selecting Print Settings Source Database, Symphony enters a looping process. It prints the contents of the Main range; then it looks to the Database range to fetch the next record (the second record), placing its contents into the Main range and printing the new Main range. This same step is repeated for each succeeding record of the database; and when the last record is printed, Symphony prints the Below range and ends the report.

This automatic looping process does not begin until you issue the Print Go command. Before the command is issued, the Main range must contain formula references to the first record of the database. The Main range that Symphony automatically creates as a function of the FORM Generate command is already set up with the correct references. Before you attempt the database report, let's see exactly how Symphony configured the Main range.

1. Move to cell A33, the first cell of the Main range.

The Main range displays the information pertaining to J.S. Bach, the first record of the database. With the pointer on A33, you can examine the formula contained in that cell. The formula, +LAST NAME, refers to a range name of a cell that contains a label, in this case "J.S. Bach." You did not create such a range name, of course; Symphony did it as another product of the FORM Generate

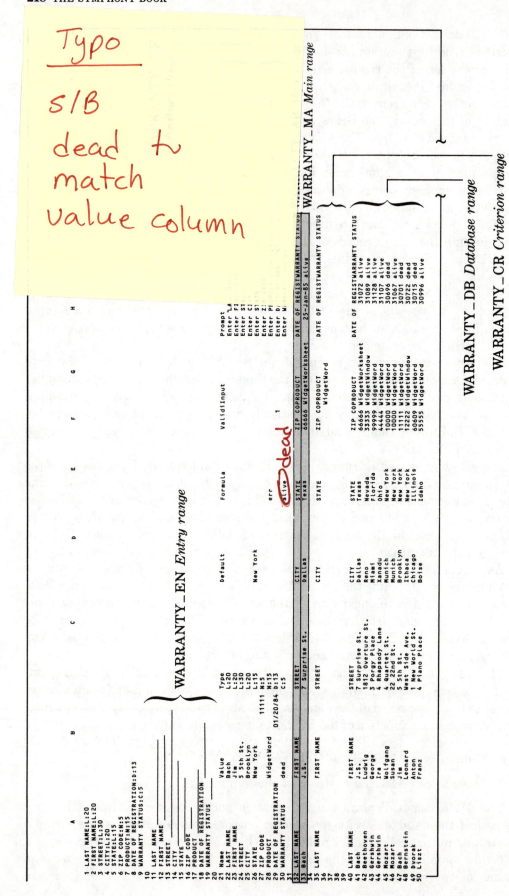

Figure 16-2. Ranges created by the FORM Generate command

command. What cell is this range name assigned to? One way to find out is to use the Range Name Create command.

2. Press the MENU (F10) key and select Range Name Create.

3. Type **LAST NAME** (or move the menu pointer to LAST NAME in the control panel).

The control panel tells you that the range name LAST NAME refers to cell A41, which is the LAST NAME field of the first record of the Database range.

4. Press RETURN to move back to cell A33.

Way back when you used the Generate command, Symphony predicted that you would need to develop a Main range containing formula references to the first record of the database. At that time, Symphony assigned range names to the fields of the first record, using the field names themselves as the range names. It was an easy next step for Symphony to store formulas in the Main range, using these range names to reference the first record of the database. And because the Main range is already set up with the correct references to the first record, Symphony is ready to perform its automatic looping process for the database report.

5. Press the right arrow key to move to cell B33.

The second cell of the Main range contains the formula +FIRST NAME. The range name FIRST NAME is assigned to the FIRST NAME field of the first record of the Database range (cell B33). If you move farther right, you will find that Symphony has filled the Main range with references to each of the other fields in the database.

By the way, Symphony did not create a Below range with the Generate command. It creates an Above range because it is usually desirable to print field names at the top of a report. However, it is harder to make assumptions about the information most users will want at the bottom of a database report, so Symphony leaves it up to you to create the Below range if you want one. You would do so by selecting the Below option of the FORM Settings sheet and designating a range on the spreadsheet as the Below range.

Printing the Database

Once the database settings sheet contains the correct settings for the Above and Main ranges, you need only issue the Print command to obtain the report. The margins have already been adjusted in the previous Print exercise; so other than the Source, there are no new Print settings to communicate to Symphony.

1. Press SERVICES (F9) and select Print Settings Source.

This time, instead of specifying a range,

2. Select Database.

Symphony wants to know which database you want to print from, and displays a list of active database settings sheets.

3. Select WARRANTY.

4. Select Quit to leave the Settings menu.

LAST NAME	FIRST NAME	STREET	CITY	STATE	ZIP CO	PRODUCT	DATE OF REGIST	WARRANTY STATUS
Gershwin	George	3 Porgy Place	Miami	Florida	99999	WidgetWord	22-Mar-85	alive
Gershwin	Ira	4 Rhapsody Lane	Xanadu	Ohio	44444	WidgetWord	01-Mar-85	alive
Mozart	Wolfgang	4 Quartet St.	Munich	New York	10000	WidgetWord	15-Jan-84	dead
Mozart	Susan	22 22nd St.	Munich	New York	10000	WidgetWord	20-Jan-85	alive
Bach	Jim	5 5th St.	Brooklyn	New York	11111	WidgetWord	20-Jan-84	dead
Dvorak	Anton	1 New World St.	Chicago	Illinois	60609	WidgetWord	03-Feb-84	dead
Liszt	Franz	4 Piano Place	Boise	Idaho	55555	WidgetWord	10-Nov-84	alive

Figure 16-3. A printout using the Database print option

If the paper is not positioned at the top of a new page, issue the Page-Advance command. If you have to turn the printer's carriage manually in order to move to the top of a page, select the Align option to let Symphony know that it is at the top of a page.

Now you are ready to print.

5. Select Go; then select Quit.

Figure 16-3 shows the results. Notice that the DATE OF REGISTRATION appears in correct format, unlike the spreadsheet printout that you generated earlier in this chapter. When you specify Database as the print source, Symphony uses the formats assigned to the cells of the Main range. When Symphony created the Main range with the Generate command, it assigned formats based on the field types listed in the Type column of the Definition range. Since DATE OF REGISTRATION is a date-type field, Symphony used Date format for the Main range.

There is another difference between Figures 16-1 and 16-3. Whereas the spreadsheet printout includes all ten database records, the database report has only seven. Why is this so? In the previous chapter, you issued a selection criterion that selected the seven registered WidgetWord customers. The criterion was saved with the worksheet and is still in use. This affects the Print command when you use the Database option and explains why the report is restricted to the seven selected records.*

The sensitivity of the database report to selection criteria is a powerful feature. It means that you can use criteria to print reports of specific groups of records from the database.

The output from both forms of the Print command are very similar. Printing with the Range option is easier, both conceptually and functionally. The Database option offers greater flexibility, however, because it provides selective printing. As you will soon discover, the Database option can deliver much more than the simple report you have just developed.

Remember to save the database file with the File Save command. The print settings you just used will be saved with the file.

In the remainder of this book, you will be developing a form letter based on the WARRANTY database. The database-reporting concepts that you've just put to use are central to the form-letter system. Before you return to database reporting, though, you must create the prototype letter that will be mailed to the customers in the database. And to create this letter, you will need to become familiar with one of the most powerful yet easy-to-use environments of Symphony: word processing.

---

*If you did not want to use the selection criteria in the report, you would have to use the spreadsheet's Erase command to erase the range that contains the selection criteria (WARRANTY_CR).

Chapter 17
Introduction to Word Processing

You may be wondering why so many chapters have been devoted to the spreadsheet and database environments, whereas the word processing environment has not even merited a single chapter. The reason is that word processing in Symphony is virtually as easy as using your typewriter. The command structure is similar to that of the other environments; moreover, typing documents is a much more intuitive activity than is calculating formulas or manipulating databases.

This chapter will familiarize you with the word processing environment. By the time you begin Chapter 18, you will be ready to put your word processing skills to use in a complex application that integrates a word-processed document with the spreadsheet and database. Before you continue, retrieve the WARRANTY file and make sure that the system date is April 1, 1985.

Bridgeotte Fidget, the Marketing Director of Widget-Ware, would like to send a letter to each of her customers announcing the company's newest software offering, Widget Digit. As her assistant, you will use the Symphony word processor to create an announcement letter addressed to a particular customer, J.S. Bach. Later, you will expand the document into a general form letter to be sent to all customers. This document will introduce you to the most often-used commands and techniques of word processing. Once you have completed this exercise, you will be able to create word-processed documents of all types and sizes.

Creating a Word Processing Window

Since word processing is a unique Symphony environment, it has its own window type, called DOC (short for "document"). It is here that you type in your document. As you type, Symphony stores the document in the worksheet, the common storage area where the information you enter is accessible in Symphony's other environments.

One of the most important advantages of windows is that they allow you to separate individual aspects of your work. To keep things organized, you will be adding a new window to your collection, exclusively assigned to word processing. For this purpose, you use the Window Create command.

1. Press the HOME key to move the pointer to A1. (This is not required to create the window, but it will make a difference later on.)

2. Press the SERVICES (F9) key and select Window Create.

In response to the prompt for the window name,

3. Type **LETTER** and press RETURN.

Symphony offers you a menu of work environments.

4. Select DOC.

Now Symphony highlights the entire screen and waits for you to determine the shape and location of the DOC window. If you do not want a full-screen window, you can alter the shape and location of the window at this time, or you can do so later with the Window Settings Layout command. For letters, it is usually most convenient to use the full screen so you can see as much of the document as possible, at least initially.

5. Press RETURN to accept the full-screen window size.

Symphony displays a Settings menu so you can alter the current settings of this window:

Name Type Restrict Borders Auto-Display Quit

You will eventually need to alter one setting. In order to see why, you must first inspect the DOC environment and see how it fits into the general scheme of Symphony environments. For now, let's complete the initial step in creating the DOC window.

6. Select Quit to exit from the Window Settings menu.

The DOC Window

The display changes to show the word processing screen, which consists of a window frame and a control panel. The top of the frame is a *format line* that shows the margins and tab stops that are set by default for the document you are about to create. The margins and tabs work as they do on a typewriter, except that in a DOC window you can see exactly where the margins and tabs are at all times. The << at the left of the format line denotes the left margin, the >> at the right denotes the right margin, and the ▶ characters represent tab stops.

Although you have not typed anything in the DOC window, it already contains information. This is the same data that is stored in the top left area of the spreadsheet; only now, instead of viewing this information as spreadsheet cells, you view it as part of a document, as if it were written on a blank sheet of paper. The SHEET and DOC windows are looking at the same data storage area in different ways.

The relationship between the DOC and SHEET environments is important to understand. Consider a large warehouse that has numerous windows.* You are standing on the outside, peering in from a large, rectangular window at the northwest corner of the warehouse. You see several piles of rainbow-colored widgets.

Suppose you turned the corner and peered in through a yellow glass window. Through it you see the same area of the warehouse and the same piles of widgets, but the widgets look different because you are looking at them in a new way.

The worksheet is analogous to the warehouse, and the information stored in the worksheet is like the widgets. Windows allow you to look at the worksheet's contents in different ways. But the data is still the same collection of letters and numbers housed in Symphony's workspace. The DOC window gives you a different perspective of the same data.

Windows also allow you to manipulate data in different ways.The SHEET window has its own unique set of commands, which are invoked with the MENU (F10)

---

* Metaphor courtesy of Steve Miller, Lotus Development Corporation.

key. Likewise, the DOC window has a set of commands specific to word processing, which are invoked with the MENU key in the DOC environment.

Window Restrict Ranges

Because you can manipulate and change worksheet information through the DOC window, you must be very careful if you begin word processing on a worksheet that already contains important information.

Notice the top of the screen. It tells you where in the document (the line number and the position in that line) the pointer is presently located. It also tells you that the pointer would be located at cell A1 if you were in the spreadsheet environment. This means that any information you might type at this point would be stored in cell A1; and if you switched to the SHEET window, you would find that you had overwritten the original cell contents.

The point is that you must take care not to overwrite important worksheet information when you use the word processor. Of course, if your application involves a single document, you do not have to worry about what you might accidentally do to the rest of the worksheet. In the WARRANTY example, however, you would want to take measures to ensure that your document will not interfere with other information. With the Restrict option of the Window Settings menu, Symphony gives you the ability to limit the access of any window to particular areas of the worksheet. The range of cells over which a window can have access is called the *Restrict range.*

You could have specified a Restrict range at the time you created the DOC window. However, it is easy enough to do it now — you only need to change one item in the Window settings sheet.

1. Press the SERVICES (F9) key and select Window Settings.

When you create a window, it inherits the settings of the window in which the pointer was located before you issued the Window Create command — unless you instruct Symphony otherwise. The pointer was in the SHEET window called MAIN. Since MAIN did not have an assigned Restrict range, neither does the new window. Therefore, both windows have access to the entire worksheet, from cell A1 to cell IV8192. In the settings window you will notice that the Restrict setting contains the range A1..D8192. To change this setting,

2. Select Restrict.

3. Select Range to change the Restrict range setting.

The entire window appears in reverse video, and Symphony is ready for your instructions. You have three options: to use the arrow keys to expand or shrink the Restrict range; to type a new Restrict range; or to press RETURN to accept the current Restrict range setting. The current Restrict range is displayed in the control panel.

Your aim is to restrict the window to an unused area of the worksheet. Anything to the right of column N would be appropriate. Therefore, let's change the Restrict range to P1..IV8192 by typing this range.

4. Type **P1..IV8192**, press RETURN, and select Quit twice.

Since the new Restrict range goes into effect immediately, the window now peers into the new range. The control panel tells you that cell P1 underlies the current position of the cursor. Anything you type will be stored in this region of the spreadsheet, not in the area of A1.

Remember that Restrict ranges are not always necessary. If your application only involves word processing, you probably won't need to use Restrict ranges. It is good to be familiar with the Restrict capability, however, for tasks that involve several environments.

Entering Text in a DOC Window

Now you are ready to begin word processing. The first step will be to type the name and address of the customer, as follows:

> J.S. Bach
> 7 Surprise St.
> Dallas, Texas 66666

No special ritual is required to begin typing. Do not worry about typing errors yet; you'll learn how to correct them shortly. Begin typing at the cursor's current position (line 1, character 1).

1. In order to type in lower- and uppercase letters, make sure that the "CAP" indicator does not appear in the bottom right of the screen. If it does, press the CAPS LOCK key to "toggle off" all-capitals typing.

2. Type the name and address as shown, pressing RETURN at the end of each line.

Pressing RETURN at the end of the third line brings the cursor to character position 1 of line 4, as indicated in the control panel. Notice the ◀ character that Symphony places at each point where you pressed the RETURN key. This character will not be printed as part of the document; it is there for your reference only.

Correcting Errors

If you make a typing error, use the arrow keys to position the cursor on the first incorrect character. For example, suppose you entered the address as

> V.S. Boch
> 7 Surprse St.
> Dallais, Texxas 66666

To change the initials V.S. to J.S., use the arrow keys to move the pointer to the "V." Then press the DEL key, which deletes the character that the cursor is highlighting, and type the correct letter, "J." The DEL key works just as it does in Edit Mode in the spreadsheet and FORM environments.

Another way to make corrections is with the BACKSPACE key. Pressing BACKSPACE causes Symphony to delete the character to the left of the cursor. Characters inside and to the right of the cursor are shifted to the left when you press BACKSPACE. To change Boch to Bach, you could position the cursor on the "c" in Boch, press BACKSPACE (which yields Bch), and type an "a" to insert the correct letter. You can remove the "i" in Dallais and an "x" in Texxas with either DEL or BACKSPACE.

If you place the cursor in the middle of a word and begin typing, the keystrokes you type will be inserted at the location of the cursor. The letter the cursor is on and the letters to the right of the cursor are shifted right to make room for the inserted characters.

The second line of the address was mistakenly typed as 7 Surprse St. The letter "i" must be inserted into Surprse. Move the cursor to the letter "s," which is the first letter that you want to push to the right when you make the insertion. Then type the letter "i," to change Surprse to Surprise. Again, insertion works the same as it does in Edit Mode.

Word processing is normally done in Insert Mode: when you place the cursor in the middle of a word and type, the keystrokes are inserted without overwriting text that is already there. If you prefer to overwrite instead of insert, press the INS key to toggle off Insert Mode. An "OVR" indicator will appear on the screen, indicating that if you begin typing in an area where text already exists, that text will be overwritten by the new characters. Pressing INS again removes the "OVR" indicator and reinstates Insert Mode.

The important editing keys are listed in Table 17-1. Make any necessary corrections in the address.

Table 17-1. DOC Editing Keys and Their Functions

Key	Effect
JUSTIFY (F2)	Justifies current paragraph
INDENT (F3)	Indents text in current paragraph (for example, use for extended quotes)
SPLIT (ALT-F3)	Pushes text following the cursor down one line, without inserting a hard carriage return
ERASE (F4)	Erases specified block of text
CENTER (ALT-F4)	Centers the current line between left and right margins
WHERE (ALT-F2)	Displays what page and line numbers of current line would be if document were printed using current print settings
INS	Toggles between Insert Mode and Overstrike Mode
TAB	In Insert Mode, inserts spaces up to next tab stop; in Overstrike Mode, moves cursor to next tab stop
RETURN (↵)	Types a hard carriage return
BACKSPACE (←)	Deletes preceding character
DEL	Deletes character at cursor position

Typing the Form Letter

The next step is to compose the form letter. Begin the salutation two lines below the address:

1. Move the cursor to line 5, character 1. (Check the location of the cursor in the control panel.)
2. Type **Dear J.S.**, and press RETURN twice.

Before you begin typing a paragraph, note that you don't have to press RETURN when you reach the right margin at the end of a line. Symphony knows exactly where the margin is, and it automatically "wraps around"—fits as many words as possible onto the line without going beyond the margin—and then begins the next line. This means that the only time you press RETURN is at the end of a paragraph.

3. With the cursor on line 7, character 1, press the TAB key to indent and then type the following paragraph:

```
As a customer of WidgetWorksheet, we thought you might like to
receive advance notice about a new product that will be released next
month.  It's a numerical analysis program named Widget Digit.
```

Remember to press RETURN at the end of the paragraph.

Notice how Symphony automatically wrapped the lines. It also *justified*, or aligned, the paragraph on the left but not on the right. You may control justification as you will see momentarily.

Pressing RETURN at the end of the paragraph you just composed brought you to line 10, character 1.

4. Press RETURN again.

Symphony advanced the cursor to line 11. Notice that pressing RETURN at the leftmost character position of a blank line does not cause the RETURN character, ◄, to appear. Instead, it has the same effect as the down arrow key.

At this point, Ms. Fidget would like to use an attention-grabbing sentence, in all-capital letters.

5. Press the CAPS LOCK key to turn on all-capital typing.
6. Type **NOW IS THE TIME TO BUY WIDGET DIGIT!**, but do not press RETURN at the end of the line. (If you do so, move the cursor to the RETURN character and press the DEL key to remove it.)

Centering a Line of Text

The letter might look better if this line were centered within the margins. The CENTER key is made up of only one keystroke combination: ALT-F4. The cursor may be located anywhere in the line that you want to center. The current position of the cursor is fine.

1. Hold down the ALT key and press F4.

Instantly, the line is centered. The CENTER (ALT-F4) key is a convenient feature to remember.

2. Press RETURN to place a RETURN character at the end of the line and advance the cursor to line 12.

Inserting Text and Using The HOME Key

You may have noticed an omission in the letter: Widget-Ware's address does not appear anywhere. It should be at the very beginning, above the customer's address.

To insert lines into a document, you first move the cursor to the place where you want to make the insertion. In this case, you want to go to the beginning of the letter. Instead of using the arrow keys to move the cursor to line 1, character 1, you can press the HOME key as a shortcut.

1. Press HOME.

Notice that pressing HOME in the word processor has the same effect as in both the SHEET and FORM environments: it transfers you to the top left corner of the area you are working in. Here is another instance of keystroke integration, where pressing the same key in different contexts produces a similar result.

The cursor now rests on the first character of the customer's name in the address. First let's insert a blank row above the customer's name. The SPLIT keystroke sequence (ALT-F3) splits a line at the place where the cursor is. If the cursor is at the beginning of a line, SPLIT (ALT-F3) pushes the current line down and inserts a blank row into the document. If the cursor is in the middle of a sentence when you press SPLIT, the line will be split at the point where the cursor was; everything at or to the right of the cursor's position will be bumped down to the next line. Note that pressing SPLIT differs from pressing RETURN. Whereas pressing RETURN inserts the RETURN symbol in the document, SPLIT splits the line without inserting the RETURN symbol.

2. Press SPLIT (ALT-F3) to insert a blank line at the top of the document.

With the "CAP" indicator still on, type the following two lines:

3. Type **WIDGET-WARE** and press RETURN.
4. Type **55 WEST WIDGET WAY. WEAVER, WASHINGTON** 77777 and press RETURN.

The sender's address does not seem to stand out because it is left-justified. Perhaps it would look better if it were centered.

5. Move the cursor to any character in the first line and press CENTER (ALT-F4). Do the same for the second line.

Moving the Cursor Quickly: The END-Key Combinations

Now you can continue the body of the letter. First, press the CAPS LOCK key to toggle off the "CAP" indicator.

The END-HOME key combination provides a shortcut for moving the cursor to the end of the document,

1. Press the END key; then press the HOME key.

As in the spreadsheet environment, END-HOME moves the cursor to the end of the active area—in this case the RETURN symbol at the end of the last line you typed.

2. Press the down arrow key to move the cursor to line 15, character 55.

You now need to move to the beginning of this line. To do so quickly,

3. Press END and then press the left arrow key.

This brings the cursor to character 1. Pressing END and then the left arrow moves the cursor to the first character in the line of text. Pressing END followed by the right arrow moves the cursor to the last typed character in the line.

Other convenient END sequences are END with the up arrow (which transfers the cursor to the beginning of the paragraph) and END with the down arrow (which moves it to the end of the paragraph). Pressing END and then a character moves the cursor forward to the next occurrence of that character. For example, END followed by an "e" would move the cursor to the next occurrence of the letter "e".

The CTRL-left arrow and CTRL-right arrow sequences are also convenient. Holding down the CTRL key and pressing the left arrow key causes the cursor to move to the beginning of the previous word. CTRL-right arrow moves the cursor to the space after the next word.

4. Press RETURN to advance to line 16.

Keystrokes and keystroke combinations that quickly move the cursor around a document are summarized in Table 17-2.

Creating Format Lines

The next paragraph in the letter will describe the new software. Ms. Fidget would like this paragraph to stand out without detracting from the previous line, which was capitalized. One way to accomplish this would be to create narrower margins for this paragraph.

With Symphony, you can create documents that have multiple format lines. As you may recall, format lines specify settings for margins, tabs, line spacing, and text justification. Text appearing between two format lines is subject to the format specifications of the top format line.

Until now, you have word processed without the use of a command menu. However, multiple formatting is a special function, so it requires the menu.

1. Press the MENU (F10) key to invoke the word processing command menu.

2. Select the Format command.

The Format menu displays these options:

Create Edit Use-Named Settings

Table 17-2. DOC Environment Cursor-Movement Keys

Key	Description
Left arrow	Move left one character in current line
Right arrow	Move right one character in current line
Up arrow	Move up one character in current column
Down arrow	Move down one character in current column
CTRL-left arrow	Move left to previous word
CTRL-right arrow	Move right to next word
END-left arrow	Move to beginning of line
END-right arrow	Move to end of line
END-up arrow	Move to beginning of paragraph
END-down arrow	Move to end of paragraph
PG UP	Move to previous screen in current column
PG DN	Move to next screen in current column
GOTO *number* or *name*	Move to specified line location, named line marker, or named format line
HOME	Move to beginning of document window
END-HOME	Move to end of document

With SCROLL LOCK on (press the SCROLL LOCK key):

Key	Description
Left arrow	Move screen right 1/4 of window width
Right arrow	Move screen left 1/4 of window width
Up arrow	Move screen down one line
Down arrow	Move screen up one row

With permission copyright 1984 Lotus Development Corporation.

The *Create command* adds a new format line. The *Edit option* changes the settings of an existing format line; the *Use-Named option* creates a format line using the settings of a different format line; and the *Settings option* displays a settings sheet of the format line that you are currently working with. You will create a new format line.

3. Select Create.

Symphony asks where you want to place the format line, suggesting the current location of the cursor, line 16. This is your intention, so

4. Press RETURN to accept Symphony's recommendation.

Pressing RETURN causes Symphony to insert the format line into the document and to bring the menu of format settings to the control panel:

Margins/Tabs Justification Spacing Line-Marker Use-Named Reset Quit

The newly created format line is shown in Figure 17-1. The left margin is represented by the letter "L" on the left side of the format line. Tab stops are denoted by the letter "T." On the right side of the format line, "R" represents the

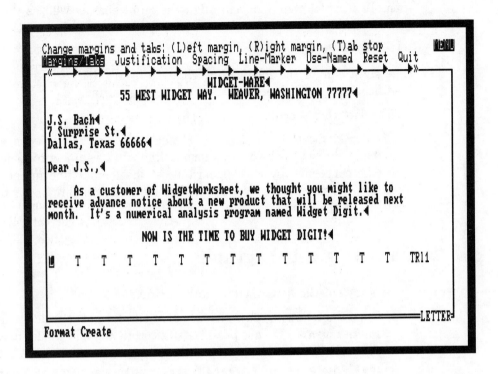

Figure 17-1. The format line

position of the right margin, followed by "l" (lowercase "L"), which signifies that the text beneath the format line will be left-justified, followed by "1" (one), which indicates that the text will be single-spaced when it is printed.

To change the margins,

5. Select Margins/Tabs.

Pressing the space bar or the TAB key pushes the left side of the format line toward the right.

6. Press the TAB key twice to push the "L" of the format line to character 11 of the line.

7. Press the right arrow key (hold it down) until the cursor is stationed at character 61.

Now you must make the format line shorter by deleting a section of it.

8. Press the DEL key (hold it down) until the letter "R" appears in character 61.

9. Press RETURN.

The new margins are now set at 11 and 61.

While you are in an editing mood, let's try a new justification setting.

10. Select Justification.

Right now, the lowercase "l" at the end of the format line indicates left justification. To instruct Symphony to align the right side as well as the left, use even justification.

11. Select Even.

The right side of the format line changes from "Rll" to "Rel", indicating even justification. You're done with the format line settings, so

12. Select Quit.

The cursor moves to the first character under the new left margin. From now on, whatever you type below this format line will be subject to its format settings. Don't be concerned by the appearance of the format line in the middle of the document on screen. When you print the letter, Symphony knows to omit the format line in the printout.

Justifying a Paragraph

Let's try out the new margins and justification.

1. Type the following paragraph, being careful not to indent the beginning of the paragraph. Do not press RETURN until the end of the paragraph:

```
Widget Digit is an advanced electronic calculator custom
designed for the widget industry.  It features unlimited
rows and columns, unlimited field widths, unlimited
formatting, and unlimited speed, at an unlimited price.
```

The text conforms to the new, narrower margins. But what happened to the even justification? Even after you change the justification in a new format line, Symphony continues left-justifying the text until you instruct it to reformat the text using the new format settings. To reformat a paragraph, place the cursor in the paragraph you want to reformat and press the JUSTIFY key (F2).

2. Move the cursor up into the paragraph you just typed and press the JUSTIFY (F2) key.

You now have an even block of text. Anything new that you type will also be evenly justified, unless you create a third format line that resets the original margins and justification.

Resetting Margins and Completing
The Letter

Since you don't want the remainder of the letter to be indented and right-justified, you will need a new format line. As before, you create the format line by moving the cursor to the line where you want to start the new format and invoking the Format Create command.

1. To move to the end of the paragraph, press END and then the down arrow key. This brings the cursor to line 21.

2. Press the down arrow key twice; then press END and the left arrow key to move the cursor to line 23, character 1.

3. Press the MENU (F10) key and select Format Create.

4. Press RETURN to insert the format line on line 23, the current line.

There is no need to reset the margins and justification yourself. Selecting the Reset option does this automatically, using the default settings that were active when you first brought up the DOC window. (These settings are still displayed in the Format settings sheet.)

5. Select Reset; then select Quit.

The new settings, indicated by the "Rl1" at the end of the format line, left-justify the text on a single-spaced 72-character line.

There is one more paragraph to type before you close the letter.

6. Type the following paragraph, pressing TAB at the beginning and RETURN at the end:

```
        The list price of Widget Digit is $10,500.  However,
if you order now, Widget Digit can be yours for only $10.50.
Order now, and Widget Digit will be sent directly to you at
7 Surprise St.
```

The paragraph margins on your screen will differ slightly from those shown here.

The GOTO Key and the Copy Command

Ms. Fidget feels that a repetition of the line, NOW IS THE TIME TO BUY WIDGET DIGIT!, would be effective before the close of the letter. Instead of typing the line over again, you can copy the line from the beginning of the letter to the bottom. This is done with the Copy command.

The DOC Copy command operates very much like the spreadsheet Copy command, replicating a range, or *block*, of text in another area of the document. Unlike the SHEET Copy command, however, the DOC command lets you copy text either to a blank area of the document or to an area that already contains text. If you use the DOC Copy command to copy to an area where text already exists, Symphony will not overwrite the original material. Instead, the copied material will simply be inserted into the text line, moving the original material down to make room for the insertion. Then Symphony will automatically reformat the paragraph by adjusting its margins.

As in the spreadsheet, the first step in using the Copy command is to move the cursor to the beginning of the text that you want to copy. In this example, the original sentence is in line 14 of the document. Instead of using the up arrow key to get to line 14, you could use the GOTO (F5) key to move directly to line 14. Although this does not save you much time in this case, GOTO is very useful in documents of greater length.

1. Press the GOTO (F5) key.

Symphony asks "Go to where?" You answer with the line number you want the cursor to move to.

> 2. Type **14** and press RETURN.

The cursor jumps directly to line 14, character 1. Here is the beginning of the text to be copied. If you copy from here to the end of the line, Symphony will copy the spaces that precede the first letter of the sentence. If you want to center the copied sentence in its new location, you should begin copying at character 1.

It would be a good idea to save the worksheet at this point. That way, if you make an error during the Copy procedure, you won't have to do any retyping to get back the original version. Once you've saved the file (using the same File Save command sequence as in the SHEET and FORM environments), you can proceed with the Copy procedure.

> 3. Press the SERVICES (F9) key; select File and then Save. Use the same WAR-RANTY file name to save the file.
>
> 4. Press the MENU (F10) key; select Copy.

Now you must tell Symphony exactly what portion of the document you want to copy from.

As the control panel indicates, Symphony assumes that the range of text you want to copy is 14,1..14,1 (which means the range of text beginning in line 14, character 1, and ending at line 14, character 1). You want to copy more than a single character, and as you might expect, you can expand this range by expanding the pointer. To expand the pointer quickly to the end of the line,

> 5. Press END; then press the right arrow key.

This expands the highlight from the first character of the line to the first letter of the sentence. To get to the end of the sentence,

> 6. Press END again; then press the right arrow key and press RETURN.

The FROM range now extends from 14,1 to 14,55 and includes the RETURN character at the end of the line.

Now Symphony wants to know the destination range. As in the SHEET environment, you only need to point to the beginning of the destination range. This will be two lines below the last line of the letter, at line 28, character 1. You may not use the GOTO key here, because you are in the middle of another command. However, you may quickly get to the correct spot by other means.

> 7. Press END; then press HOME to transfer the cursor to the last character of the document.
>
> 8. Press the down arrow key twice to move to line 28.
>
> 9. Press END; then press the left arrow key to move to character 1 of line 28.
>
> 10. Press RETURN to complete the Copy command.

That concludes the body of the letter. To sign off,

> 11. Press END, press HOME, press the down arrow key twice, press END, and then press the left arrow key.
>
> 12. Press the TAB key seven times to move to line 30, character 36.
>
> 13. Type **Sincerely,** and press RETURN.
>
> 14. Press the TAB key seven times to move to line 31, character 36.

15. Type **Bridgeotte Fidget** and press RETURN.

Actually, there should be four lines inserted between "Sincerely" and Bridgeotte's name to allow room for a signature. The SPLIT (ALT-F3) key will do the trick.

16. Move the cursor up once, to line 31, character 1.

17. Press the SPLIT key sequence (ALT-F3) four times.

The Page Command

When you are ready to produce a printed copy of this letter, you will want Symphony to print the text and then advance the printer paper to the top of the next page. This is the function of the *Page command*. At any point where you want the paper to advance to the next page, issue the Page command. Page stores a special code, ::, in the document, which instructs the printer to advance the paper.

```
                         WIDGET-WARE
              55 WEST WIDGET WAY.  WEAVER, WASHINGTON 77777

        J.S. Bach
        7 Surprise St.
        Dallas, Texas 66666

        Dear J.S.,

             As a customer of WidgetWorksheet, we thought you might like to
        receive advance notice about a new product that will be released next
        month.  It's a numerical analysis program named Widget Digit.

                     NOW IS THE TIME TO BUY WIDGET DIGIT!

             Widget Digit  is an advanced  electronic calculator
             custom  designed  for  the  widget  industry.  It
             features  unlimited  rows  and  columns,  unlimited
             field widths,  unlimited formatting,  and unlimited
             speed, at an unlimited price.

             The list price of Widget Digit is $10,500.  However, if you order
        now, Widget Digit can be yours for only $10.50.  Order now, and Widget
        Digit will be sent directly to you at 7 Surprise St.

                     NOW IS THE TIME TO BUY WIDGET DIGIT!

                     Sincerely,



                     Bridgeotte Fidget
```

Figure 17-2. The form letter, first draft

1. Press END and then HOME to move to the last character of the letter.

2. Press the down arrow key, press END, and then press the left arrow key.

3. Press MENU (F10) and select Page.

Your letter should look like Figure 17-2.

The Move Command

Ms. Fidget is not quite satisfied with the letter. She would like it to begin with the capitalized "NOW IS THE TIME" line.

The change is easy to implement, because Symphony includes a Move command in the word processing environment. The *Move command* transfers text from one area of the text to another. Whereas Copy duplicates the text in one area and moves the duplicate to another area, Move removes the text from its original position and inserts it somewhere else.

The change that Ms. Fidget wants can be accomplished either by moving the first paragraph below the capitalized sentence or by moving the sentence above the first paragraph. Let's choose the first method.

Symphony will need to know what block of text you want to move. Suppose you begin the block at the first character of the blank line above the first paragraph and end the block at the end of the paragraph. Then you instruct Symphony to move this block to the area beginning at line 15, the blank line below the sales pitch. The first paragraph and the blank line above it will be removed from their original location, so that the salutation will be followed by a blank line and then the centered sales pitch. Next comes the moved block of text, followed by a blank line and the remainder of the letter.

To begin the Move procedure,

1. Point the cursor to the beginning of the block to be moved by pressing GOTO (F5), typing **9**, and pressing RETURN.

2. Press the MENU (F10) key and select Move.

To expand the highlight over the entire paragraph,

3. Press END and then the down arrow key to move to the end of the first paragraph.

The control panel indicates a range of 9,1..12,54.

4. Press RETURN.

Now move to the destination of the block you wish to move, the line below the sales pitch.

5. Use the down arrow key to move to line 15, character 1.

6. Press RETURN to activate the move.

The new version of the letter looks much better. It almost meets Ms. Fidget's needs.

The Erase Command

The letter boasts of a program that has an unlimited price. With a list price of $10,500, Ms. Fidget is afraid that this may be a bit overstated. To be safe, you should erase that part of the letter.

Earlier you used the DEL key to delete characters. You could do the same here. However, when you have to erase more than a few characters, it is usually faster to use the *Erase command*. The Erase command deletes a block of text.

There are two ways to invoke the Erase command. You may choose the Erase option of the DOC command menu, or you may press the ERASE (F4) key. Pressing the ERASE key is faster, since it requires only one keystroke.

Figure 17-3 shows the block of characters that you must remove from the letter.

```
                              WIDGET-WARE
                55 WEST WIDGET WAY.  WEAVER, WASHINGTON 77777

        J.S. Bach
        7 Surprise St.
        Dallas, Texas 66666

        Dear J.S.,

                   NOW IS THE TIME TO BUY WIDGET DIGIT!

            As a customer of WidgetWorksheet, we thought you might like to
        receive advance notice about a new product that will be released next
        month.  It's a numerical analysis program named Widget Digit.

                Widget Digit  is an advanced  electronic calculator
                custom  designed  for   the  widget   industry.  It
                features  unlimited  rows  and  columns,  unlimited
                field widths,  unlimited formatting,  and unlimited
                speed, at an unlimited price.

            The list price of Widget Digit is $10,500.  However, if you order
        now, Widget Digit can be yours for only $10.50.  Order now, and Widget
        Digit will be sent directly to you at 7 Surprise St.

                NOW IS THE TIME TO BUY WIDGET DIGIT!

                        Sincerely,



                        Bridgeotte Fidget
```

Figure 17-3. Text to be deleted with the Erase command

1. Move the cursor to the beginning of the block to be erased (line 21, character 16).
2. Press the ERASE (F4) key.

To expand the highlight over the text to be erased,

3. Press the right arrow key until the highlight extends to the "e" in price (character 38).
4. Press RETURN.

Symphony deletes the phrase and automatically reformats the paragraph.

The Search and Replace Commands

There is only one more correction to make. As you know, Widget-Ware is a subsidiary of Fidget Widget Manufacturing. The corporation is having an image problem, and so it would like to establish its name more firmly in the market. Since company officials expect the new line of software to be an industry favorite, they feel that changing the name of the software from Widget Digit to Fidget Digit will benefit the corporation. Fortunately, Symphony provides two commands, *Search* and *Replace*, that make it easy to adjust the letter.

Using the Search Command

First let's see how this change will affect your letter. To do this, you will conduct a search for all occurrences of the words Widget Digit. The Search command allows you to search for any occurrence of a string of characters (such as Widget Digit).

You may search forward or backward in relation to the position of the cursor. (You may not search both forward and backward with the same command.) To search through an entire document, you should place the cursor at the beginning of the first line before invoking the Search command.

1. Press the HOME key.
2. Press MENU (F10) and select Search.

In response to the "Search for what?" prompt,

3. Type **Widget Digit** and press RETURN.

Symphony will locate the string if it exists. Otherwise, it will beep and tell you that it could not find a match. If there is a match, Symphony will give you the opportunity to search further for additional occurrences, either forward or backward in relation to the occurrence it just found.

4. Select Forward. Continue to select Forward to see how many times the words Widget Digit occur in the letter.
5. Select Quit when you're done.

Notice that Symphony located all occurrences of the string, disregarding variations in capitalization.

Using the Replace Command

It is also possible to replace all occurrences of a particular string with a different string. Replace is a very useful command. If you repeatedly misspelled a word in a long document, Replace allows you to correct the entire document with a single command. You may opt to replace some or all occurrences in the text. The command works like Search, except that it replaces strings as it locates them.

The Replace command is what you need to change all occurrences of Widget Digit to Fidget Digit.

1. Press the HOME key so that the replacement search will begin at the beginning of the text.

2. Press MENU (F10) and select Replace.

Symphony prompts for the string you want to replace. If you had previously issued a Search or Replace command, Symphony will guess that you want to replace the string that you specified before. To override Symphony's guess, you may type a different string. In this case, the recommendation is what you want.

3. Press RETURN.

To specify the replacement string,

4. Type **Fidget Digit** and press RETURN.

After locating the first occurrence, Symphony displays a menu:

Once Continue Skip All-Remaining Quit

Selecting "Once" replaces the one occurrence and terminates the command. "Continue" replaces the occurrence and finds the next. "Skip" does not replace the occurrence but tells Symphony to seek out the next occurrence. "All-Remaining" instructs Symphony to replace this and all remaining occurrences automatically, without asking the user about each one. You should use "All-Remaining" only when you are confident that you want to replace each and every occurrence.

Symphony duplicates the replacement string exactly as you type it, in this case with upper- and lowercase letters. In contrast, when it searches for an occurrence in either the Search or Replace commands, Symphony disregards both upper- and lowercase. This means that it is not always prudent to use the All-Remaining option. To see why,

5. Select All-Remaining.

6. Press HOME.

Look at the sales pitch line. Symphony located an occurrence of Widget Digit, but that occurrence was in all-uppercase letters. Replacing this occurrence (and the one in the second sales pitch line at the end of the letter) was not what you intended. To rectify the error, you must replace Fidget Digit with FIDGET DIGIT. This time, you should use the Continue and Skip options so as not to change all occurences to uppercase.

7. Press MENU (F10) and select Replace.

8. Type **Fidget Digit** and press RETURN.

9. Type **FIDGET DIGIT** and press RETURN.

10. Select Continue to replace the first occurrence, in the first sales pitch line.

11. Select Skip five times so as not to capitalize the next five occurrences.

12. Select Continue to replace the next occurrence, in the second sales pitch line.

13. Select Quit to end the command.

Now the letter is in the right form. Having satisfied the needs of management, you are ready to print the letter in Chapter 18. Before proceeding, don't forget to save the file under the same WARRANTY file name. All of the settings, including the page-advance marker, will remain in effect when you next retrieve the file.

Chapter 18
A Form Letter
Using Data Fields

In the last several chapters you have built a database application that incorporated form generation, criteria selection, sorting, querying, reporting, and word processing. This chapter provides a "grand finale" to this application. You will convert the letter designed in Chapter 17 to a form letter into which Symphony will substitute information about the different customers in the database. Then you will print the letter using the Print command in the DOC environment.

Before beginning, you will need to retrieve the WARRANTY file. Make sure you are in the DOC window.

Using the WHERE Key
For a Page Count

It is often useful to know how long a document will be before you start printing it. In the case of your form letter, for instance, you should know whether the entire letter will fit on a single page. A one- or two-line overflow to a second page would look awkward.

Symphony has a WHERE key sequence that allows you to ascertain a document's length before you print it out. Pressing the WHERE (ALT-F2) key causes Symphony to convert the cursor's on-screen location to a printed-page position, which it displays as page and line numbers in the bottom left corner of the screen. It uses the page format settings that are currently in effect (including margins, vertical spacing, and justification) to calculate the printed-page position.

By moving to the bottom of a document and pressing WHERE, you can determine how long that document will be when it is printed. To find out the length of the letter,

1. Press END; then press HOME.

2. Type the WHERE key sequence (ALT-F2).

The page and line numbers appear on the bottom left of the screen. Your letter will fit on a single page. Note that to use WHERE, the cursor must be positioned somewhere within a line that contains text. WHERE does not work outside the text area.

Printing the Letter

Now you're ready to print a copy of the letter on paper. First, make sure your printer is turned on and the paper is properly aligned. Next,

1. Press the HOME key.

2. Press the SERVICES (F9) key; select Print.

3. Select Settings; then select Source.

Because you have already printed portions of the WARRANTY worksheet, the settings sheet indicates a range to be printed. This is not the range you want. To cancel the previous range,

4. Select Cancel.

The Source range setting is now blank. Unlike the SHEET and FORM environments, the DOC environment does not require a new Source range in order to print. Unless you explicitly tell Symphony to print only part of the text (by specifying a Source range for only part of the document), Symphony assumes you want to print the entire document.

5. Select Quit.

To commence printing,

6. Select Go; then select Quit.

After printing, the paper should advance to the next page (as specified by the Page command that you issued in Chapter 17).

Preparing a Generalized Form Letter

J. S. Bach's form letter is ready to be mailed, but there are several more potential Fidget Digit customers. The letter must be personalized and printed for each of them.

If you had a secretary who would manually type the letters on a typewriter, you might approach the task in a manner that is quite similar to Symphony's. You might compose a sample letter for the first customer, as you have already done; then you would make a copy and mark the places that have to be changed in each letter. These places are indicated in Figure 18-1.

```
                        WIDGET-WARE
            55 WEST WIDGET WAY.  WEAVER, WASHINGTON 77777

J.S. Bach
7 Surprise St.
Dallas, Texas 66666

Dear J.S.,

            NOW IS THE TIME TO BUY FIDGET DIGIT!

    As a customer of WidgetWorksheet, we thought you might like to
receive advance notice about a new product that will be released next
month.  It's a numerical analysis program named Fidget Digit.

        Fidget Digit  is an advanced  electronic calculator
        custom  designed  for  the  widget  industry.  It
        features  unlimited  rows  and  columns,  unlimited
        field widths,  unlimited formatting,  and unlimited
        speed.

    The list price of Fidget Digit is $10,500.  However, if you order
now, Fidget Digit can be yours for only $10.50.  Order now, and Fidget
Digit will be sent directly to you at 7 Surprise St.

        NOW IS THE TIME TO BUY FIDGET DIGIT!

            Sincerely,




            Bridgeotte Fidget
```

Figure 18-1. Form letter showing variable strings

Proceeding one by one through the records on the customer list, the secretary would type a letter for each customer, substituting the correct information into the highlighted areas in the form letter.

To create a form letter in Symphony, you must switch to the spreadsheet environment. The letter is stored in the spreadsheet as a column of labels, with each line stored in a separate cell. Wherever information from the database must be substituted in the letter, you insert a spreadsheet formula referring to appropriate cells of the first record in the Database range. Thus, if you look back at Figure 16-2, you will see that the FIRST NAME field of the first record is stored in cell B41 of the spreadsheet. Thus, you would substitute a formula reference to cell B41 for J.S. (which is the FIRST NAME field) in the first highlighted cell of the letter.

Once the formulas have been put in place within the letter, you designate the form letter as the Main range of the report, and then use the Print Settings Source Database command to instruct Symphony to print all of the letters. When Symphony sees the formula references to the fields of the first record, it infers that you want to process a report for each record, and it will substitute the values of each successive record into the formula cells.

Preparing the Form Letter
In a Spreadsheet Window

You will need to switch to the spreadsheet window in order to make the necessary adjustments. Instead of going into a separate spreadsheet window, you can simply switch the LETTER window from word processing to the spreadsheet environment.

1. Press HOME.

2. Press the TYPE (ALT-F10) key sequence and select SHEET.

The pointer is positioned on cell P1, and the control panel displays the contents of the cell. Recall that you created the first line of the letter by typing WIDGET-WARE and pressing the CENTER (ALT-F4) key sequence. In the spreadsheet this line is stored as a label. Thus, the cell entry shown in the control panel begins with an apostrophe, the left-justify label-prefix. Symphony figured out how many spaces it would need to insert before WIDGET-WARE to center the word. The label consists of these spaces, followed by WIDGET-WARE.

If you move down once, to cell P2, you will see that the second line is also preceded by an apostrophe. Indeed, all lines of the letter have been stored the same way.

3. Move the pointer to cell P4.

This cell contains the addressee's first name, followed by a space and then the last name. To accomplish the necessary substitutions, you must replace these names with references to the corresponding FIRST NAME and LAST NAME fields of the first record of the Database range. The references are separated by a space. You can use the string functions to store this combination of strings in a single formula.

Converting String Labels to Formulas

J.S. Bach's last and first names are stored in cells A41 and B41, respectively. You will need to convert J.S. Bach into a formula that is a combination of three character strings: the string contained in B41 (first name), the space between the first name and last name, and the string contained in A41 (last name).

Recall from Chapter 9 that you can create a formula using the & (ampersand) string operator to combine two strings. The formula to derive the first line of the customer address would be +B41&" "&A41, which concatenates the first-name string with a space and the last-name string. You need not use cell addresses, though, since Symphony has already given range names to the fields of the first record of the Database range. As Figure 18-2 indicates, the range names that Symphony assigned to the fields of the first database record are the database's field names themselves—the names listed in the NAME field of the Definition range that have become the column headings in the Database range. An alternative formula entry to +B41&" "&A41 would be +FIRST NAME&" "&LAST NAME.

1. Type **+first name&" "&last name** and press RETURN.

If you do not notice any difference in the display, you have done well. The control panel confirms that the cell now contains a formula instead of a label. But the formula produces the same result as the former contents of the cell, and that is just what you want.

The next replacement in the form letter is the second line of the address, which is simply the STREET field.

2. Move the pointer to cell P5; type **+street** and press RETURN.

Again, if the cell display remains unchanged, you have done well.

The third line of the address is a little more complicated. It begins with the CITY field, followed by a comma and a space, then the STATE field, two spaces, and the ZIP code. If all of the fields were character fields, the formula would be

+CITY&", "&STATE&" "&ZIP CODE

ZIP CODE is not a character field, however. It is a number, and you cannot concatenate a numeric field with a label field. Instead, you must first convert the numeric field to a string, using the @STRING function. The syntax of this function is @STRING (*cell address, number of decimal places*). The second argument tells Symphony how many decimal places to include in the converted string. Since ZIP codes are integers, the *number of decimal places* should be 0.

The string equivalent of the numeric cell named ZIP CODE can be obtained from the formula @STRING(ZIP CODE,0). To combine it with the CITY and STATE strings,

3. Move to cell P6 and type

+city&", "&state&" "&@string(zip code,0)

4. Press RETURN.

	A	B	C	D	E	F	G	H	I
40	LAST NAME	FIRST NAME	STREET	CITY	STATE	ZIP	COPRODUCT	DATE OF REGISTR	WARRANTY STATUS
41	Bach	J.S.	7 Surprise St.	Dallas	Texas	66666	WidgetWorksheet	31072	alive

Figure 18-2. Range names in the spreadsheet Database range

Combining Strings and Label Cells

The salutation is different from the address lines. It combines one string ("Dear "), which you want to use in every letter, with the FIRST NAME string, followed by a comma. In this case, you must break up an already existing string and insert the reference to the FIRST NAME field.

Currently, the cell contains the label'Dear J.S.,. This label must be converted to a concatenation of three strings: "Dear ", the FIRST NAME field, and ",". The formula +"Dear "&FIRST NAME&"," will do the trick. Rather than type the string from scratch, you can use Edit Mode.

1. Move to cell P8 and press the EDIT (F2) key.

Notice that the formula in the control panel includes the RETURN character at the end of the label, even though this symbol is not displayed in cell P8.

To change the beginning of the string from 'Dear to +"Dear " (note the space after the word Dear),

2. Press the HOME key to move the edit cursor to the beginning of the label.

3. Press the DEL key to remove the apostrophe.

4. Type a + and then a " (double quote) to insert the beginning string indicator.

5. Press the right arrow key five times to move the edit cursor beneath the letter J.

6. Type a " to insert the ending string indicator here.

7. Type an **&**.

The control panel now shows + "Dear "&J.S., followed by the RETURN character.

8. Press the DEL key four times to delete J.S.

9. Type **first name&**.

10. Type a ".

11. Press the END key to move the edit cursor to the space after the RETURN character, and type " to end the line of text.

12. Press RETURN.

The control panel should show "Dear "&FIRST NAME&",". (It displays a space instead of the RETURN character.) The salutation is ready.

Completing the Other String References

The first full paragraph makes reference to the package currently owned by the customer. This product name should be made variable, to be substituted by the PRODUCT field for the record being processed.

1. Move the pointer to cell P12.

2. Press the EDIT (F2) key.

Here, too, you must break up the label into three strings, replacing WidgetWork-sheet with a reference to the cell named PRODUCT.

3. Press the HOME key.

4. Press the DEL key to remove the apostrophe; then type a + and ".

5. Press the TAB key four times; then press the right arrow key twice to move the cursor beneath the W of WidgetWorksheet.

6. Type a "; then type **&product&**.

7. Press the DEL key 15 times to delete WidgetWorksheet, making sure to leave the comma that follows.

8. Type a ", press the END key to move to the end of the formula, and type a ".

9. Press RETURN.

Row 26 of the spreadsheet contains the last substitution, the STREET field in the sentence "Order now, and Fidget Digit will be sent directly to you at . . . ."

10. Move the pointer to cell P26; press the EDIT (F2) key.

11. Press the HOME key; press the DEL key; type a + and ".

12. Move the edit cursor beneath the 7 in 7 Surprise St.

13. Type "; then type **&street&**.

14. Press the DEL key 13 times to remove 7 Surprise St, leaving the period at the end of the formula to end the sentence.

15. Type a "; press the END key; type a "; then press RETURN.

Your job is nearly done. You are ready to print.

Printing the Form Letter

When you print a form letter for the entire database, you must use the Print Settings Source Database command. First, though, you must make sure that the Above, Main, and Below ranges have been set correctly. In Chapter 16, you assigned an Above range and a Main range to produce a simple report of the database's contents. Printing a form letter requires a different Main range. Instead of using the Main range shown in Figure 16-2, you must designate the form letter itself as the Main range. This tells Symphony to make the field substitutions to the formulas in the form letter.

Symphony will begin by substituting the proper fields of the first database record into the formulas of the Main range. It then prints the Main range, goes to the next record, substitutes the fields into the Main range, and prints the Main range, repeating this procedure until the entire database has been processed.

No Above or Below range is required here. You will only be printing letters, and they require no additional messages, column headings, or summaries. Since the report-related database ranges set in Chapter 16 are no longer suitable, the easiest thing to do is cancel them and reassign the Main range to the form letter. To do this, invoke the database settings sheet.

1. Press the HOME key.

2. Press the MENU (F10) key; select Query Settings.

To cancel the Report ranges,

3. Select Cancel; then select Report.

To reassign the Main range,

4. Select Report; then select Main.

Highlight the entire form letter, including all columns that display text:

5. Type a . to anchor the range.

6. Move to cell W36.

7. Press RETURN.

8. Select Quit three times to exit from the Query menus.

The Print command is the same command you used to print the database report in Chapter 16.

9. Press the SERVICES (F9) key and select the Print command.

10. Select Settings Source Database.

11. Point to WARRANTY to select the WARRANTY database as the source for the printing.

12. Select Quit to exit from the Settings command.

13. Select Go to commence printing.

Your printer will now begin processing letter after letter to the customers in the database, substituting the appropriate strings of information as it prints. Thanks to the page advance marker you inserted at the end of the letter, the printer paper advances to the next page as soon as each letter is completed.

Seven letters in all should be printed out. Why not ten letters, since there are ten customers in the database? Remember that you established criteria to select WidgetWord customers. Because this is a database report, it will select only the records that pass the criterion selection. (To print letters for every customer listed in the database, you would first have to erase the WARRANTY_CR criterion range.)

14. Select Quit.

Having finished the report, you should save the worksheet.

15. Press SERVICES (F9), select File Save, press RETURN, and select Yes.

Developing this form letter has required a broad understanding of Symphony. You have used the FORM, SHEET, and DOC environments, as well as windows, criteria, string functions, and a host of other features. Nonetheless, there is much more to learn. You will be sharpening your skills further as you apply them in your everyday use of Symphony. To explore advanced techniques, you may wish to read *Symphony™Master: The Expert's Guide* (Edward Baras, Osborne/McGraw-Hill, 1985), which picks up where this book leaves off.

Appendix A
Keystroke Macros

How to Create a Macro

A Macro Example

Developing a Purchase Order
    Macro

Invoking the Macro

Computer applications often involve repetition. You may well come across a Symphony project that requires you to execute repetitively a particular procedure or sequence of commands and keystrokes. Performing the same procedure time and again can become tedious and is prone to error. Even if it is not, there are instances when you'll want to make an application easier to use by automating a procedure—storing the commands and entries somewhere and invoking the procedure by merely pressing a key or two. A *keystroke macro* is just such an automated procedure.

A macro is a column of cells that stores the keystrokes of Symphony commands and entries exactly as you would have typed them yourself. You assign the macro a unique name; when you later invoke it by simply entering its name, Symphony executes the macro all at once. An entire set of commands can be run automatically and repeatedly by using macros.

Macros execute procedures much more quickly than you can type them. Macros can help you eliminate typing errors and reduce the tedium of long and repetitious typing sequences. Perhaps the most important advantage of macros is their ability to reduce an entire procedure to a couple of keystrokes. This feature lets you automate or customize your work for a specific task or application.

This appendix shows you how to create and invoke a macro. The macro you will develop relates to the purchase order tracking model in Chapters 8 and 9. Bear in mind that the macro feature is so powerful and sophisticated that this appendix only serves as an introduction.

Symphony includes an entire language—the *Symphony Command Language*—specifically for the purpose of developing powerful macros. This appendix does not cover the Symphony Command Language. However, macros and the Command Language are covered at length in *Symphony Master: The Expert's Guide* (Edward Baras, Osborne/McGraw-Hill, 1985).

How to Create a Macro

How do you create a macro? The easiest way is to use *Learn Mode*. As its name implies, Learn Mode permits Symphony to learn the keystrokes that you teach it. Symphony stores what it learns in the *Learn range*, the column of cells that will comprise the macro. Learn Mode works like a tape recorder. You turn it on, and Symphony records whatever you type until you turn it off. Once you record your keystrokes, you can "play them back" by invoking the macro. The keystrokes that you record can be commands, data entries, anything that you would normally type in Symphony.

Before turning on Learn Mode, you specify the Learn range so that Symphony knows where to store the macro keystrokes. After you turn on Learn Mode, you go through a "dry run" of the procedure you want Symphony to learn. When you are done teaching the procedure to Symphony, you turn Learn Mode off, which tells Symphony to stop learning—that is, to stop recording keystrokes in the Learn range.

Once you have created the column of macro cells, you must give the macro a name, which will be used later to *invoke*, or execute, the macro. To name a macro, you assign a range name to the first cell of the macro, using the Range Name Create command. Standard macros have special names consisting of two characters.* The first character is \ (the backward slash key). The second character is a letter. Thus, \A and \B are valid macro names.

Once the macro has been created and named, you can invoke it. This is done by holding down the ALT key (not the backward slash key) and pressing the letter assigned to the macro. To invoke macro \A, for example, you would hold down ALT and press A.

The instructions for using Learn Mode to create a keystroke macro are detailed in "Steps for Creating a Keystroke Macro" (see box).

---

*You can name macros with nonstandard names. See the Symphony *Reference Manual* for details.

A Macro Example

Let's look at a simple example of a macro before you proceed to the purchase order macro discussed in the remainder of this appendix. Suppose you saved a worksheet file called TEST on your disk, and you wanted to create a macro to resave this file. Such a macro would be useful if you update the file often. Without a macro, you would

1. Press SERVICES (F9) and select File Save.

If you were already working in the TEST worksheet, Symphony would recommend TEST as the name of the file to be saved. You would then

2. Press RETURN.

Next, Symphony would ask whether you wanted to replace the old file with the current worksheet. You would

3. Type **Y** to select Yes.

This would save the file. The keystrokes you would have typed to perform this procedure are F9 FS RETURN Y.

Symphony stores the keystrokes in the Learn range exactly as you type them, except that it translates certain special keystrokes into macro notation. For

---

STEPS FOR CREATING
A KEYSTROKE MACRO

- Place the pointer on the cell it should be at when the dry run begins.
- Select a column of cells in which to store the macro, in an area that does not interfere with the parts of the worksheet already in use. This column of cells will be the Learn range.
- Press the SERVICES (F9) key and select Settings Learn Range to specify the Learn range. Expand the pointer over the range or type the cell addresses of the range; then press RETURN. The range should include at least enough room to house the entire macro.
- Turn on Learn Mode by selecting Yes from the Learn menu.
- Go through a dry run. Symphony will record your keystrokes in the Learn range automatically, translating special keystrokes as needed. When you're done,
- Press LEARN (ALT-F5) to end Learn Mode.
- Move the pointer to the first cell of the macro (which is the first cell of the Learn range).
- Use the Range Name Create command to name the macro. The macro name must be composed of the \ (backward slash) character followed by a letter (for example, \A and \Z).
- To invoke the macro, hold down the ALT key and press the letter of the macro name. For example, to invoke a macro named \A, hold down ALT and press A.

instance, Symphony stores F9 in the macro as the notation {SERVICES}. Similarly, Symphony translates RETURN into ~ (a tilde). Symphony automatically translates these keys in a macro when you use Learn Mode. The translated macro procedure would be {SERVICES}FS~Y. Table A-1 summarizes the special keystroke notations used in macros.

To name the macro \A, you would use the Range Name Create command, assigning the name only to the first cell of the macro. You invoke the macro by holding down ALT and pressing the A key. Symphony executes the macro and saves the file, just as if you had typed the keystrokes yourself.

Developing a Purchase Order Macro

The remainder of this appendix will show you how to develop a more sophisticated keystroke macro. The macro will relate to the purchase order tracking system of Chapters 8 and 9, so you will need to retrieve the file named PURCHASE. You should also set the system date to April 1, 1985. Make certain that the "CAP" indicator is on.

The Purchase Order Tracking System

Recall that the purchase order tracking system uses a spreadsheet to store information about the purchases of Fidget Widget, Inc. Figure A-1 shows the

Table A-1. Keystroke Notations Used in Macros

{ABS}	{ERASE}	{PGUP} or {BIGUP}
{BACKSPACE} or {BS}	{ESCAPE} or {ESC}	~(the RETURN key)
{BIGLEFT} (control-left)	{GOTO}	{RIGHT}
{BIGRIGHT} (control-right)	{HELP}	{SERVICES} or {S}
{BREAK}	{HOME}	{SPLIT}
{CALC}	{INDENT}	{SWITCH}
{CAPTURE}	{INSERT}	{TAB}
{CENTER}	{JUSTIFY}	{TYPE}
{DELETE}	{LEARN}	{UP}
{DOWN}	{LEFT}	{USER}
{DRAW}	{MENU} or {M}	{WHERE}
{EDIT}	{PGDN} or {BIGDOWN}	{WINDOW}
{END}		{ZOOM}

layout of the spreadsheet as it looked when you completed it in Chapter 9. When you record a purchase in the spreadsheet, you enter the item name, the date ordered, the date received (if it has been received already), and the quantity ordered. Based on this input, the model uses formulas to look up the unit price of the specified item in the supplies lookup table in the far left portion of the spreadsheet. It then calculates the total price, looks up the vendor's name in the supplies table, creates a purchase order code, and determines the purchase order status (CLOSED, OPEN, or LATE). For each purchase, you enter the inputs and then copy the formula from a previous purchase order entry to the current one.

This procedure works well as long as the information contained in the supplies lookup table remains unchanged. The model uses this table to determine the unit price, total price, and vendor information for each entry.

The first item you recorded in the spreadsheet was an order for pencils. The spreadsheet's formulas determined that the UNIT PRICE was $2.50 (cell P6), the TOTAL PRICE was $125.00 (Q6), and the VENDOR was PENCIL PUSHER (R6). This was true as of the date you created the entry.

However, suppose that tomorrow the price of pencils goes up from $2.50 to $3.00 per case. Any pencils that you order after tomorrow should be logged in at the new price, so you would change the price in the supplies lookup table. However, you wouldn't want this change to affect previously recorded pencil orders in the spreadsheet.

A Problem With the Model

Here's the problem. If you make a change in one cell of the spreadsheet, all formulas that depend on the changed cell will be recalculated and will reflect the change. Since the formulas in the original pencil entry depend on the supplies table, changing the price in the table would change the related items in that entry, even though the pencils were purchased before the price change went into effect.

Try an example.

1. Move to cell B7 of the supplies table, which contains the UNIT PRICE of pencils.

2. Type **3** and press RETURN.

3. Move to cell P6, the UNIT PRICE of the original pencil order.

The UNIT PRICE has changed from $2.50 to $3.00, and the TOTAL PRICE has changed from $125.00 to $150.00, even though you do not want these cells to change.

4. Move back to cell B7 and change the price back to $2.50.

You are going to have to make a change in the model. Somehow, you will have to remove the formulas from purchase order transactions that have been entered but leave the values of the formulas in place. That way, changing the supplies table won't affect existing spreadsheet entries, because the existing entries will no longer depend on the table; they will no longer contain lookup formulas. What you want to do is "freeze" the UNIT PRICE, TOTAL PRICE, and VENDOR entries, after they have been calculated, by replacing the formulas with their resulting values. You can accomplish this with the Range Values command.

A	B	C
	UNIT	
ITEM	PRICE	VENDOR
CLIPS	$0.50	YANKEE CLIPPER
PAPER	$2.00	PAPER TIGER
PENCILS	$2.50	PENCIL PUSHER
STAPLES	$1.50	STAPLETON

FIDGET WIDGET SUPPLIES ANALYSIS   01-Apr-85   12:55:52 AM

	DATE ORDERED			DATE RECEIVED				UNIT	TOTAL
ITEM	M	D	Y	M	D	Y	QUANTITY	PRICE	PRICE
PENCILS	2	1	85				50	$2.50	$125.00
PAPER	3	27	85	3	29	85	30	$2.00	$60.00
CLIPS	3	6	85				100	$0.50	$50.00
STAPLES	1	3	85				75	$1.50	$112.50

	PURCHASE ORDER		P.O.	ORDER
VENDOR	PREFIX	SUFFIX	CODE	STATUS
PENCIL PUSHER	JPEN	1	JPEN1	LATE
PAPER TIGER	JPAP	2	JPAP2	CLOSED
YANKEE CLIPPER	JCLI	3	JCLI3	OPEN
STAPLETON	JSTA	4	JSTA4	LATE

Figure A-1. The purchase order tracking system

The Range Values Command

The *Range Values command* replaces the formulas of a range of cells with their resulting values. You may use Range Values to copy the values to another part of the spreadsheet or to overwrite the formulas with their values (which is what you will do).

To see how Range Values works, you will convert the UNIT PRICE, TOTAL PRICE, and VENDOR formulas already in cells P6 through R6 to their values. Then you will change the price of pencils in the supplies table and see how the Range Values command solves certain problems but creates other problems that you can solve with a macro.

1. Move the pointer to the first UNIT PRICE entry in cell P6.

Notice that the content of this cell, shown in the control panel, is a formula: @VLOOKUP(H6,$A$5..$C$8,1). This formula looks up the ITEM (stored in H6) in the lookup table (range $A$5..$C$8) and retrieves the corresponding cell one column to the right.

2. Press MENU (F10) and select Range Values.

To expand the pointer over the three formulas you want to convert,

3. Press the right arrow key twice.

To expand the range to the other records,

4. Press END; then press the down arrow key.

5. Press RETURN to finish designating the range of formula cells to be converted to values (P6..R6).

Symphony asks where you want to put the resulting range of values. To overwrite the formulas of the range you just designated,

6. Press RETURN.

Notice that the formula in cell P6 has been changed to a value (2.5). The same conversion has happened to the rest of the range. Now let's make a change to the supplies lookup table.

7. Move to cell B7 of the supplies table, which contains the UNIT PRICE of pencils.

8. Type **3** and press RETURN to change the UNIT PRICE to $3.00.

Next,

9. Move to cell P6, the UNIT PRICE of the original order for pencils.

The UNIT PRICE has not changed because it is a value, not a formula. Thus, each day as you make new entries into the spreadsheet, you can convert the UNIT PRICE, TOTAL PRICE, and VENDOR to values so that changes in the supplies table will only affect future purchase order entries, not existing ones.

A Problem With New Entries

But now you have an even bigger problem. Suppose you wanted to make a new entry for an order of 50 cases of pencils at the new $3.00 price. Let's try it.

1. Move to cell H10, where you'll make the next purchase order entry.

2. Input the data for a purchase of 50 cases of pencils ordered on March 15, 1985. Leave the pointer on cell O10.

The next step would be to copy the formulas of the remaining items (UNIT PRICE, TOTAL PRICE, VENDOR, PURCHASE ORDER PREFIX and SUFFIX, P.O. CODE, and ORDER STATUS) to the current one. But there are no formulas for the first three, because you just replaced them with values!

You must come up with some way of storing the calculated values of new records and then freezing them after they have been calculated. One tedious but functional way of achieving this goal is to reenter the formulas for UNIT PRICE, TOTAL PRICE, and VENDOR. For each new record, you would first enter the inputs (ITEM, DATE ORDERED, DATE RECEIVED, and QUANTITY); next, reenter the formulas for UNIT PRICE, TOTAL PRICE, and VENDOR, and freeze their values; and then copy the remaining items (PURCHASE ORDER PREFIX and SUFFIX, P.O. CODE, and ORDER STATUS) from the previous record.

This procedure would work, but it would certainly not be convenient. Every time you entered a new record, you'd have to enter three formulas, issue the Range Values command, and copy the remaining formulas. That's a lot of work to do for each and every purchase order entry. Even if you could remember the three formulas, you'd probably make typing errors more often than you could bear. Worse still, it would take forever to enter a batch of new purchase orders.

...ro for the Purchase
... System

...ro is an excellent solution to the problem. Let Symphony do all of the ... you. A macro can perform the entire procedure quickly, efficiently, and ... time after time. Once you create the macro, all you have to do is enter ...s (as you have done so far) and then invoke the macro.

... for Creating a Keystroke Macro" outlines the procedure you will follow. ...eginning, you should turn on Learn Mode and go through a "dry run" of ...rokes you want the macro to perform.

...st step is to choose a column of cells in which to store the macro label ... will store them to the right of the model, in column W. A Learn range of ... will be more than enough to hold the entire macro.

...nform Symphony of the location of the Learn range that you just selected.

1. Press the SERVICES (F9) key and select Settings Learn.

2. Select Range.

Next, type the range coordinates (or you could simply point to the range).

3. Type **W1.W30** and press RETURN.

The Learn menu returns. Next, turn on Learn Mode.

4. Select Yes from the Learn menu.

Recording the Macro in Learn Mode

Now you are back in the spreadsheet. On the bottom left of the screen, the "LEARN" indicator tells you that Symphony's "tape recorder" is on. Until you press the LEARN key sequence (ALT-F5), Symphony will store your keystrokes in the Learn range, W1..W30. Now go through a dry run of entering the calculated fields of your purchase order for pencils. When you're done, you will press the LEARN (ALT-F5) key sequence again and inspect the Learn range to see how Symphony recorded your keystrokes.

Entering the Unit Price Formula

The pointer is currently on the QUANTITY cell of your new purchase order record.

1. Press the right arrow key to move to UNIT PRICE (cell P10).

The lookup formula for UNIT PRICE is @VLOOKUP(H10,$A$5..$C$8,1). To enter this formula,

2. Type **@VLOOKUP(**.
3. Point to the ITEM entry in cell H10.
4. Type a **,** and then type **$A$5.$C$8,1)**. Press RETURN to conclude the formula entry.

To format the result in Currency format,

5. Press MENU (F10), select Format Currency, and press RETURN twice.

Entering the Total Price Formula

Total price is equal to QUANTITY multiplied by UNIT PRICE.

1. Press the right arrow key to move to TOTAL PRICE (Q10).
2. Type + to begin the formula.
3. Point to the QUANTITY cell (O10).
4. Type a * to indicate multiplication.
5. Point to the UNIT PRICE cell (P10) and press RETURN.
6. Press MENU (F10), select Format Currency, and press RETURN twice.

Entering the Vendor Formula

The lookup formula for VENDOR is @VLOOKUP(H10,$A$5..$C$8,2).

1. Press the right arrow key to move to VENDOR (R10).
2. Type **@VLOOKUP(**.
3. Point to the ITEM in cell H10.
4. Type a **,** and then type **$A$5.$C$8,2)**; press RETURN.

Applying the Range Value Command

Now that you have entered the formulas for UNIT PRICE, TOTAL PRICE, and VENDOR, you must convert the formulas to their values in order to make them immune to changes in the supplies table.

1. Press the left arrow key twice to move to UNIT PRICE (P10).
2. Press MENU (F10) and select Range Value.
3. Press the right arrow key twice to expand the pointer over the three formulas.
4. Press RETURN twice to complete the command.

Copying the Remaining Formulas

Now you are ready to copy the other items from the previous line.

1. Press the right arrow key three times to move to the PURCHASE ORDER PREFIX (S10).
2. Press the up arrow key once to move to the previous record (S9).
3. Press MENU (F10) and select Copy to begin the Copy command.
4. Press the right arrow key three times to expand the pointer to the ORDER STATUS column.
5. Press RETURN to finish specifying the FROM range.
6. Press the down arrow key to point to S10, the beginning of the TO range.
7. Press RETURN to complete the command.

Examining the Learn Range

You have completed the procedure to store the calculated items in the new record. Now you can turn off Learn Mode and see what Symphony did. Without further ado,

1. Press the LEARN key sequence (ALT-F5).

The "LEARN" indicator disappears. To see the Learn range,

2. Press the GOTO (F5) key, type **W1**, and press RETURN.

Your screen should look like Figure A-2. Symphony has recorded your input keystroke for keystroke, except that it has translated the special keys like RETURN and MENU into the macro notation listed in Table A-1.

The macro label cells are in place. However, the macro cannot be used until it has been named. Let's name this macro \A. Recall that the macro's name must be assigned to the first cell of the column of macro labels. With the pointer on this cell (W1),

3. Press MENU (F10) and select Range Name Create.
4. Type **\A** and press RETURN twice.

```
            W                 X          Y          Z
   1   {RIGHT}
   2   aVLOOKUP({LEFT}{LEFT}{LEFT}{LEFT}{LEFT}
   3   {LEFT}{LEFT}{LEFT},$A$5.$C$8,1)~
   4   {MENU}FC~~
   5   {RIGHT}
   6   +{LEFT}{LEFT}*{LEFT}~
   7   {MENU}FC~~
   8   {RIGHT}
   9   aVLOOKUP({LEFT}{LEFT}{LEFT}{LEFT}{LEFT}
  10   {LEFT}{LEFT}{LEFT}{LEFT}{LEFT},$A$5.$C$8
  11   ,2)~
  12   {LEFT}
  13   {LEFT}
  14   {MENU}RV{RIGHT}{RIGHT}~~
  15   {RIGHT}
  16   {RIGHT}
  17   {RIGHT}
  18   {UP}
  19   {MENU}C{RIGHT}{RIGHT}{RIGHT}~{DOWN}~
```

Figure A-2. A listing of macro \A

Invoking the Macro

The macro is now ready to be used when you make the next entry. To try it out,

1. Move to H11, the first cell of the next purchase order entry.

2. Enter the input for purchasing ten boxes of paper on March 24, 1984.

The macro will only work if the pointer is on the QUANTITY cell. Making sure that the pointer is in the right place (O11), invoke the macro.

3. Hold down the ALT key and press **A**.

Watch how quickly and accurately Symphony completes the purchase order entry. Your macro has reduced a very tedious and error-prone procedure to a matter of two keystrokes. It also makes the data entry process easy to teach; you can teach a beginner to enter data and invoke a macro in a matter of minutes. Macros allow you to disguise the underlying complexity of an application in a veil of simplicity. They may take time to develop, but the end result is a streamlined system well worth the effort.

Index